Welcome to the *EVERYTHING*® series!

These handy, accessible books give you all you need to tackle a difficult project, gain a new hobby, comprehend a fascinating topic, prepare for an exam, or even brush up on something you learned back in school but have since forgotten.

You can read an *EVERYTHING*® book from cover-to-cover or just pick out the information you want from our four useful boxes: e-facts, e-ssentials, e-alerts, and e-questions. We literally give you everything you need to know on the subject, but throw in a lot of fun stuff along the way, too.

We now have well over 100 *EVERYTHING*® books in print, spanning such wide-ranging topics as weddings, pregnancy, wine, learning guitar, one-pot cooking, managing people, and so much more. When you're done reading them all, you can finally say you know *EVERYTHING*®!

FACTS
Important sound bytes of information

ESSENTIALS
Quick handy tips

ALERT
Urgent warnings

QUESTIONS?
Solutions to common problems

THE EVERYTHING Series

Dear Reader,

You want to sail because it's fun, relaxing, and seems so very romantic. The trouble is, once you've done a little investigation, you quickly discover that it'll take more than a whim to get you on the water and safely to your destination. With any type of sailing, there's a lot of science, budgeting, decision-making, learning, and frustration to get through before you're proficient enough to sail happily and safely into the sunset.

By now you've probably also realized that there is a mountain of reference materials that cover every aspect of sailing in excruciating detail, but very few that tell you what you need to know in a fun and concise way.

We recognize that you don't want to be hunkered down with endless pages of reading when you'd much rather get out there on the water and enjoy yourself, so we've worked extra hard to craft *The Everything® Sailing Book, Second Edition*, with all the most important information you'll need right up front. While writing the book, we formalized our own thoughts about sailing, conducted up-to-date research on new developments in the field, and had hours of discussions with others. This commitment to detail has certainly taught us a variety of new techniques and reinforced a tremendous wealth of invaluable advice—all of which we've recorded here.

We do hope that you thoroughly enjoy reading this book at least as much as you enjoy the many thrills that await you out on the water.

Nikki Smorenburg

Michael Smorenburg

THE
EVERYTHING®
SAILING
BOOK

Second Edition

From rigging to reaching—all of the
information you need to set sail

Michael and Nikki Smorenburg

Adams Media Corporation
Avon, Massachusetts

EDITORIAL
Publishing Director: Gary M. Krebs
Managing Editor: Kate McBride
Copy Chief: Laura MacLaughlin
Acquisitions Editor: Bethany Brown
Development Editors: Kelly Ewing
Michael Paydos

PRODUCTION
Production Director: Susan Beale
Production Manager: Michelle Roy Kelly
Series Designer: Daria Perreault
Layout and Graphics: Arlene Apone,
Paul Beatrice, Brooke Camfield,
Colleen Cunningham, Daria Perreault,
Frank Rivera

An Everything® Series Book.
Everything® is a registered trademark of Adams Media Corporation.

Published by Adams Media Corporation
57 Littlefield Street, Avon, MA 02322 U.S.A.
www.adamsmedia.com

ISBN: 1-58062-671-8
Printed in the United States of America.

J I H G F E D C B A

Library of Congress Cataloging-in-Publication Data
available from the Publisher.

**Some aspects of sailing are dangerous. This book is not a substitute
for expert advice or personal sailing instruction.**

This publication is designed to provide accurate and authoritative information with regard to the subject matter covered. It is sold with the understanding that the publisher is not engaged in rendering legal, accounting, or other professional advice. If legal advice or other expert assistance is required, the serv-ices of a competent professional person should be sought.

—From a *Declaration of Principles* jointly adopted by a Committee of the
American Bar Association and a Committee of Publishers and Associations

Illustrations by Barry Littmann, Eric Andrews, and Terrel V. Broiles.

*This book is available at quantity discounts for bulk purchases.
For information, call 1-800-872-5627.*

Visit the entire Everything® series at everything.com

Contents

Introduction

Sailing places humans in an environment that is not only exciting but hazardous. Because oceans and waterways are unpredictable, you need as much knowledge as you can get before you actually venture into the water. Not only will this approach save you time, but it may even save your life.

If you're looking for a comprehensive guide to sailing, you've come to the right place. This book is a snapshot of the sport, packaged in a fun-to-read manner. You'll find valuable information that will help you put the elements of wind, water, equipment, and skill to practical use.

We start with the basics and lightheartedly walk you through each element of sailing with straightforward descriptions and explanations. You can read the book cover to cover, if you'd like, or use the index to go straight to the information you need.

Whether you're sailing a tiny dinghy on small lakes or cruising around the ocean, you'll find something in this book. We not only cover the basics such as buying a boat and docking, but we cover information such as proper etiquette and racing as well. If you're a first-time sailor, you won't want to miss a chapter.

CHAPTER 1
Learning to Sail

As you watch sailors gracefully navigate their way in and out of ports, you may forget that water is not a natural human environment. Because of the inherent dangers involved around water, it's not a good idea to master sailing simply through trial and error. This chapter tells you what you need to know to sail safely and efficiently.

Consider a Sailing School

Assuming that you're entirely new to the sport, you may want to invest your time and money in a sailing school. A basic keelboat course generally requires you to attend four to six hours of classroom instruction and seven to ten hours of on-the-water instruction in a moderate-sized sailboat. Although you're not going to become an expert sailor in a week, you will learn the basics. You should also get a good grounding on how to communicate and work with the crew and passengers.

U.S. Sailing and the American Sailing Association (ASA) are among the most widely recognized schools. Both organizations carry nationally recognized sailing certification and accreditation programs, which qualify you for several levels of certification, including small dinghies and basic keelboat handling. In addition, the U.S. Coast Guard Auxiliary and the U.S. Power Squadron both teach courses that range from elementary navigation right through to basic engine maintenance.

ALERT

The five most important tips for a first-time sailor:

- Always wear your life jacket.
- Leave a float plan listing when you'll leave and when you'll return.
- Know the rules of the road.
- Watch out for boats with inattentive drivers.
- Obey boating rules.

If no commercial sailing or navigation schools are in your area, don't despair. Local clubs, volunteer organizations, or informal groups may provide you with the skills you need. Another option is to turn your vacation into a learning experience. The Caribbean, the Mediterranean, and the South Pacific are all brimming over with good schools and willing captains.

No matter what type of program you decide on, you need to ask some questions before signing up:

- What is the length of the program?
- How much time commitment is involved?

- How flexible are the hours of instruction?
- What types of boats and sailing are covered?
- Is the school certified?
- Is this certification accepted everywhere?
- Is the class introductory only?
- Are private lessons available?
- Does the school offer free introductory lessons?

You can expect the price to range from a few dollars per course at local clubs to around $1,000 per course for more intensive and advanced levels. Naturally, prices fluctuate enormously depending upon on region, season, and demand.

FACTS

The United States Power Squadron teaches boating courses in more than 500 areas. Although the courses and instructions are free, students pay a nominal fee to cover the costs of a workbook and chart. For more information or to order the course on video, call ✆ (800) 828-3380.

Join a Sailing Club

Once you've graduated from a sailing school, joining a sailing club is the next step toward honing your skills. Certain sailing clubs consistently produce top-notch sailors, so you'll want to do your homework before signing up with a club. To receive a comprehensive list of clubs and schools, contact U.S. Sailing or ASA.

When selecting a sailing club, you'll want to ask questions that will help you get a feel for the various levels of member involvement and determine whether the club has a strong core that will likely prosper and grow for many years.

For starters, you'll want to find out whether the club organizes social events, such as barbecues, dinners, dances, and races. If the club sets up group trips to classic sailing destinations, that's even better. You'll be able to check out new venues at reduced travel rates. You'll also want to ask whether the club offers seminars. Visiting celebrities and on-site equipment manufacturers give you the opportunity to discuss techniques and problems.

FACTS

- The in-flowing Atlantic Ocean keeps the Mediterranean Sea from drying up.
- Frigid descending water at the Poles causes slow-moving, ultra-deep sea rivers thousands of miles long that keep the planet habitable.
- No ocean wave is higher than 100 feet from trough to crest. Most so-called mountainous waves are only 30 to 40 feet high.

Also be aware that some clubs have membership restrictions. Some clubs are community-based, while others force you to jump through a bunch of screening before accepting or rejecting your application. Finally, find out whether the club has any reciprocal membership affiliations where you can receive benefits at other organizations.

Study the Wind

Wind can make things aboard a vessel behave unexpectedly: An unexpected jibe can cause the boom to whip around, seriously damaging the skull of an untrained sailor. Often, these things occur simultaneously and even set off an uncontrollable chain of reactions. When these events occur around other vessels or near reefs, breaking waves, or sandbars, their effects quickly become magnified. That's why your first sailing lessons need to be on land, where you learn how to observe the way wind moves and how the currents and tides ebb and flow. Although technology has made sailing simpler, you need to be able to predict the wind's effect on your boat long before you put your hand on the tiller.

Start with a Small Boat

You wouldn't learn to drive a car by hopping in an eighteen-wheeler truck; sailing is no exception. Dinghies are a great way to learn sailing because they really take you back to the basics and fundamentals of the discipline. You get an instant sense of what is happening to the vessel and benefit from feeling the reaction of the boat to minute adjustments you make to the rigging. The fact that any error on a small boat is magnified allows you to know instantly what went wrong so that you can avoid making the same mistake in the future.

Aside from the enormous benefits and the exhilaration of dinghy sailing, some rather obvious differences exist between keelboats and dinghies. First, there is the question of ballast. A keelboat has a heavily weighted keel that counteracts the force of the wind and the tendency to capsize. Dinghies rely on the weight of the crew to stay upright in a blast of wind. From the moment you set foot into the dinghy, your body and how you use it become part of the delicate balance between water, wind, and upright forward motion. With the right instruction and a little practice, you'll quickly master the art of counterbalancing against the wind and get the reward of instant performance for every slight adjustment you make.

ALERT

A Small Craft Advisory Alert lets sailors of small boats know of potentially hazardous sea conditions that are either present or forecast. This advisory is usually issued for conditions of eighteen knots of wind or hazardous wave conditions.

Sailing dinghies is also the greatest way we know of to build teamwork and to acquire the ability to command your crew. Although dinghies are not very forgiving of mistakes, the amount of damage you can do or trouble you can get into is only a fraction of the problems you might encounter in a keelboat.

Practice, Practice, Practice

Like any other sport, sailing requires all the practice you can afford to give it. In return, you'll be rewarded with rapid progress every time you go out and apply yourself. What you're trying to do is build a foundation of second-nature reaction to the sailing environment. Like driving a car or riding a bicycle, what initially requires a lot of mental processing will quickly become a reaction that you hardly even have to think about.

We find that the best approach is to pick a particular maneuver and perform it over and over again until you're able to hold an intelligent conversation while doing it. Repeatedly tack the boat thirty or forty times in a row. Approach a buoy over and over again, practicing your gentle approach as though you're making a wharf landing.

ESSENTIALS

Learning sailing doesn't just end once you've mastered the basics. To stay on top of the sport, you'll want to take a sailing safety class, as well as a CPR class. Also make sure that you've kept current with the boating rules.

Once you're confident of your feel for the wind and the vessel, see how close you can come to capsizing the vessel and then repeatedly practice recovering from the position. Admittedly, this maneuver is somewhat intimidating to think about in the early days, but by the time you're experienced enough to attempt it, you'll probably find it quite stimulating. The point of the exercise is that you can pick your time and place to rehearse crises in the safest conditions possible. At some time in your sailing career, you'll probably have to recover from a near capsize, so you might as well do it on your chosen turf.

In addition, don't forget to drill yourself and your crew with man-overboard recovery. Learn to take a quick bearing on the spot, safely bring the boat around in the fastest possible time, and make a new heading to intercept the party with all haste. This particular skill is one you might use during a real life-and-death crisis. If you're ever unlucky enough to have to execute it under adverse and emotionally draining circumstances, you'll be happy that you practiced it early on in your career.

CHAPTER 2

Getting Familiar with Different Boats

In sailing, the voyage is at least as important as the destination, if not more so. Matching the boat to your needs is an important first step to a successful voyage. In this chapter, you find out about the different types you will encounter.

The Categories

Boats that are good for families fall into an enormous range. Narrowing the categories down really depends on the main activity a family intends using the boat for—sport, camping, fishing, cruising, racing, training, and so on. Most family boats are built to traditional design, use a simple rig, and are constructed of low-maintenance and durable materials such as fiberglass.

Of course, as with selecting any craft, the primary questions to be answered relate to price, what category of water conditions will be encountered, whether a cabin is necessary, whether sleeping aboard will be a requirement, and so on. The following table describes each of the main categories of boats.

TYPE	CREW	LENGTH (FT)	NOTES
Trailer sailer	4	20	Retracting centerboard allows for trailer. Good for weekends and short trips.
Small cruiser/racer	6	30	Good all-round boat. Popular boat and therefore easy to buy and sell. Not good for prolonged cruising.
Long-distance cruiser	6+	33+	Requires experienced skipper and crew. Good water storage and food storage facilities.
Family cruiser	6+	38+	Wide beam makes for spacious accommodations. Should be easy to handle for a family.

Try to stay with traditional designs from well-respected manufacturers and look for a boat that is reasonably versatile. That way, if you start out with the idea that racing will be your ultimate focus but discover that cruising is much more your style, you'll have a boat in which you can experience the cruising lifestyle for a time before you make up your mind to upgrade into a more specialized rig.

Single-Mast Rigs

Although very large boats require more than one mast in order to carry the amount of sail area they require to power them, the type of boat the average family or sport sailor needs will be well served by the lower cost, lower maintenance, and relatively simple-to-operate single mast.

Remember that a single mast doesn't mean a single sail. On a downwind run, a single-mast sailboat can actually have three sails rigged at the same time: The mainsail might be set in its normal position sternward of the mast, the jib can be set toward the bow, while the spinnaker can be unfurled out over the bow.

Most modern designs fall into the single-mast rig category. Typically, single-mast rigs are easier to handle, less expensive, and smaller than multimast vessels. A single-mast rig will probably be the first boat you'll learn how to sail or own.

Single-mast boats are divided into several categories, including sloops, cutters, and catboats. The location of the mast determines the boat's category. Single-masts are built anywhere from 10- to 70-plus feet in length and span the full gamut of sailing types, from ocean racing to lake cruising.

A sloop's mast is positioned slightly forward of amidships—or closer to the bow than to the stern. On the bow side of the mast, you should find the jib sail; while on the stern side, the mainsail is usually rigged to a horizontal boom that protrudes sternward from the mast.

When the mast is brought slightly closer to the stern and protrudes amidships from the deck and supports two sails on its bow side, the boat is labeled a *cutter*. By contrast, if the mast is rigged well toward the bow and only carries a mainsail, it is classified as a *catboat*.

In the hands of experienced sailors, even tiny, simply rigged, single-mast sailboats are capable of astonishing feats. Several boats not much larger than the average family sedan have repeatedly crossed the world's greatest oceans and even achieved circumnavigation single-handedly.

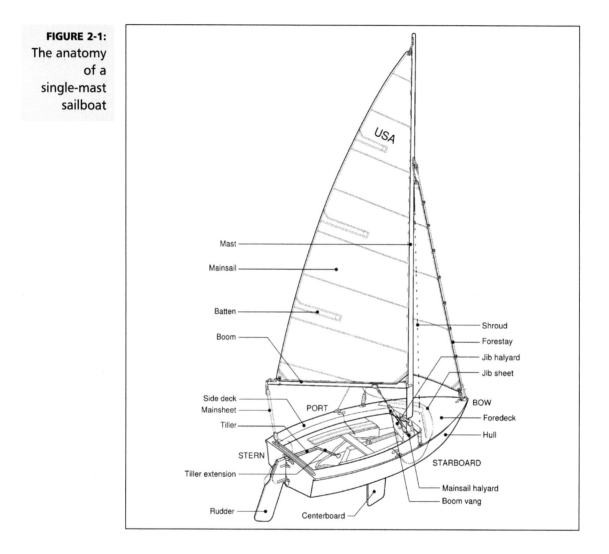

FIGURE 2-1:
The anatomy of a single-mast sailboat

USA

Mast
Mainsail
Batten
Boom
Side deck
Mainsheet
Tiller
PORT
STERN
Tiller extension
Rudder
Centerboard

Shroud
Forestay
Jib halyard
Jib sheet
BOW
Foredeck
Hull
STARBOARD
Mainsail halyard
Boom vang

Two-Mast Sailing

It stands to reason that the longer and larger a boat, the more power it will require to make it perform. For obvious reasons of stress and leverage, it's not appropriate to design excessively tall masts and massive sails. Rather, when a boat's length exceeds 40 feet, it makes more sense to gain additional square footage of sail area by erecting additional masts either fore or aft of the main mast.

The larger ocean cruisers use this configuration and gain the additional safety feature of remaining mobile in the event of losing a mast out in the vastness. Two-masters might well exceed 100 feet, and the sight of one of these majestic vessels can be breathtaking.

Again, it's the way the masts are positioned and rigged that creates the subdivisions of this category. Two-masted sailboats include schooners, ketches, and yawls.

ESSENTIALS

Running lights are required on all boats over five meters. They are white to the stern, red to the port, and green to the starboard. The colored lights are visible from all sides of the boat, as well as from forward.

Once the most popular arrangement for larger boats and traders, the schooner's mainmast is set well to the stern and is always taller than either the single or multiple masts that are positioned closer to the bow.

Ketch rigs are two-masted vessels that have a taller mainmast toward the bow, and a mizzen or smaller mast toward the stern and in front of the wheel or tiller. Though a rare configuration these days, a variation of this rig is the yawl, where the mizzenmast is located behind the wheel or tiller.

Multihull Sailboats

The hull is the basic tub or shell that makes flotation possible. Traditionally, because the vast majority of boats are mono- or single-hulled, we tend to think suspiciously of any variation. From the perspective of many people, catamarans or cats (two hulls—not to be confused with catboats) and trimarans (three hulls) seem somewhat experimental and not really an option to own. However, depending on your needs, these alternative designs might well be just what you're looking for.

Although length for length multihulls are more expensive to build and buy than monohulls, cats and trimarans are becoming increasingly popular. Admittedly, their wider beam can create more strife when trailing and storing, but in the water, that broadness translates into much more deck room for relaxing and much more stability in waves and chop.

Another major advantage of the multihull over the monohull is its speed. This quickness comes from their power-to-weight ratio. They can carry a lot of sail power and have relatively little weight. Multihull boats also tend to have much less drag than monohull sailboats. Multihull sailboats are becoming more popular for families because they provide a lot of deck area, good accommodations, and are stable even in relatively rough water.

FACTS

Examples of multihull boats are pontoon boats, some houseboats, catamarans, and trimarans. The multihull boat gives a smooth ride, and its wide stance gives it great stability. It is a great hull for family and friends and for those who are prone to seasickness.

The geometry of multihull vessels interacting with the unforgiving forces of wind and ocean ask special things of engineers and building materials alike. Traditional wisdom holds that the stresses placed on the two hulls that are separated by several feet offers all kinds of promise for disaster. It sure makes sense that the twisting and buckling that can occur could cause the vessel to either behave poorly leading to the failure of the hull's integrity. But most sailing pundits are now reconsidering their positions. Modern materials and computer-aided design, manufacture, and testing methods have dispelled the worst fears.

In spite of an erroneous label of being unseaworthy and even dangerous in rough weather, cats offer a soft ride through heavy conditions. They also tend to require less energy to drive them and therefore are more efficient on both wind and fuel consumption.

There have to be disadvantages, right? Indeed, the very thing that makes the multihull so popular is possibly its greatest danger.

FIGURE 2-2:
The difference between mono- and multihull heeling angles

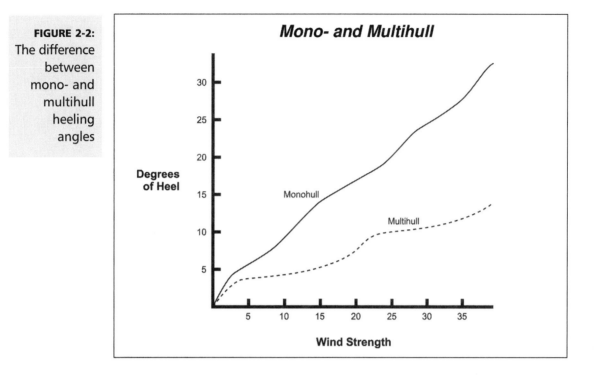

The heel, or tilt, of a monohull gives you a good clue that the wind is picking up and that you may be carrying too much sail and are overpowered. The trouble is, the heel can come too late. The greatest disadvantage of the nonheeling properties of the multihull is that you don't get the message right away, so you need to remain more aware of subtle changes. The first clue you'll get that the wind has picked up is that the multihull converts the increase in wind speed directly into forward thrust, causing the boat to accelerate sharply.

FACTS

Vee-bottom boats are popular with many runabouts at sea or inland waters. It provides a much smoother ride than a round-bottom boat because it has a sharper entry into the water. However, vee-bottom boats require more power to attain the same speed, so you need a powerful engine.

Small Day Sailboats

Many people wisely make their first vessel a small day sailboat. Small vessel is a somewhat nebulous term that's more a personal label than a class. Small boats are a broad category that encompasses a wide variety of design, rigging, and application. On the low end of the scale is the glorified rowing boat with a mast and sail. Then there's the purpose-built sportcat, right on up to day sailing vessels.

Keep in mind, however, that the mix of wind and water is not for everyone. As a beginner, it's often a good idea to cut your teeth on the sport side of sailing by investing a small amount on these more reasonably priced and cheaper-to-maintain vessels and not putting yourself through all the bother of securing sailing licenses and finding moorings. The following table gives you the scoop on the different types of small boats.

TYPE	DESCRIPTION	LENGTH (FT)	CREW	SKILL LEVEL
International Optimist	Youth	7' 7"	1	Basic
International Cadet	Youth	10' 6"	2	Basic
Topper	Youth	11'	1	Basic
Mirror	General	10' 10"	2	Basic
Wayfarer	General	15' 10"	3	Intermediate
International 420	Racing	13' 9"	2	Advanced
International Laser	Racing	13' 10"	1	Advanced
International 14	Racing	14'	2	Advanced
International Enterprise	Racing	13' 3"	2	Intermediate
International 505	Advanced	16' 6"	2	Very Advanced
Olympic Star	Advanced	22' 8"	2	Very Advanced
Drascombe Lugger	Family	18' 9"	2	Intermediate
Hobie 14	Catamaran	14'	2	Intermediate
International Tornado	Advanced Catamaran	20'	2	Very Advanced

Small day sailboats give the family an opportunity to find the most suitable sailing conditions on any given day, transport the boat to the location, and spend the day or weekend playing in relatively safe conditions. Being small and manageable also means that this class of sailboat is the ideal rig for children to learn sailing at an early age.

On the other hand, the more Spartan and boisterous nature of smaller boats simply cannot offer the same luxury and seclusion that larger vessels can, so the choice to go small has to be tempered with this expectation.

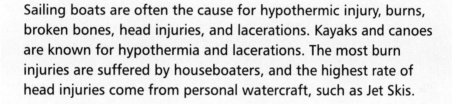

ALERT

Sailing boats are often the cause for hypothermic injury, burns, broken bones, head injuries, and lacerations. Kayaks and canoes are known for hypothermia and lacerations. The most burn injuries are suffered by houseboaters, and the highest rate of head injuries come from personal watercraft, such as Jet Skis.

Cruisers

Larger sailing boats, usually with full-length ballast keels for stability, are called *cruisers*. Cruisers are generally fitted for comfort and usually include facilities for overnight accommodation below decks that might be bare and Spartan or sport all the plush trimmings of home, including carpets, television, stereo, and, these days, even computers.

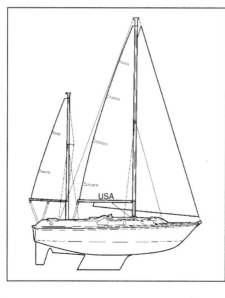

FIGURE 2-3:
Family cruiser

When it comes to choosing a full-sized ocean cruising boat for the family, the stakes go up considerably because of the financial outlay. Because the secondhand market for family-type boats is well developed, finding a boat to buy, and then selling it once you decide to upgrade, is relatively easy.

Cruising covers a wide spectrum of activities, from short trips with family and friends, to long offshore legs in personally unexplored territory. In this regard, size alone is not as important as how the boat is constructed, laid out, and fitted.

Racing Boats

If you're intending to race, chances are you'll target a particular class that is both popular in your region and that grabs your interest. When selecting the type of racing boat, you need to first think about the physical size of the racer. Small boat racing is a bit like horse racing in

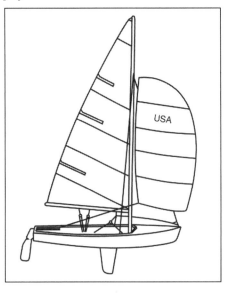

FIGURE 2-4:
Racing boat

that the boats are greatly affected by the load and its distribution on board. Tall and lanky sailors with weight distributed toward their upper torso can, pound for pound, exert a much greater leverage out over the beam than a shorter squat sailor. The skill and age of the sailor will also be a factor when deciding whether to choose a mainsail rig only or one with a jib. A final factor to look at will be how easy the vessel is to trail, rig, and launch.

The Sabot and the Optimist are excellent choices for children who wish to either race or simply learn to sail. Both are very stable and easy to rig and have active one-design classes across the country. In addition, they're light and easy to transport atop your car. Along the same lines, you might also consider the Vanguard Pram and JY Club Trainer.

ESSENTIALS

The following are some simple do's and don'ts for boating safety: Do always wear a lifejacket, do observe all the rules-of-the-road, do check the weather forecast before setting sail, and do always keep a good lookout. Don't drink alcohol while sailing, don't stand in small boats, and don't ever overload your boat.

Generally, Optimist or Sabot sailors stay with the class for two to four years, which makes a very active used-boat market. After four years, most sailors have generally grown too large or have become more skilled and wish to move on to a more challenging class, which they find in the Laser or Club 420. Buying and selling these boats is quite easy and risk-free.

And at the extreme end of the spectrum are the high-performance ocean racers. What Formula One cars are to automobiles, ocean racers are to sailing. With no penny saved on go-fast equipment and instrumentation, these incredibly costly, extremely Spartan flat-bottomed craft have short, deep keels. These boats are the ones that appear in the America's Cup race.

FACTS

Flat-bottom boats may be small utility boats or even high-speed runabouts. They have a shallow draft and are pretty cheap to build. However, the water conditions need to be very calm because these boats tend to give a rough ride.

Sport Cats

Many a sailing world speed record has been set by this class of craft. These are the catamarans we see pulled up on the beaches of tropical islands. Best known in this industry is the Hobie Cat. In fact, Hobie has pretty much been coined as the generic name for the entire class.

With their incredible acceleration and excellent maneuverability in breezes that are barely more than a puff, these cats can get up on the plane like a powerboat and race in and out through waves. With no solid structure other than some rigging and a trampoline made from mesh fabric connecting the two lightweight hulls, they offer little resistance to the water and are exhilarating to play with.

The broad beam of the cat allows for more sail area and more transference into speed. In addition, because the hulls can be kept extremely narrow, they have an extremely slim profile to the water and can attain remarkable performance, even in high winds. By standing out on the windward hull, the crew can leverage their weight and keep the boat from capsizing. Often, these cats can be seen riding or "flying" up on one hull with the experienced crew keeping their balance by finely adjusting their weight, the amount of wind spilled from the sail, and the rudder direction.

FIGURE 2-5:
Catamaran

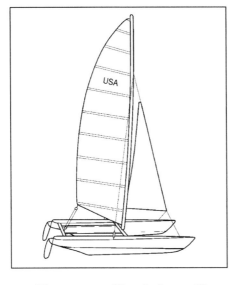

Sport cats are highly affordable playthings that can be trailed and launched easily. Because they draw a very shallow draft, they can get in and out through sandbars and reefs. Although they offer little in the way of comfort, they are ideally suited to young families and those competitive in nature.

The largest of the class are in the 18- to 20-foot region. These often have centerboards or daggerboards that help the trailing rudder keels to maintain stability and direction.

Of course, sailing being sailing, there are two subcategories that refer to the type of mast rig. Where a jib system is set up, we call it a sloop-rigged catamaran. However, smaller catamarans won't have a jib and are termed cat-rigged catamarans.

CHAPTER 3
Buying a Boat

You may decide that you love sailing so much that you want to invest in a boat. But such a big decision is not one you should make rashly. In this chapter, we walk you through the buying decision and process.

Making the Decision to Buy

Buying a boat doesn't always make economic sense if you're just starting out or if circumstances make it more worthwhile to rent, lease, or charter one. Although you may be tempted to consider only a boat's price tag, you need to consider other factors as well, such as the mooring, insurance, upkeep, and licensing. After you factor in all the peripheral costs, divide that figure by the number of days (or even hours) per year that you make use of the boat. It's not uncommon for the ultimate figure to be in the thousands of dollars per day that boat owners actually spend when they break it down this way. Often, for a fraction of this amount, you could pay for an air ticket to a new venue every year and vacation in some paradise on somebody else's boat—and still come out of the deal with change.

To help you figure out just how deep and wide the hole in the water is that you're considering investing in, here's a short worksheet:

ITEM	ANNUAL COST
Monthly payments × 12	$
Registration fees	$
Equipment amortization and replacement	$
Insurance	$
Trailer registration	$
Dock fees	$
Maintenance/repairs	$
Taxes	$
Fuel and oil	$
Sail upgrade and repair	$
Hull, motor, and electronic maintenance	$
Total	$

Ouch . . . ! Makes you wish you'd never done the sums. Yet an awful lot of very smart people are still investing in the habit, so there's obviously much more to buying a boat than the simple economics. It's an indefinable pride and a return to the simple pleasures of nature and a diversion from an otherwise hectic world. Owning and caring for the right boat that really suits your pocket, family, and lifestyle can be a very pleasant experience.

Fortunately, boats also last a long time and don't go out of fashion, so financing is reasonably easy to find. You should be able to negotiate a deal with up to a fifteen-year repayment schedule.

Deciding Between New and Used

Who wouldn't like a new boat? Of course, the moment you take delivery, you experience an immediate devaluation because it's suddenly a "used" or "pre-owned" boat. On the other hand, reputable manufacturers offer warranties and payment plans that soften the blow to a degree. You'll also, theoretically, enjoy a few months and even years when you won't have to spend time and money on maintenance, and that's a big instant gratification bonus. But that doesn't mean that things won't go wrong after delivery, especially since boat building isn't a big industry like automobiles. Sometimes a small problem can take quite a bit of repeated and time-consuming exploration and excavation to solve.

FACTS

When buying a secondhand steel boat, you need to check whether rust is on the hull and whether the zincs have been eaten away evenly or only on one side of the hull. You may want to pay for ultrasonic testing to determine the thickness of the plate.

It goes without saying that used boats offer much more bang for your buck. However, unlike used motorcars, boats are subject to much more destructive elements, so inspection and insight to design and materials is a much more important part. The intrinsic design of a boat and its watery environment means that inspection of hull, bulkheads, and moving parts is not a simple matter. This all adds up to the fact that maintenance can be expensive and often difficult. Some boats are neglected in ways that are not readily apparent just by looking at them, yet an experienced eye will spot and uncover the telltale signs.

You may even be considering a third option: building your own boat. We strongly suggest that you not even consider this option. Back when people had more time and had the tools and experience in craftsmanship, building boats was a hobby. The economic realities of today more or less dictate that you'll probably get a much better deal if you shop around or buy a hull and fit it yourself.

Determining Your Needs

Once you're ready to make an investment in a boat, you need to get realistic about your desires. After the boat's initial and ongoing cost, you should consider the vessel's safety, physical condition, options and accessories, visual appeal, and actual performance.

In our experience, any boat on the water is some kind of compromise. You're either making do with less boat to suit your budget, forgoing space so that you can trail the boat behind your car, or trying to force your cruising vessel up to racing speeds because your lust to win is stronger than your cruising lifestyle. The list of compromises rolls on forever.

The point is that every purchase requires balancing items you really *want* against items you *need*. In addition, boats are not tennis racquets; you don't discard them, and you stand to make or lose significant money in any deal.

FACTS

Hull design falls into two categories: displacement and planing. Displacement vessels ride comfortably because they have a large underwater profile, and they're designed to travel with minimum propulsion. Planing vessels require more horsepower to get the boat up because they're designed to rise up and ride on top of the water.

Two of the most important issues in selecting a boat are cost and level of expertise. The larger the boat, the more masts, sails, and expense it will entail. First-time sailors are well advised to start with small craft and professional lessons before even contemplating the purchase of a vessel.

The main reason for unhappy boat owners is lack of planning and forethought. We could write volumes of theory on this subject, but the quickest way to help you focus on the right boat for you is to ask yourself a few questions:

- How much can you afford to spend on your boating hobby?
- Do you want to tow your boat or moor it?
- Will you operate the boat in lakes, rivers, or oceans?
- Will you use the boat for racing, day cruising, weekend stay-overs, or more extended excursions?
- When, and how often, will the boat be used?
- Who will use the boat?
- What type of boat suits your personality and temperament?
- How many people will you sail or cruise with?
- Must it have overnight capacity?
- How many bunks do you need?
- How large a vessel do you need?
- How long do you plan to keep the boat?
- How big a cockpit do you want?
- What are the draft limitations of your intended sailing area?
- Are you in a warm or icy climate?

In addition, try to become familiar with your boating options. Spend time at a boat club or in an Internet chat room. Ask lots of questions so that you can become familiar with the problems and frustrations you may encounter. Then transpose yourself mentally into those circumstances and try to imagine how you'd react and whether you feel comfortable taking on similar challenges. Keep in mind that the realities of cost, adverse weather, rules and regulations, and other compromises are not for everyone.

If you still don't know what type of boat to buy, we suggest you go for a dinghy class. Not only are dinghies cheap, but they give you a really good hands-on feel for the most basic elements of wind and water.

Wherever you go, collect boat brochures, which provide specifications that will help you narrow the field. Don't forget to find out about fuel and water tank capacities and maximum sail area.

Tracking Down a Boat

If you're hooked and decide to buy a boat, first hire a boat that is similar to your intended acquisition. Once you're confident about the type of boat and your needs, you're ready to start your search. You can find a boat through several venues, with each offering inherent advantages. Remember that one of the best ways to get the inside track on the trade of boats is simply to ask anyone involved in the type of sailing you're interested in.

FACTS

Many sailboats, canoes, and even trawlers have round bottoms. The round-bottom boat needs to be outfitted with a deep keel or a stabilizer, or it may roll and capsize. These boats move easily through the water, especially at slow speeds. They are great for excursions and for casual cruising. They allow for a lot of leeway in terms of water conditions and are very robust.

Once you've tracked down a potential boat, you need to make sure that it really meets your wish list. Take a walk around the boat—outside, around the deck, and inside—to get an overall impression. Record your comments as you walk. It's not necessary to have a detailed picture here—all you want to do is get that all-important overview and note issues, both good and bad, that'll warrant later review. Besides noting details for later review, keep a running commentary of layout, aesthetics, materials, features, and general condition or appropriateness to your requirements. List the questions you have for the seller. The issue you should constantly have in mind is how well the vessel matches up to your expectations and needs.

Boat Shows

Most major cities have regular boat shows where you'll find a wide variety of vessels on display. Spend some time visiting these shows and take along a notepad and carry bag so you can collect information to analyze and follow up on later. If you're planning to attend the show for more than one day or if you'll attend more than one show, use the first show day to form general impressions and collect literature. Also, only concentrate on boats that are apt to fit your needs.

Shows are also the ideal place to check out what's really available. Check what's new, compare deals, and take a reality check of your own needs in light of what you find. Don't feel hustled into making a rapid decision. In our experience, with such a high-priced item as a boat, you'll be able to take a rain check and still negotiate a discount deal a month later.

Besides the retailers you'll meet at the boat show, your local telephone directory will most likely have a listing for boating retailers. Naturally, anyone active in sailing will probably know of reputable stores. In addition, some boat builders will sell direct to the public. Again, check your local telephone directory or ask around where sailors meet.

Agents

Like real estate, boats are sold through agents who list them in various publications. Whether you're a buyer or a seller, you'll find a list of agents in your local telephone directory or through other interested parties. The Internet is becoming a prime marketing environment for agents, and a simple search using any search engine of your choice will probably swamp you with more agents than you can check out.

Media Advertisements and Auctions

Most major newspapers list a column for boats offered. A better bet is to find a dedicated "for sale" publication that lists only boats or yachts. If you know what you're looking for, this is the place where you can really find bargains, but be careful. Know what you're doing or have someone with you who does.

What is true for media advertisements is equally valid for auctions. In fact, you'll be certain to find auctions listed in media advertisements.

Becoming a Boat Detective

When buying a secondhand boat, the first question you should ask is why the seller is selling. Good excuses are as numerous as boats for sale, so try to verify and see whether the reason makes sense. There are enough good boats with sufficient diversity that if you instinctively feel something is wrong, walk away—it's far cheaper than going with your emotions and making a mistake.

If you're spending considerable amounts of money, consider finding yourself a qualified marine surveyor, whose job is similar to a professional home inspector. Ask for recommendations at the local club or marina and insist on proof that the individual is a member of a bona fide marine surveyor association. You also may want to call the National Association of Marine Surveyors (NAMS) or the Society of Accredited Marine Surveyors (SAMS) to recommend a surveyor in your area.

Regardless of whether you retain a surveyor, you need to look for certain signs when buying a boat. The first lesson is to open your eyes and ears—if it doesn't sound or look right, chances are it's not. The following list, although not complete, is a good place to start:

- Check for soft or hollow spots on the decks and hull area that are dramatically different from the areas around; bubbling or bulging areas are the most obvious signs.
- Look for evidence of water damage or waterlines inside the hull or engine compartment.
- Look for evidence of rust or for buffing and abrasion, which may be an attempt to hide rust; if you see a line of rust in the engine compartment, it's reasonable to assume that the engine has experienced some flooding.
- Look for any evidence of rust stains around bolts and screws or from behind paneling, which is a big red flag for misuse of nonmarine quality materials.
- Make sure that the drive shaft turns true and doesn't wobble or is misaligned.
- Wiggle the propeller back and forth to look for damage and evidence of repair; too much play may mean that the bearings are worn.

- Visually inspect the steering mechanisms for obvious signs of wear or abrasion to control wires and pulleys (especially make sure that the mechanism moves freely and with smooth articulation throughout its entire range of movement).
- If you can see it, take a look at the keel and ensure that it runs true in both the horizontal and vertical planes.
- Review all safety equipment for compliance with code, for date specifications, and for signs of poor storage or other neglect.
- Watch out for upholstery stains and abuse, either openly displayed or covered and concealed, which can be signs of a broader neglect for the vessel.

SSENTIALS

To close your boat deal, you need to agree on the price to pay and the payment method. You then need to get a survey for insurance needs and make sure that you get insurance that suits your needs.

- Look for signs of water damage and stains around the edges of hatches and windows, as well as their immediate environment.
- Beware of the musty smell of mold, which is a giveaway to leakage and prior water damage or neglect.
- Make sure that the railings are bolted right through surfaces, not simply screwed on, and that they don't squeak or groan when you tug them.
- Look for hull and other identification numbers and ensure that they match registration and title information.
- Haul out all the sails onto a nice open area and inspect them for any deterioration of seams, paneling, and sun exposure and other stress and stretch marks; do the same for all ropes, chains, cables, and stanchions.
- Even if the engine has few hours on it, check all rubber for signs of deterioration such as cracking, discoloration, or nicks and tears. Engine belts and hoses are particularly vital to keep new and well installed.
- While in the motor component, check the oil dipstick with your fingers and feel for grit and check the color and smell for evidence of burning; give the transmission fluids the same treatment as the oil.

- Ask to see any maintenance records; well-kept ones are a plus.
- Check for mismatched paint, which is a classic sign of repair.
- Measure the vessel on sight and test-sail it.

Beware of sellers who don't readily volunteer information, try to avoid talking about it, or assert that something is somewhat normal or of no consequence. They're probably not playing their hand from the top of the deck. If they don't give you this kind of obvious information, what else are they hiding?

If the boat was pre-owned before the seller bought it, try to reach the previous owner and ask them all you can about the boat. They're not invested in the sale and might give you some good leads.

Before you move toward an offer, boat dealers and banks that make boat loans subscribe to BUC and NADA, two reference books that you should definitely consult to determine the value range for your boat model and year.

By this point, you've probably successfully frustrated the seller and done a reasonable job of making him or her think twice about concealing information from you. The seller should also be about as soft as he or she is going to be for negotiating the best price.

Taking a Test Sail

With all of your questions satisfactorily answered, it's time to give her a test run. You will be able to do this right away, or you may have to schedule a time that is convenient. The more serious the seller gauges your intentions to be, the more likely you'll be able to set up a proper run.

First, note the weather conditions, such as the wind velocity, its consistency, and the state of the sea. Clouds or rain won't have much of a bearing on the boat's performance, so disregard this type of element. If your test day happens to be dead still and flat calm, you'll be left with very few clues as to how the boat will react when things are a little perkier.

If you've got some equipment such as GPS or a decibel meter, periodically take readings and record any unusual variation. With the engine running at various speeds, check and record noise readings in all cabins and in the main saloon. Also, recheck these readings when the engine is idling and the boat is halted so that you have an idea of what it might sound like if you have to charge the battery while at anchor.

Once you're underway, make sure that you have enough room to move around the deck while lines are being handled and fenders shipped. Notice how the boat accelerates, handles, and turns and whether it has any special techniques involved with regard to throttle and wheel handling. Also observe how quickly the boat can stop and come about, as well as how smoothly the winches operate.

ALERT

Whenever you fuel your boat, you'll want to switch off the engine; close all ports, hatches, and doors; secure the boat to the dock; and have all passengers go ashore. Don't use electrical switches and don't overfill the tank. If you do overfill the tank, make sure that you wipe up all spillage. Finally, refuel any portable tanks ashore.

Also, make sure that you literally take the boat in hand. Handle the various lines yourself, get behind the wheel, and conduct every other aspect of the sailing routine that you typically would in all conditions. At the helm, put the boat on a close reach and feel the wheel or tiller. Try sitting and standing and put your body in every conceivable physical position that you might ever be forced to be in. Notice whether there are any blind spots and how well the instruments function. Observe the boat's reaction to wind and watch out for excessive motor vibration, smoke emission, or an oily film on the water. To find out whether the boat has any steering deficiencies, execute a few short tacks.

In some boats, sailing to windward can be a long and slow process. To discover if this is one of those vessels, sail close to the wind, note the compass bearing, and then come about onto the other tack. Maintain the course awhile and note whether any wind shifts might be altering your speed or handling and then recheck the compass. Then subtract the two compass headings from each other (taking any wind shifts into account).

If the angle is greater than 95 degrees, then the boat is not happy sailing close to the wind.

With the sails stowed, you can get a really good feeling of how the boat feels under power. Correlate that rpm with the speed and you'll be able to calculate what her optimum cruising speed will be. Correlate this with the seller's claims and get a feel for what your instinct says about the vibration and sound at that rpm pitch. You'll also be able to get an idea of what the top end should be under full throttle and what your range would be if you were forced to motor somewhere in a hurry.

ESSENTIALS

Don't buy your dream boat today unless you have endless money. You will find that your needs may change after your first boat, and you can always change your boat to adapt to your needs. Start conservatively; you can always buy bigger and faster.

Remember that the way a boat feels is one of the main turn-ons for any sailor. This is the ultimate acid test. Forget the instruments, what the salesperson has said, and everything else for the moment. If you're not blown away and happy at this moment, then this boat isn't for you.

If you've noticed anything odd about the way the boat handles, ask why this is so. After you've been through the docking and stowing procedure, it's probably a good time to give the seller your honest impressions and hear what their comments are and how they counter any objections you might have.

CHAPTER 4

Taking Care of Details after the Sale

Once you've purchased your boat, you need to take care of a few odds and ends. If you're not the superstitious type, you may decide to rename your boat. But no matter what, you need to document, register, and insure your boat, as well as stock it with the proper boating equipment.

Renaming Your Boat

Since time immemorial, the renaming of a vessel has carried a superstitious awe that mariners have observed with fanatical dread. The fear stems from a belief that the most unlucky ships are those that change their name and offend the gods.

Legend holds that Poseidon, god of the oceans, records the name of every seafaring vessel in the Ledger of the Deep. So, to reduce the possibility of annoying the mighty god of the seas by changing your vessel's name, you must first expunge its record from the Ledger.

When you're done reading the advice that follows, you might agree that it's much easier to simply leave the name as it is. However, perhaps the old name is so horrendous that you just can't live with it, so here's how you need to proceed.

You begin by obliterating every trace of the boat's current identity. According to legend, this must be done thoroughly. No log record, identification marking on any equipment, or other reference can afford to survive the ceremony. If you do miss a reference to the old name, begin the ceremony again. Whatever you do, do not bring aboard any item that bears the new name of the boat until every reference to the old name is expunged.

FACTS

To remove your boat name, use a rag with denatured alcohol and some fine rubbing compound.

Check the logbooks, engine stickers, maintenance records, and other warranty documents for all references. Inspect all key chains; throw away all garments, caps, or other paraphernalia embossed, printed, or embroidered with the name. Use correction fluid on paper references to the old name and paint over old names on the hull and equipment, life rings, transom, and sails.

Denaming

Once you've deleted all references to the old name, you need to stock up on some supplies. You'll need a good bottle of champagne and a metal tag with the old name of the boat written in water-soluble ink. Next you'll need witnesses, in the form of good friends or common passersby. Then you're ready to dename the boat:

1. Begin the ceremony to invoke the powers by chanting the following rite: "O, mighty and great ruler of the seas and oceans, to whom all ships and we who venture upon your vast domain are required to pay homage, we implore you in your graciousness to expunge for all time from your records and recollection the name *<insert your vessel's old name here>*, which has ceased to be an entity in your kingdom. As proof thereof, we submit this ingot bearing her name to be corrupted through your powers and forever be purged from the sea."
2. Drop the metal tag from the bow into the sea and say, "In grateful acknowledgment of your munificence and dispensation, we offer these libations to your majesty and your court."
3. Pop the bubbly and pour at least half of the bottle into the water, starting from east to west. Your witnesses can drink whatever remains in the bottle.

Renaming

Now you're free to rename the vessel whatever and whenever you like. Of course, renaming will require more good champagne. Usually, the renaming ceremony occurs immediately after the purging ceremony, although it may be done any time later. Here's how you rename your boat:

1. Call on Poseidon by saying, "O, mighty and great ruler of the seas and oceans, to whom all ships and we who venture upon your vast domain are required to pay homage, we implore you in your graciousness to take unto your records and recollection this worthy vessel hereafter and for all time known as *<insert your vessel's new name here>*, guarding her with your mighty arm and trident and ensuring her of safe and rapid passage throughout her journeys within

your realm. In appreciation of your munificence, dispensation and in honor of your greatness, we offer these libations to your majesty and your court."

2. Pop the first bottle of champagne, remove one glass for the master and another glass for the mate, and then pour the balance into the sea from west to east.

Asking for Fair Winds and Smooth Seas

If you're hoping for fair winds and calm seas, you've got to appease the gods of the winds, and there are four of them. Fortunately they're brothers, so it's possible to invoke them all simultaneously:

1. Address each by name as follows: "Oh, mighty rulers of the winds, through whose power our frail vessels traverse the wild and faceless deep, we implore you to grant this worthy vessel *<insert your vessel's new name here>* the benefits and pleasures of your bounty, ensuring us of your gentle ministration according to our needs."

2. Face to the north and pour a generous dollop of champagne into a champagne flute. Toss the contents to the north and recite the following: "Great Boreas, exalted ruler of the North Wind, grant us permission to use your mighty powers in the pursuit of our lawful endeavors, ever sparing us the overwhelming scourge of your frigid breath."

3. Face west, pour the same amount of champagne, toss the contents to the west, and recite the following: "Great Zephyrus, exalted ruler of the West Wind, grant us permission to use your mighty powers in the pursuit of our lawful endeavors, ever sparing us the overwhelming scourge of your wild breath."

4. Face east, repeat the champagne-tossing maneuver, and say, "Great Eurus, exalted ruler of the East Wind, grant us permission to use your mighty powers in the pursuit of our lawful endeavors, ever sparing us the overwhelming scourge of your mighty breath."

5. Face south, repeat the ceremony, and say, "Great Notus, exalted ruler of the South Wind, grant us permission to use your mighty powers in the pursuit of our lawful endeavors, ever sparing us the overwhelming scourge of your scalding breath."

6. Now it's time to open the remaining champagne bottles and celebrate with your witnesses! Only at this point may you bring aboard any articles that make reference to the new name.

Documenting and Registering Vessels

With a few exceptions, all vessels of five or more net tons that are used in coastal waters, in Great Lakes waters, on the navigable internal waterways of the United States, or in the Exclusive Economic Zone must be documented. A recreational boat, owned by a U.S. citizen, may (at the option of the owner) also be documented if it weighs more than five net tons. The Coast Guard is the issuing authority for a Certificate of Documentation.

FACTS

Vessel documentation is one of the oldest functions of government. It is a national form of registration and provides evidence of nationality for international purposes, admits certain vessels to restricted trades, and provides for unhindered commerce.

Federal law requires any undocumented vessel equipped with propulsion machinery to be numbered in the state in which it is principally operated. The law allows for states to create their own numbering systems so long as they meet or exceed federal requirements. At the time of this writing, only Alaska falls outside of the approved numbering system. In Alaska, the Coast Guard performs the numbering function.

Advantages and Disadvantages

If the owner has a choice between the two forms of registration, what are the advantages or disadvantages of documenting the boat? The main benefit of documentation versus numbering is that a documented vessel may be the subject of a Preferred Ship Mortgage under 46 United States Code Chapter 313. In practical terms, this means that lending institutions regard a documented vessel as a more secure form of collateral. For larger and more expensive boats, it may be easier to obtain bank financing if the boat is documented rather than just numbered.

Another benefit is that the certificate of documentation may make customs entry and clearance easier in foreign ports, so if you're planning international cruising, you may wish to take the extra step. The document is treated as a form of national registration that clearly identifies the nationality of the vessel.

The main disadvantage of documenting rather than numbering is the greater cost. The initial documentation fee for a recreational vessel is $100. The numbering fee varies from state to state, but averages about $25. In addition, documented vessels are not exempt from state or local taxes or other boating fees. Some individual states require a registration fee even if a boat is documented.

All about the HIN

The law states that all boats manufactured or imported on or after November 1, 1972, must have a hull identification number (HIN) on their hull. The HIN is a twelve-character serial number that uniquely identifies a vessel. A HIN is not the same as the state registration number described earlier in this chapter. The HIN must be shown on the state certificate of registration.

More than just a number, the HIN serves an important safety purpose. It enables manufacturers to get in touch with boat owners if their boats are part of a defect notification or recall campaign.

The regulations dictate the format of the HIN. The first three characters are a MIC (Manufacturer Identification Code) assigned by the Coast Guard to the manufacturer. Characters four through eight are a serial number assigned by the manufacturer. The last four characters indicate the month and year the boat was built, and the model year. Before August 1, 1984, the manufacturer could have expressed this in the form of a model year designation.

THE HIN MONTHLY CODE FORMAT PRIOR TO AUGUST 1, 1984					
AUG	A	DEC	E	APR	I
SEPT	B	JAN	F	MAY	J
OCT	C	FEB	G	JUNE	K
NOV	D	MAR	H	JULY	L

FIGURE 4-1:
HIN,
old format

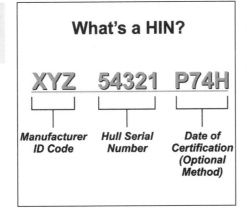

Boat manufacturers must ensure the display of two identical hull identification numbers, one-fourth of an inch high or more, on every boat sold. The primary HIN must be affixed in a publicly viewable location on the starboard side of the stern or transom and within two inches of the top of the transom, gunwale, or hull/deck joint, whichever point is lowest.

For boats without transoms or on boats on which it would be impractical to put the HIN on the transom, it must be displayed on the starboard outboard side of the hull, aft within one foot of the stern and within two inches of the top of the hull side, gunwale, or hull/deck joint, whichever is the lowest point. On catamarans and pontoon boats, the HIN is placed on the aft crossbeam within one foot of the starboard hull attachment.

THE HIN MONTHLY CODE FORMAT AFTER AUGUST 1, 1984					
JAN	A	MAY	E	SEPT	I
FEB	B	JUNE	F	OCT	J
MAR	C	JULY	G	NOV	K
APR	D	AUG	H	DEC	L

FIGURE 4-2:
HIN,
new format

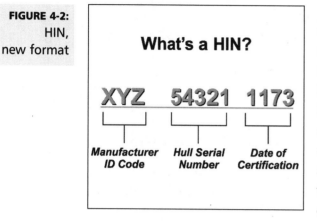

What's a HIN?

XYZ   54321   1173

Manufacturer
ID Code

Hull Serial
Number

Date of
Certification

Boats manufactured or imported after August 1, 1984, must have a duplicate secondary HIN displayed on an unexposed place inside the boat or beneath a fitting or piece of hardware. This HIN is used to help authorities identify your boat if vandals remove or damage the primary and publicly viewable HIN on the transom. It is illegal for anyone to change or remove a HIN without written permission from the Coast Guard.

If you're interested in checking the validity of a HIN of any vessel, the Coast Guard maintains a searchable database online at *www.boatsafe.com/links/index.htm.*

If you build boats for your own use (not to sell), you must still obtain a HIN from your state boating agency. The MIC at the beginning of the HIN for a home-built boat is the state's abbreviation, followed by a Z.

Finding the Right Sail

We'd like to be very emphatic that the reliability of sailing equipment is vital if you're to avoid worst-case safety scenarios. Because you'll pretty much get what you pay for, it's very important that you not be penny-wise and pound-foolish. Invest the extra money and get the best.

The sail is the first obvious big-ticket item. It will be the ultimate determiner of how well your boat performs. Sailmaking is a large industry, and you'll have to choose from an awful lot of materials, designs, and makers. Depending on whether you're a weekend warrior, a serious racer, or a blue-water cruiser, you'll want to choose an appropriate specialist, design, and material.

You can judge a sail's value based on its inherent design and quality of cut, its construction material, its ability to withstand abuse, and its condition if it's secondhand. It's interesting to note that technology and computer-aided design have resulted in ever better sail design and material. For this reason alone, if performance is a factor, you'll probably want to look at new or fairly current designs only.

FACTS

If you want to know the time anywhere in the world, don't sweat. Just surf on the Internet to ✐ *www.time.gov*. This site will give you the official time for any location in the United States, accurate to within one second.

The following sections give you an elementary overview of sail design that should be applicable to your chosen interest. It's by no means a final word on the matter, and you should consult with various parties—though not necessarily salespeople—who can help you focus a little better on what would best suit your particular needs.

For Weekend Warriors

If you're mainly interested in day sailing and stick close to home, you probably won't have a big budget to spend on fancy extras. You won't need state-of-the-art designs, so pick good-quality and well-constructed sails from respected sailmakers. You're looking to buy sails in this order of priority:

* *Mainsail:* Woven-polyester crosscut—standard or economy-grade fabrics will do—with conventional battens and one reef line.
* *Headsail:* 150 percent overlap woven-polyester crosscut—again, standard or economy-grade fabric with leech and foot ultraviolet covers.
* *Cruising spinnaker:* It should be a .75-ounce radial-head cruising spinnaker with dousing sock.

For Racer Cruisers

You're one of the lucky ones among us who can take off on weeklong jaunts to race or cruise over courses of hundreds of miles. So that you can cram more sightseeing into less time and get where you're going quicker, you'll need to invest a little more money in performance sails that can deliver maximum thrust over a wide range of conditions and maintain their form for a long period of time.

- *Mainsail:* Woven-polyester crosscut of standard or high-tenacity fabric, and fill-oriented, with full-length battens or at least top-two-full battens; two reefs; and lazyjacks or Dutchman system (for racing) or built-in sail cover if you're into cruising.
- *Headsail:* Radial-paneled laminate or fiber-oriented if you're into racing, but if you're into cruising, 135 percent or racing-specific overlap; foam luff flattener; and head and tack reefing patches or extended reinforcing; leech and foot ultraviolet covers for cruisers.
- *Cruising spinnaker:* Again a .75-ounce, though tri-radial construction, dousing sock.
- *Storm jib:* Non-overlapping roller-reefing/furling laminate jib with foam luff flattener.

For Blue-Water Buffs

If you're into ocean crossing or spending lazy months cruising through harsh tropical regions where UV eats everything it can lay its rays on, make sail longevity your top priority. In addition, you can't afford problems out in the deep, so durability is everything. Here are some guides for a minimum sail inventory:

- *Mainsail:* Woven-polyester crosscut of high-tenacity, fill-oriented fabric that is one ounce heavier than standard. Select either full-length battens if your budget can withstand a top-quality luff-car system, or, if boat performance can afford a reduction in mainsail area, go for battenless two reefs with extended two-ply head and clew areas and triple-stitched "Seam-kote" plastic-coated seams. Try to ensure extra reinforcing in batten areas, tablings, and luff and foot slides. Go for top-quality hardware.
- *Primary headsail:* Woven-polyester crosscut of high-tenacity fabric that is one ounce heavier than standard, with 135 percent overlap, triple-stitched "Seam-kote" seams, two-ply head and clew areas, extended patching or head and tack reefs, extra reinforcing in leech and foot tablings, and foam luff flattener.

- *Jib or staysail:* Constructed of woven-polyester crosscut of high-tenacity fabric that is one ounce heavier than standard with extra reinforcing, foam luff flattener, storm trysail, and storm jib with two-ply sections along leech.
- *Cruising spinnaker:* Tri-radial construction, 0.75-ounce with 1.5-ounce luff panels, or entirely 1.5-ounce if possible.

Choosing Hardware Equipment

It's absolutely vital that the peripheral equipment you add to your vessel is both good quality and, where applicable, professionally installed. Here are the details of gizmos and items that'll make your sailing a lot smoother and more comfortable.

Mechanical Goodies

The mechanical goodies you'll want to buy include winches and blocks. Because not all winches are made equal and there is such diversity in size, function, load capacity, and quality, it's important that you have expert advice before deciding to buy.

A block is a pulley or a system of pulleys that is set into a casing. You've probably heard the term *block and tackle*; in nautical terms, this refers to the system whereby line is fed through a rigging of blocks in such a way that a gearing effect can be achieved. With so much wind power in huge sails, it makes a lot of sense to have good-quality, purpose-built blocks installed in appropriate places. They might be carrying quite a load, and you don't want to leave any margins for error.

Finding-Your-Way Goodies

Some navigational aids you'll want to consider include navigation instruments, marine sextants, night-vision goggles, binoculars, and a navigation computer.

When it comes to navigation instruments, all of the fancy bells and whistles installed at the helm of a modern cockpit are generally available in portable versions. If you've got the surplus funds, it's not a bad idea to double up on some items such as a Global Posistioning System, or GPS, because it's something you can take with you if you're ever marooned.

The marine sextant measures the altitude of celestial bodies from which you can fix your position on the globe. Although not in common use today, it's nonetheless a vital piece of hardware when modern technology lets you down. However, without knowledge of how to use it and some hands-on experience riding out the waves while squinting through the sighting mechanism, it'll be about as much use to you as an unattached faucet fitting in the desert. If you buy one of these—and for oceangoing craft we seriously suggest that you do—ensure that you get some lessons and practice with it from time to time.

FACTS

Charts are not only used as the nautical road map, but they also give you the water depth at low tide, pinpoint shipwrecks, warn you about shallow water with mud banks, and show lighthouses, prominent landmarks, buoys, and bridges.

Night-vision goggles are a wonderful toy and one of the latest additions to the modern sailor's array of goodies. The technology can run you anywhere from a little over $100 on up to several thousand dollars. For your money, you'll get a pixilated twilight view of the world even on the blackest of nights. Of course, there's an incredible application here for spotting hazards and assisting rescuers in blackout conditions, but it's still a luxury item and will probably remain so for some time into the future.

Don't overlook buying binoculars. Because you'll generally be using them onboard a rocking and rolling platform, do consider that too narrow a field of view will seriously affect your ability to hold station on a desired object.

FIGURE 4-3:
Compass

Lastly, navigation computers vary from control-room-sized monsters right down to calculator-sized LCD displays. Nobody can say exactly where this technology is headed or how fast it will get there, but based on the past ten years of observation, you can bank on there being an extraordinary time ahead for technophiles.

Then there are all the other wonders in a box, such as radios, a depth-sounder, weather monitoring equipment, and compasses and other plotting tools.

Consider what type of boating you will do when you shop for the right personal flotation devise. Try it on before buying. Is it comfortable? Will the color be visible when you are in the water? Can you adjust it for a snug fit?

Safety Equipment

As the skipper, you're responsible for your crew's safety, so you need to make sure that all required safety equipment required for the class of vessel is on board and in good order. More than simply auxiliary safety equipment such as flares or life jackets, navigation lights and radios probably fall into the must-have category. Find out what they are and don't go to sea without them.

Besides meeting the legal requirements, prudent boaters should carry additional safety equipment. We suggest the following items of equipment, depending on the size, location, and use of your boat. Some of them might be somewhat obvious; others, like sunburn lotion, just make you go "Wow . . . good idea."

- VHF radio
- Chart and compass
- Boat hook
- Visual distress signals
- Spare anchor
- Spare propeller
- Heaving line
- Mooring line
- Fenders
- Food and water
- First-aid kit
- Binoculars
- Flashlight
- Spare batteries
- Mirror
- Sunglasses
- Searchlight
- Marine hardware
- Sunburn lotion
- Extra clothing
- Tool kit
- Spare parts
- Ring buoy
- Alternate propulsion (paddles)
- Whistle or horn
- Dewatering device (pump or bailer)
- Fuel Tanks
- Spare Fuel
- Anchor
- Pumps (must work or have manual bailer)
- AM/FM radio

Securing Your Boat

Boating is not without theft. You'll be surprised just how much of it occurs in circumstances that seem wholesome and trustworthy. The first thing to do is reduce opportunity by properly stowing equipment and keeping it under lock and key. You can't make things absolutely theft-proof. All you're trying to do is dissuade the amateurs and opportunists who will pick on softer targets if your boat is always properly squared.

If your boat was manufactured after 1972, find the HIN stenciled on the hull and permanently mark your boat, trailer, all your equipment, electronics, and other personal items with it. Don't make the mark discreet; make it obvious so that the thief or the individual whom the thief attempts to sell it to will immediately see it. It should dissuade both the theft and, we hope, the subsequent sale, too. In addition, follow these tips to keep your boat safe and sound:

- Keep a copy of your registration numbers and documentation on dry land in a safe place. In a world of photocopiers, it's crazy not to stash several copies in several places.
- Take photos or video footage of all your items with numbers displayed and catalogue them. Record brand and model names and numbers, as well as serial numbers.
- Close the curtains if you have them. If thieves can't see it, they're unlikely to look for it.
- If you can't remove it or lock it up below decks, ensure that the latches and locks on hatches and other opening ports are intact and firmly secured.
- Consider alarm systems; they're cheap, wireless, and worthwhile. Try to get a marine-grade system from a boating store. A smoke alarm system is another great addition.
- Cover and secure all exposed areas that are not behind locked doors.
- Installing secretly hidden kill switches and fuel shutoff valves or removing motor parts such as the coil wire will keep a would-be thief entertained long enough to be discovered.

Boats on trailers pose even easier targets because the thief is exposed to a brief window of discovery before racing off with all your neatly packaged bounty. Wherever possible, try to store your boat and trailer in a locked garage, secured boat storage facility, or mini-storage warehouse. If that's not an option, keep the boat out of sight, deep into your yard.

Make sure that you turn the trailer so that the hitch is inaccessible and will require some manhandling to hitch it to a vehicle. If you can, park another vehicle in front of the trailer to block it in. If you're storing the boat long term, remove a trailer wheel. High-tensile strength chains and locks that are fixed to a permanent fixture like a large tree or post will help, too. You can also purchase a trailer hitch lock, which effectively incapacitates the hitch. Also check to see whether your hitch dismantles easily; you can simply remove the working parts and keep them with you.

If You Can't Secure It, Insure It

Insurance is just an augmentation to a theft protection plan. When you take the cost of a deductible to be met, the intangible value that insurance can't cover, the downtime, inconvenience, and aggravation value associated with a theft, and replacement of the missing items into account, you start to realize how important theft prevention is.

Besides, insurance companies just don't like to be on the losing end of a bargain. The very first claim sends rates skyward, while a history of claims will disqualify policy renewals outright.

While on this note, do look into local conditions and storage facilities ahead of time because premiums will depend on where and how you use and store the boat and its equipment. Very often, a boating safety course can really help to get your insurance rates down.

ALERT

To avoid theft, take the fuel line from the portable tank or the battery with you if you are going to leave the boat unattended for an extended period. Never leave the keys in the ignition and store all equipment out of sight.

If It's Stolen

The first step for victims of marine theft is to immediately report your loss to your local law enforcement agency, the United States Coast Guard if on federal waters, your insurance company, and the marina or storage facility manager. When a loss occurs, all the trouble you went to marking your goods and having the ability to positively identify your property is crucial to its recovery and the prosecution of thieves and dealers in stolen goods.

CHAPTER 5

Cleaning and Maintaining Your Boat

U nkempt boats are seen as a reflection of the owner in the boating community. That's one reason fiberglass boats are popular; they're easy to clean and repair. In this chapter, you find out how to keep your boat in tip-top shape, and prepare it for winter.

Keeping Your Boat Shipshape

Your cleaning job will be much easier if you select a vessel constructed from low maintenance material in the first place. Because the innate structure of fiberglass is so stable and resistant to all kinds of attrition, from prolonged exposure to the elements to organic infestation, fiberglass boats don't take a lot of care—hence its popularity in pleasure craft. By contrast, wood is beautiful, but it's a constant battle against the elements and microscopic fauna and flora that would make your plaything their home and grub.

Hardy materials aside, your boat is a major investment, one that offers you a wonderful return—if only in personal value of sport and entertainment. However, to keep everything functioning well and to avoid becoming an eyesore for guests and onlookers, regularly washing the vessel down with fresh water and occasionally scrubbing with mild detergents is a must.

ESSENTIALS

Even in relatively small doses, detergents and cleaners can devastate a local marine ecosystem. Wherever possible, try to conduct the following chores with your boat on land. In addition, try to select cleaning materials that are ecosensitive and biodegradable.

Much like washing a car, a sponge and bucket will be all you'll need for smooth surfaces, but for nonslip decking and crevices, rivets, and screws, you'll need a hard-bristle brush. Wash metals well because even chrome and stainless steel will eventually feel the effects of their salt-brine home.

Algae also loves to build up around the water line, and anti-algae solutions are available to take care of this situation. In addition, in particularly polluted harbors, an oily scum buildup may also be present and need appropriate treatment. If you're battling algae, cruise the marina and seek out a vessel of similar era and construction to yours and then ask the owner how he or she keeps everything shipshape. The person will certainly appreciate your compliments and most likely be overjoyed to help.

Live fish aren't too relaxed when you bring one aboard. Even if you release it, the scales it will jettison will cover everything and eventually make your boat look and smell like a trawler. And if you decide the fish is a keeper, you'll also discover that it won't submit easily, resulting in a further splatter of scales, blood, and offal. A mild solution of bleach will normally remove the worst with quite little effort. In addition, common kitchen cleanser spray bottles that contain bleach are very handy for spot cleaning.

When cleaning fiberglass, avoid using abrasive powders, as even the dullest surfaces don't like them. If you want to try to lift a gleam, move to a microabrasive or cleaner like Soft-Scrub, which can be used with gentle pressure.

FACTS

Most boat-cleaning products contain *oxylic acid,* which is great to use for cleaning teak decks, fiberglass, and rust. Purchase oxylic acid in its pure form from any pharmacy. You get it much cheaper because you are not paying for any filler substances. Then, when you clean, wear rubber gloves to apply, leave it on for ten minutes, and then wipe it off with fresh water.

Because of the intricacy in design and lots of nooks and crannies for salt to do its corrosive job, your rigging calls for special attention. Neglect will ultimately lead to a weakened structure and the possibility of disaster when under pressure in the most hostile of circumstances. Weekly freshwater hosing and periodic scrubs with soap and brush will be a good preventive measure.

About once or twice per year, purchase a purpose-designed wax, and apply it after washing and drying the boat. Make sure that you don't use a slick wax on deck areas; if you have doubt whether the wax you have will turn slippery when wet, test it in an out-of-the-way but representative surface. If you're satisfied, try it on another limited area of low traffic. Wet it down, and test your footing with various footwear and bare skin.

Mildew can be a curse. Whenever possible, bring upholstery, life jackets, and any other susceptible fabrics into the sun to allow the UV rays to kill off the pesky microscopic critters. Try to dehumidify the below decks in whatever ways you safely can.

ESSENTIALS   To maintain your PFD, don't place objects on it and don't dry it in a dryer, heater, or any other direct heat source. Instead, rinse with fresh water after each use and let it drip dry. Also make it a habit to check for rips, tears, or holes.

Beyond having a clean profile, the deck should also be clear. In addition to it being unsightly to have clutter and rope lying around, it is a real safety hazard. Be meticulous about not letting clutter build up in the first place. Don't turn your schooner into a junk. If you must dry garments on deck, try to keep them as low as possible.

Also draw all awnings and covers taut and as close to horizontal as possible. In addition to being more attractive, it will stop them from flapping and therefore making a noise while rubbing to threadbare destruction.

On this note, besides loud and raucous guests and blaring radios, do know that the clinking and clanking sounds of halyards against masts can be a major source of irritation. Whenever possible, secure these away from the mast or give them a wrap around it.

Cleaning below the Line

The water line is the point where air and water meet. Keeping the lower half clean is more important than you might at first realize. From the point of view of a crustacean or other aquatic creature, the underside of your hull is a reef. In fact, it's a wonderful reef that delivers a regular variety of tasty delicacies that they can filter out of the passing water whenever you're on the move.

If you're feeling benevolent, you might be inclined to allow them this prime piece of submarine real estate. However, it's only fair of us to warn you that—apart from being unsightly and ultimately damaging to the value of your vessel—their lumpy and bumpy profile does nothing for the performance of your sailing.

FACTS

Sailing superstitions:

- To help you see safely through all conditions, paint an eye on the bow of the ship.
- Dolphins are considered good luck symbols to all sailors.
- Never count the miles you have sailed.
- Children are considered a blessing to have on board.

Algae and seaweed is one thing, but when you graduate to a hardy barnacle invasion, you're dealing with a much tougher customer. And, don't think that these little devils are only a scourge in oceans; their prevalence in fresh waterways is growing all the time.

In some areas, within just a week of immersion, you'll already feel the sandpapery grittiness of their telltale calcium deposit beginning to build on your highly polished hull. The longer you allow them their reign, the more extensive their hold will become. By the time they're dime-sized, they'll require power-sanding and concerted scrapping—a messy, difficult, and expensive undertaking.

The trick is to make your hull inhospitable from the outset. Certain paints, available at specialty marine hardware stores, contain elements that are toxic to marine organisms. The toxin is not DDT. Most of the modern active ingredient is copper, which evidently makes for a bad neighborhood so far as barnacles and their like are concerned.

ALERT

A few tips can make navigating your boat much easier. For starters, use a tricolor light. It will increase visibility on open water and use less energy since it only has one bulb. Use gift wrapping cardboard rolls to store your charts. Use Plexiglas to cover your cabin table on top of the relevant chart. You can make notes with markers and erase when done and not worry if you spill anything over them.

Maintaining Your Major Equipment

Your boat is a valuable asset that is exposed to among the harshest of earth's elements. To keep its value, you need to maintain a regimen of maintenance. Maintenance is particularly important in climates where winters are harsh. Ideally, the best place for a boat during winter is out of the water, under cover, in a climate-controlled storage unit. Chances are, your boat will be too large for all but covering.

Remember that neglect will ultimately cost you money, reduce the performance and value of your vessel, spoil your enjoyment of sailing when equipment fails prematurely and at inopportune moments, impact your insurance payments and ability to claim, and ultimately not even save you time.

The first step in a good maintenance regimen is to commit to a written checklist and schedule calendar. Start out by checking your owner's manuals for the boat, motors, and other equipment you might have purchased. It's well worth organizing all of the various recommendations into a single checklist and schedule. The time you invest up-front, while you're still enthusiastic and intimately aware of the value and cost of each item, will come back to you over and over again.

The following sections give you a generic outline of some of the items and issues you need to consider when you store your boat for a prolonged period, such as over the winter. You can also find entire books devoted to maintenance and scan the Internet for specific information and recommendations.

ESSENTIALS

To maximize your boating experiences, you need to keep each system working properly. You should perform preventive maintenance according to the manufacturer's suggestions on the following systems: air-conditioning, refrigeration, freshwater, electrical, waste, generator, and fuel. Don't forget to maintain your batteries and cooking facilities as well.

Fuel

You'll want to change fuel filters and water separators when you store the boat. To prevent condensation from building up during winter storage, top the fuel tank(s) and add commercially available fuel stabilizers. In addition, check all hoses and clamps to and from the tank for wear and fit. Repeat this checkup when you next use the boat.

Outboard Engines

The cooling systems of the engine are exposed to sediments and corrosive deposits of salt. To combat short-term blockage and promote engine longevity, you need to flush an outboard every time you use it in salt water, and as often as possible in freshwater lakes and river with heavy sediment.

Flushing an outboard is simple. Muffs, which look very much like stereo headphones, attach to any garden hose. Slide the muffs over the water intake, turn the hose on, and run the engine for a minute. Never run the outboard without providing water into the cooling system because it will rapidly overheat and seize. Let the water drain from the system after you've killed the engine and removed the muffs.

You'll want to make sure that you wash down the external parts of the engine with soap and water. For long-term stowage, you also need to minimize deposit buildup in the carburetor of the fuel system when the fuel evaporates. Read your engine manual for details on how to do so. Disconnecting the fuel line and running the engine till it quits is one method, but some manufacturers recommend various fuel treatment processes with conditioning chemicals.

In addition, apply a film of grease to propeller shafts and threads, change transmission oil, lubricate moving parts per manufacturer's recommendations. Briefly remove the sparkplugs to spray a fogging oil into the cylinders to lubricate the cylinder walls, pistons, and rings.

Inboard Engines

For inboard engines, you should warm up the engine before you change the oil. Change the transmission fluid and install new oil filters as well. Use fresh water to flush the engine.

When you return from any trip, check your inboard engine for any problems. When the boat is unattended, close the cooling water inlet valves and switch off the main power insolator. Place your outboard engine in an upright position to let water drain away. Tilt the engine before towing. Spray the engine with water repellent. Check the propeller for dents.

Grease the drive shaft and threads, lubricate moving parts per manufacturer's recommendations, and briefly remove sparkplugs in order to spray a fogging oil into the cylinders in order to lubricate the cylinder walls, pistons, and rings.

If you're storing for the winter in a cold climate, circulate antifreeze into the cooling system if at all possible. Also wipe the engine down with a towel sprayed with WD-40. That lubrication will help keep the moving parts functioning smoothly.

Batteries

Don't overlook your battery when storing your boat. First, disconnect the cables and remove the battery. Using a water and baking soda solution, clean the terminal ends and battery, and then make sure to rinse the solution residue off with clean water.

Lightly grease the terminal ends and cable fittings. Always store the batteries in a cool, dry place and connect a trickle charger to ensure battery is properly charged for next use. Do not expose the battery to open flame or excessive heat, and never charge it in a confined area.

Bilges

It is important to pump the bilges dry and ensure that they are clean before storing your boat. Use a good scrubbing brush with a soapy solution to remove any oil spillage. After the bilge has been cleaned and is thoroughly dry, lightly spray it with a moisture-displacing lubricant and apply a small amount of antifreeze if the climate calls for it.

FACTS

Keeping your bilge clean eliminates bad odors and prevents bacteria growth, corrosion, and rust. You can use a liquid laundry detergent such as Tide to clean your bilge. If you will use a lot of cleanser, try to choose a natural cleaning product.

Fresh Water System

Completely drain all water reservoirs, including freshwater and hot water tanks. To isolate the hot water tank, you can disconnect both in and out lines and connect them to one another to ensure that nothing can crawl into the system. If you're in a freezing climate, use a nontoxic antifreeze in all water systems to preserve their integrity.

Head

In case you're not yet familiar with the term, the head is the toilet. Clearly, you don't need much imagination to realize that it's something you'd rather deal with at the end of a season rather than several months later!

Start by evacuating the holding tank by pumping it dry at an approved facility. Introduce a flow of fresh water into the bowl while pumping and flush through four or five times.

Consult your owner's manual for recommendations on cleaning chemicals you can run into the system. Once you've flushed chemicals through, add fresh water once more and pump again. If required, run antifreeze through the system. Alcohol-based antifreeze can harm some systems, so check your manual to see whether it is safe to use in yours.

ALERT

Never have a water tank that overflows anywhere onboard. Not only does it spoil anything that it may get in contact with, but it can also damage your electrical equipment and cause untold havoc with your general stay on the boat.

Other Useful Tips

Here are a few other tips that can save you time and elbow grease:

- A small amount of cooking oil in your marine toilet every so often will lubricate the seals, O-rings, and moving parts and help resolve stiffness with pumping.
- Rice in the galley's saltshaker removes moisture that can clog it up.
- To clean sails, use a solution of warm water and common household dish washing liquid. If the staining is more severe, soak or drench the affected area with a mix of ½ cup nonchlorine bleach and ¼ cup mild soap for every gallon of warm water. After the soak, scrub the stain with a deck brush, rinse in cold water, and then air-dry. This is a fairly delicate operation, so take it easy on the concentration of bleach and amount of soaking and scrubbing you apply, since you can easily damage the fabric. Commercial sail-cleaning agents are also available at most boat stores.
- At your local boat store, ask for cleaning agents to deal with plastic windows. UV rays are wicked at discoloring plastic, and you definitely don't want to strip away any protective films that might be present. Also, ensure that you dry plastic properly as direct sunlight will actually boil droplets and cause permanent discoloration.
- Teflon grease applied to a clean propeller will protect it from infestation by organic growths.
- Apply liquid neoprene to seal electrical connections that are exposed to moisture. This treatment both seals and insulates.

Preparing Your Interior for Winter Storage

With the major equipment and rigging taken care of, you can turn your attention to some of the other vital equipment that might have special stowage needs or could be serviced or cleaned during the layoff. These include any valuables, electronic equipment, PFDs, flares, fire extinguishers, lines, and fenders.

FACTS

Before you let the first coat of paint on your deck dry, you may want to sprinkle finely ground walnut shells over it before applying subsequent coats of paint. The walnuts will cost you about a buck or two per pound and will help make the surface nonslip.

Before securing the vessel, clean out all lockers and drawers, give the refrigerator and freezer a thorough washing, and place all cushions on end or remove them to a climate-controlled environment such as a garage. These simple chores will reduce the opportunity for mildew and mustiness to develop. A dehumidifier or odor and moisture-absorbing product available at most boat stores will be a huge bonus, and you'll thank yourself for the small investment.

To help keep the mildew out after you've cleaned the interior of the boat, add a small quantity of Mildicide powder to rinse water and wipe it onto all surfaces. If you find mildew already building up, use a solution of nonchlorine bleach in a spray bottle, apply to the affected area, and then wipe clean.

Storing Your Boat

If your boat must remain in the water for any length of time, ensure that the rudder shaft and stuffing box is free of leaks and that your bilge pumps are in good working order and free of debris. You'll also want to make sure that the float switches are properly activated. Set up a schedule to periodically check on the boat or have marina staff do this for you and report any problems they find. In regions that experience ice during winter, you might investigate a de-icing system—locals will tell you the best solution.

QUESTIONS?

What if you discover stains on your sail?
Unfortunately, mildew cannot be removed. Green stains can be removed by laundering the sails. Use oxalic acid crystals to remove rust stains.

It is ideal if you can get your boat up and out of the water. Once it is out of the water, open the seacocks to drain all water. After you're on dry land, you can thoroughly clean fouling such as barnacles or other flora from the hull, shafts, rudders, and propeller. Once the hull and fittings are cleaned, inspect everything for damage or deterioration. If you find problems, attack them as soon as possible because any water seepage that has occurred might need as much time as possible to drain.

CHAPTER 6
Being the Skipper

We really appreciate that you must be tired of all the cautions—the ifs, the buts, and the maybes—but there's really no way around making your sailing career a happy and safe one without first preparing you for every eventuality. In this chapter, you find out what your responsibilities are as the skipper.

Sailing Solo

Whether you sail with or without a crew depends on several factors. Size matters to a degree; a small craft is obviously designed to be handled by a smaller crew or a single sailor, while a large vessel generally isn't. However, vessel design, the type of sailing being undertaken, and the conditions will dictate the minimum and maximum crew capacity.

When you first attempt to take the boat out solo, you should take a few precautions. The first rule to follow is to wear your life jacket at all times and to pick a day when the wind is light and traffic on the water is minimal. Naturally, you'll find going downwind easier than going upwind, so be very aware of your likely destination in the event that you're not enormously successful at tacking back to your starting point. Another good idea is to ask someone to be available to assist you in case you run into trouble.

You should also factor in your competence and experience. Skill is particularly important when maneuvering in tight conditions like waterways or harbors or bringing the boat to the wharf. Even the best sailor in the world can't be at the helm, working the sails, and leaping across to tie off on the bollard all at once.

ESSENTIALS

The following are some common rhymes that we find useful in determining the depth of an area: Brown, brown, run aground. White, white, you might. Green, green, nice and clean. Blue, blue, run right through.

Remember that sailing conditions can change quite rapidly, so calm conditions are no guarantee that a minimum level of self-reliance is all you should be content with. You also need to think about whether you can raise the heaviest anchor onboard without the help of a winch, as well as what you'll do it you have engine trouble or medical problems. If you're still considering solo sailing a boat, you must answer the following question: Can you can reef or lower, smother, and get sail ties around the largest sail on board, in all kinds of weather, with no assistance?

Getting Skipper Certified

Strict rules govern the level of skipper's ticket the captain of the day holds. Local and state laws will give you specific details that govern the level of license you require in order to skipper a particular class of vessel and what those limitations might be.

When you begin carrying passengers—and boating just isn't fun without some company—the rules of charter complicate matters even more. The rules governing passengers aren't unlike those for land-based taxicabs—you can give your buddies a ride, but if you receive any form of payment or reward, you need a fully certified cabbie license. Even if your passengers are sharing fuel costs, it may be defined as consideration and require more than a simple skipper's license.

As the skipper, you'll want to follow a few guidelines:

- Never leave the boat unattended.
- Step into the center when entering a small boat.
- Don't carry equipment onto the boat, hand it on.
- Distribute the boat's load evenly.
- Don't overload the boat.
- Check the boat's capacity plate.

Authorities do have some leeway, though, in how they interpret the law. So more than likely, if you're a recreational boater, you will be allowed to share expenses for a day on the water, so long as payment is not mandatory in order to participate in the trip.

Stepping Aboard

Because boats have a tendency to move rather easily in the direction a force heaves them, the smaller the boat and the bigger you are, the tougher it will be for you and your passengers to board. And, when conditions deteriorate or the landing is wet and slippery, bridging the short gap can be positively dangerous.

Going overboard is unpleasant at the best of times and potentially catastrophic. Besides being slippery with lots of obstructions at every step, boats are full of hard materials with angular corners that seem to have been designed with the sole purpose of staving your ribs, shins, and elbows in. Also, watch your head when sails and booms are overhead. Sudden shifts in wind can literally be a headache.

When boarding, do not hurry and do not hesitate with one foot on shore and the other on the boat; the boat's rising and falling motion relative to the shore could cause you to fall into the water. With smaller boats, try to keep your weight over the keel line to prevent accidental heeling over the side. Bigger keelboats don't present as big a hazard to climb aboard, but the penalties for falling into the water between boat and dock rise in the same proportions as difficulty to ascend decreases.

As far as moving around on board, we've reduced the most important factors to a rule of three: hold on, hook in, and stay low. By moving with bent knees and keeping your center of gravity low, you're far less exposed to sudden or unpredictable movements of the deck under your feet. And on smaller craft, you'll want to be very aware of sudden shifts in weight. Wind and ballast—yes, your body is ballast—can conspire to capsize small craft.

Proceeding Once Afloat

It is the skipper's responsibility to educate his or her crew as to a particular vessel's special needs, and his or her idiosyncrasies, in terms of a docking procedure and where and how lines need to be secured. Therefore, any botched efforts that are not pure negligence or apathy on the crew's part, can only be ignorance—in which case, the skipper is solely to blame for not communicating the requirements thoroughly enough.

When waterways become very congested, some understandings beyond basic rules of navigation need to be established if a continuous barrage of radio, horn, and whistle cacophony is also to be avoided. This comes down to a few simple gestures, skipper to skipper. Waving one another through or other simple hand gestures.

ALERT

As the skipper, you need to be aware of local hazards, such as hazardous inlets, dams, locks, and shoaling and whitewater areas. You'll also want to know where abnormal tides and currents occur. Make sure that you have charts on all areas you are boating in.

While sailing in close confines, all vessels should be at absolute slow pace and keeping a lookout for possible hazardous situations. Experienced skippers literally wave one another by with gracious and friendly waves. Of course, the finest gesture any captain can make under these conditions is to see a situation developing and avoid it altogether by a timely and slight alteration in course.

Sails are designed to capture hundreds and perhaps thousands of pounds of wind pressure. If a sail is flapping wildly, stay on the windward side of it, or you'll receive a smack you won't forget in a hurry. Try to fold and collapse it onto itself to make it lose power quickly.

Do keep in mind that your sails will create a blind spot behind which obstructions and victims might be masked. Therefore, never make a turn that is not well planned and properly communicated to all parties who could be affected. In addition, synthetic sails can be slippery, so standing on them can be dangerous.

Giving Orders

The captain gets to bark the orders, but this is not the navy, and there's no guarantee that everyone aboard has boating experience or has a clue what sailing jargon means. Besides, they can't read your mind, so try to be specific with your instructions, acting them out wherever necessary. In short, don't expect anyone aboard to second-guess your wishes.

In addition, those aboard may also not have the benefit of well-practiced skills, so besides avoiding fancy sailor's language, get an idea of who knows what before you dish out responsibilities. Remember that a well-meaning passenger might think they've tied the right knot or steered the right heading, but you could be on the rocks if they've overestimated their own abilities and were too proud to admit it.

Taking the Rules Seriously

As the skipper, you need to make sure that you take the following rules seriously and ensure that your crew and passengers do, too:

- Ensure one member aboard knows how to operate the vessel in your absence.
- Never carry equipment aboard; hand it across or lift it across.
- Distribute goods and people evenly side to side and fore and aft.
- Never exceed the boat's carrying capacity.

It's also the responsibility of the operator to refrain from careless, reckless, or negligent operations on the water. Failure to operate a boat in a safe manner could endanger life or property of other persons. Again, be courteous and exercise caution.

Being Courteous

The waterways of the free world that are neither private nor restricted are like the shade of a tree—they belong to everyone, yet they belong to no one. Everybody has a right to enjoy the tranquility of the shore or open reaches in their own way, provided that their enjoyment does not encroach on the rights of another.

If you want to have a good time, as a responsible sailor, the onus is on you to uphold your end of the bargain. Remember that your wake is a very tangible impact that you leave behind. It might be fun to scream around in your motor-powered tender, but please control it. Along this line is sound pollution. Sound travels far over water, so try to keep your engine noise and general revelry to a minimum when in even surprisingly distant proximity to people.

Besides being illegal, physical pollution and littering is offensive and unnecessary. Please do respect nature and the rights of those who will follow you. Don't dump waste overboard or allow your beaten-up old engine to leak gas or oil into the drink.

In addition, private docks are like private or reserved parking bays and need to be respected. Likewise, speed postings or other restrictions need to be observed with respect. Lastly, boating is a community, and the laws of the waves dictate that you are obligated to lend your assistance to anyone in distress or in danger. Don't wait to be called to help. Keep an eye out for any signs of your fellow sailors having problems, and give them a hail to see if they want assistance.

FACTS

Make the guardrails in your cockpit area much more comfortable to lean against by cutting a hose pipe open and covering the rails with it. By cutting a PVC pipe down the side and using tape around the top and bottom, you can cover turnbuckles to prevent lines or sails from getting caught.

Knowing Who's Boss

No boat can be run by a committee. In smaller craft, the type you'll probably be sailing in, the boss is usually the one with his or her hands on the wheel or tiller arm. This person is generally the vessel's owner and the individual aboard with the most experience.

Like any leadership role, you don't have to be Captain Bligh to make things happen, but you do need to have everyone understand that, though you're not implacable, your decisions and orders need to be followed precisely as you give them. Get this message across before you cast off, and you shouldn't have a problem. Experienced crews will expect you to take this role, while inexperienced crews will probably appreciate the security of knowing that someone's taking charge.

By all means, give everyone a speech. It's a little like the aircrew routine flight crews give you on commercial airlines:

- Explain the course you'll be following, and what you'll be expecting from everyone, and certain individuals.
- Choose your second in command. In the event that you're not able to be skipper for a period, your commander will take over.

- Run through the rudiments of the boat's operation with everyone.
- On smaller boats that might be disturbed by crew movement, remind everyone to remain seated as much as possible and to move with caution. On larger boats, remind them to be aware of the pitch and roll in the swells.
- Run through a short list of emergency equipment and procedures, including proper use of radio equipment. Point out the PFDs and have everyone try them on and adjust them to fit. Do ensure that those who can't swim keep theirs on at all times.
- Tell everyone where the heads are.
- Do insist on a no-smoking policy anywhere near fuel.
- Explain good conduct and courtesy.
- Caution guests that boat surfaces can be very slippery, particularly during the morning after a sprinkling of dew.

Encouraging Common Sense

Sometimes you've just got to wonder—is this really the most common of the senses? More common than eyesight, touch, or hearing? Because it seems that an awful lot of people forget to put their brains in gear before engaging their actions.

The clue here is to pause a moment before making rash decisions. Are there consequences, and how can I reduce them? You'll find passengers who delight in hanging over the bow—*Titanic* style—feeling like they're kings of the world. Do they ever pause a moment and consider how equally exhilarating it would be to pull the same stunt on the hood of their car?

Advocating a Positive Sailing Attitude

Why the heck are you sailing? Whether you're racing, cruising, traveling, or just getting your kicks in your own unique way, we'll wager that you're sailing comes down to one word—*enjoyment*. You enjoy sailing, so smile. Remember the song ". . . even the bad times are good . . . " and take it to sea with you. When pandemonium breaks loose, hum the song to yourself; you're developing a new coping skill. Keep that fact in mind even during the bad times.

Sailors share a strong tradition of kinship. How many people do you just wave to for the heck of it while driving down the road or greet in the middle of the city? Out on the water, you'll receive plenty of greetings and always find buddies at any club you visit. More than a sport or convenience, sailing is a lifestyle. Never forget why you joined the fraternity and sustain the positive experience for others.

Conducting a Safety Check

Before you set sail, you need to do a short safety inspection. First, conduct an inventory of equipment and spares. Produce a checklist for this task and always use this list as your baseline—not your memory.

Next, check the rigging. Go aloft yourself or send the most experienced of the crew up into the rigging to inspect that everything is well secured and in good condition. Last, stow personal belongings to ensure they're not underfoot when you break out the equipment.

Developing a Sailing Strategy

In life, but especially in sailing, you'll hear the words *strategy* and *tactics* constantly being repeated. Strategy is the plan of action, while tactic is the maneuver. One is more theory, while the other is an element of its execution.

Beyond racing, knowing the difference between strategy and tactics will still be important—if only in terms of managing your crew effectively. You'll devise a strategy of how they'll work most efficiently to give everyone a safe and enjoyable ride, and you'll employ various tactics to execute these designs.

CHAPTER 7

Leaving the Dock

Y ou're ready for your first sail! In this chapter, we guide you through the most important points of leaving the dock for the first time. You also find out how to rig the rig and handle the lines.

Rigging the Rig

The first thing you need to do is rig the rig. For a change of pace, we'll do it by the numbers, but please bear in mind that rigs might differ. This description is meant to be generic in nature and to simply give you an overview of the procedure you'll go through:

FIGURE 7-1:
Sail and rigging anatomy

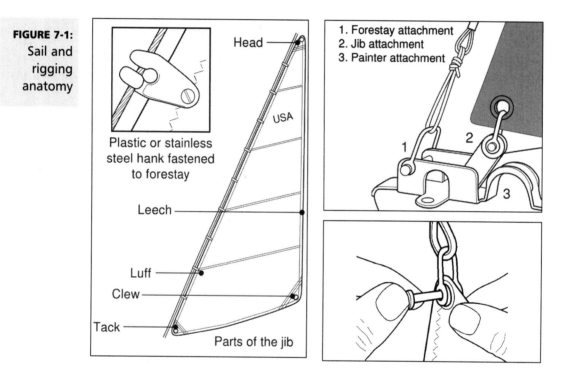

1. Forestay attachment
2. Jib attachment
3. Painter attachment

Plastic or stainless steel hank fastened to forestay

Head

Leech

Luff

Clew

Tack

USA

Parts of the jib

1. With the boat at its mooring, lay the mainsail on the deck next to the boom.
2. Locate the clew and feed it into the track that runs it along the top of the boom or into the groove designed to hold it. Get a buddy to help because this step is far more simple when one feeds and the other slides the clew along toward the outer end.
3. If the sail has batten pockets, slip in the battens. You'll probably notice they're tapered and of different lengths. Generally, the longest are near the foot and the shortest near the head, so sort them into descending length and then hold them against each pocket to get an

idea of whether they'll fit. Now, insert the thinner end in first. Don't forget to secure them with the clip or pocket provided.

4. Straighten the sail's luff and remove any twists. Then secure the tack to the fitting on the boom close to where it attaches to the mast.

5. Attach the clew to the outhaul at the other end of the boom. With the foot of the sail secured, gently increase tension on the line to stretch it out and then cleat the outhaul.

6. Inspect the main halyard and ensure that it's not snagged or twisted around any stays. Now, attach the halyard's shackle to the head of the sail.

7. Attach the luff to the mast via the slide attachments that are spaced along its edge.

8. Ensure that the rudder is functioning and that the water is deep enough. Lower the centerboard if you have one.

9. You don't want to sail until you're ready, so before raising the sails, point the boat upwind so that they luff and the boat is in irons. Double-check that the rope that controls the mainsail is slack so that the sail cannot fill with wind even if the boat drifts perpendicular to the wind.

10. Begin hoisting the sail, all the while feeding the slide into the groove in the back of the mast.

11. When the head reaches the top of its extent, cleat the halyard off on the mast, coil the remaining line neatly, and hang it below the cleat.

12. Though your first trip never should be with mainsail only, if your boat has a jib, the first priority is to locate its tack. With your own sails, it's not a bad idea to indelibly mark this corner. Sorting through bundles of sheet can be frustrating, and all corners look pretty much the same at first. A hint with the jib is that the angle this corner forms is wider than the clew.

13. Now, approach the bow and, adjacent to the forestay, you'll find a fitting that can support the jib in the same way the mast supports the mainsail.

14. With the jib attached to the forestay with the hanks or snaps along its luff, begin at the bottom of the sail and work up. That way, the bottom section will be easier to attach.

FIGURE 7-2(a):
Typical sail
and rigging
configuration

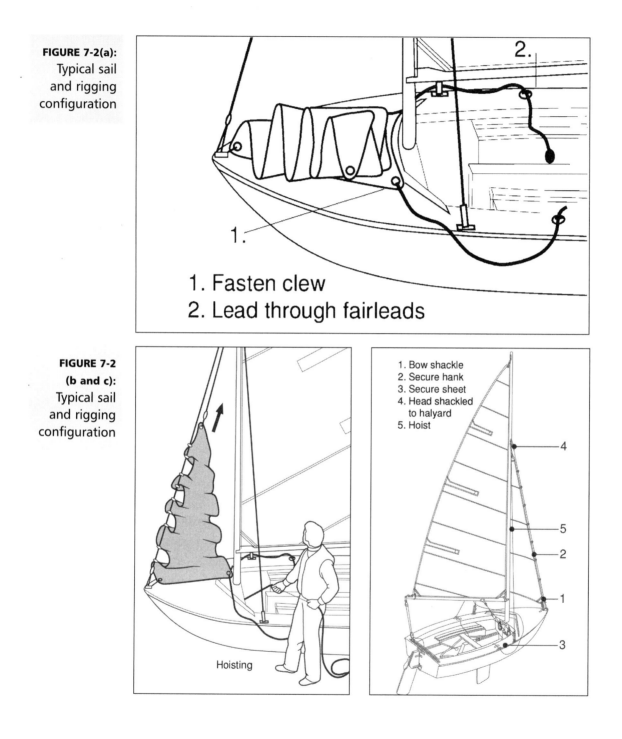

1. Fasten clew
2. Lead through fairleads

**FIGURE 7-2
(b and c):**
Typical sail
and rigging
configuration

1. Bow shackle
2. Secure hank
3. Secure sheet
4. Head shackled
   to halyard
5. Hoist

Hoisting

15. Next, find the jib's clew. The best way to find the tack is to look for the corner where the boltropes attach to the boom and the mast meet. If you see only one rope, it's the clew.

16. Using a bowline or shackles, attach the jib sheets and run the sheets through the pulleys (blocks) provided back to the cockpit. One goes to each side. Put a figure-eight stopper knot in the end of each so that they don't run back through the blocks.

17. Attach the jib halyard to the head of the jib. On a windy day, it's very easy for the jib to be blown off the front deck, so have a crew person sit on the jib until you're ready to hoist it.

That's it! You're finally ready to go.

FACTS

Before sailors had modern technology to warn them of upcoming storms, they knew they were in for a storm when the knots tightened up. The fibers in the knots absorb moisture as humidity rises, so lines shrink.

Line Handling and Marlinespike

Though the five knots you'll find most important to know are easy to tie and untie, occasionally you end up with a solidly fouled line. Enter the marlinespike, a bona fide tool designed for the job. Its pointed metal spike and heavy construction make it a fine lever to wedge into an uncooperative knot and massage the bundle loose. Alternatively, it is used to separate strands of rope when splicing.

So that you never need your spike, practice the following knot-tying techniques until you can tie them in your sleep. Then, never let just anybody tie important knots—especially if you intend to undo them at some time in the future.

Here's a bit of trivia for you: There are 38 pounds of gold, 128,000,000 tons of salt, and 4,037,000,000 tons of oxygen in a cubic mile of seawater. In addition, the world's seas have risen from six to eight inches in the past 100 years.

Bowline

The simplest and most common knot for producing a loop of any size at the end of a rope, the bowline won't jam and can quickly be undone.

FIGURE 7-3:
Bowline

Simply form a small loop (the direction is important) toward the rope's end. Pass the free end of the knot up through the loop. Take the end around behind the standing part of the rope. Now, bring the end back down through the loop. Here's a quaint allegory to help you remember: "The rabbit pops out of its hole, runs round the tree, and drops back down the hole again." The rabbit is the end of the rope, the tree is the rope itself, and the hole is the small loop.

When you use this knot to secure valuable goods or lives, really secure it by simply tying a stop knot, such as a Figure of Eight knot, in the rope's end.

To quickly identify if you have tied the bowline in a normal or left-handed configuration, check to see that the running end (rabbit) departs the knot inside of the loop.

Clove Hitch

When you've got to tie off to a pole, even if you've only got one hand available to do so, the clove hitch is the way to go. It's quick and secure and rarely jams. You'd generally use it either to start or finish a lashing. However, be aware that even if the rope is under tension, the clove hitch is a knot that can unroll if the pole turns.

FIGURE 7-4:
Clove hitch

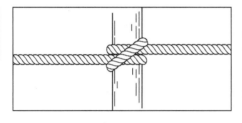

To tie a clove hitch, take a single turn around the pole. Angle the rope to cross over the top of the turn and wrap it around the pole again so it passes on the opposite side of itself from the first turn around the pole. Pass the end back under the angled cross-over. Pull the rope up tight.

To avoid unrolling, adapt the knot to a round turn and two half hitches at the start and end of lashings—it's not as neat looking, but it is effective. Here's the variation:

Don't execute the angled crossover, instead, pass the end over the top of the rope and back through the loop it forms. Repeat the looping technique.

Figure of Eight Knot

Sometimes as a stop knot, the figure-eight is invaluable, particularly when you need to bulk out the end of a rope to stop it slipping back through another knot. It's also a great way to quickly stop a rope or cord from fraying.

FIGURE 7-5:
Figure of
Eight knot

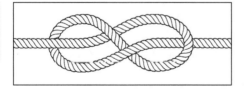

This knot is easy to remember because it looks like its name—a figure eight. Form a loop with the rope. Pass the end over itself and tuck it back under; you can see the 8 starting to form. Pass it back through itself and pull it up snugly into a tight bunch.

Reef Knot

The reef knot gets its name from the days of sailing ships, when the sails were "reefed" or rolled up and lashed to the cross spar with a reef knot. In order to release the sail, often in dangerous weather conditions and precariously balanced on the spars of the rigging, sailors had to work their way along the cross spar and tug the securing reef knot free. With no safety harnesses, they generally had only one hand free to get the job done. The weight of the sail caused the knot to slip and the sail to unfurl.

FIGURE 7-6:
Reef knot

These days, we generally use the reef knot to quickly join two pieces of rope or twine. Don't rely on it as a long-term fix or to carry heavy loads; for that, go to the fisherman's knot. Don't attempt this knot to join ropes of different thickness. Another downside is that it can slip and bind very tightly to itself, so avoid using it where life or limb are at stake! On the plus side, the reef know is a good general-purpose knot that's easy to learn and tie in a hurry.

Take an end of each rope in each hand. Pass the left strand under the right piece and simultaneously mirror the action by passing the right strand under the left side. Now, turn the ends 180 degrees and bring them back through the loop formed by the opposite cord and then pull the knot up snugly with equal pressure in opposite directions of the rope.

An alternative way to tie it is to pass the left strand under the right piece and simultaneously mirror the action by passing the right strand under the left side. Because the ends have passed each other, they're effectively in opposite hands. Now, reverse the technique by passing the right end over the left end and pulling up tight. This sounds more complicated than it is, but it's really quite easy when you try it. To help you remember the sequence, say, "Left over right and under, right over left and under" as you tie the knot.

To undo the reef knot, grip one loose end and pull it in the opposite direction back over the knot, effectively straightening that piece of rope and causing the other piece to entwine itself around the straightened piece. You'll now be able to slip the second piece of rope off the straightened piece.

Fisherman's Knot

As the name suggests, this knot comes from fishermen who typically use small-diameter twines and string. It's a great knot to quickly join together two ropes of equal thickness when you need a dependable joint.

Something to bear in mind is that friction between the ropes can build up fiber-damaging heat, which will create a weak spot in the knot. To avoid this, moisten the rope slightly before tightening it.

FIGURE 7-7:
Fisherman's knot

To tie this knot, place the strands side by side. Pass one strand over the other in a loop. Pass the end back through the loop it has formed and then repeat the technique with the other second strand. Pull the ends up tight and place equal pressure in opposing directions on either side of the knot; it should come up snugly into a neat and hold-fast knot.

Sheet Bend

To join two ropes of unequal diameter, use the sheet bend. Start by making a bight or loop in the thicker of the two ropes. Pass the thinner rope up (the shaded rope in **FIGURE 7-8**) through the bight and then twist it around the back of the bight. Now tuck the thinner cord back under itself.

FIGURE 7-8:
Sheet bend

FIGURE 7-9:
Left-handed sheet bend

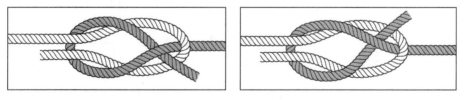

Be sure that the knot is tied in such a way that both ends come off on the same side of the bend, as illustrated in the figures.

When the ends depart the knot on opposite sides of the bend, the knot becomes much less secure and is known as a left-handed sheet bend. This should be avoided.

FIGURE 7-10:
Double-sheet
bend

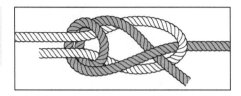

If the ropes are to be placed under a lot of strain or have very different diameters, you can vary the knot and make it a double-sheet bend. It just requires an additional twist of the thinner cord.

Rolling Hitch

The rolling hitch can be useful in instances when joining two ropes together and being able to quickly change the position of the knot simply by sliding one rope over the other before relocking the knot is important. (Note: If you give it a single turn, the knot becomes a clove hitch.)

Though the one rope can slide and be repositioned along the length of the other rope, when tension is applied to them, the ropes bind tightly together and lock into position. When tension is released, the hitch loosens, and the knot can be repositioned at a new location. In most modern configurations, adjuster clips will perform this task, but it's still a very worthwhile technique to use.

FIGURE 7-11:
Rolling hitch

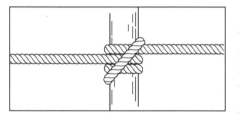

To tie the rolling hitch, pass the cord to be locked twice around the rope onto which it will lock. Pass the end diagonally over itself and wrap it back under the other rope so that it comes around on the opposite side of its initial twist. Pass the end back under its own diagonal traverse. When you're done and want to secure the knot, use a stop knot such as the figure-eight knot.

Sheepshank

Sometimes, ropes are just too long for a temporary job or have too much slack that must be reduced. Never cut the rope! The sheepshank comes to the rescue in the same way a facelift revitalizes sagging jowls; it just tucks the sag away within its own length.

Good news for the rope is that the knot simply falls apart the moment it goes slack. The knot falling apart can be very bad news for you if it happens at an inopportune moment, so the places you use the knot and the way you avoid this are all important. The first rule for keeping the knot intact is ensuring that the rope is only used in circumstances where full tension can be assured 100 percent of the time. For example, using the sheepshank to shorten a rope in order to tow another vessel would be inviting disaster. To lock the knot a little tighter and fine-tune the shortening, employ up to five half hitches on each end.

FIGURE 7-12:
Sheepshank

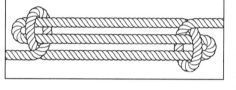

First, lay the rope in an **S** curve. Loop the end around the one bend. Mirror a loop around the other bend. Take up the slack and apply pressure until the two loops bind onto the bends. The sheepshank is now in full operation until slackness allows it to slip its own knotty embrace.

Undocking

Ahead of actually casting off, you need to establish an undocking plan. Your crew and passengers should be briefed on what, how, and when you're planning to take certain critical actions of the plan so that they can assist or accommodate your needs.

Before taking another step, don't forget to unplug and recover any electrical or telephone cables that might be linked to the shore. Your first order of business is to consider what currents are in the immediate area of your slip, the name given to the home your boat occupies along the dock. Check the depth of water on your anticipated exit path, what the current wind direction and level is, and whether there is any traffic that could possibly be a hazard. The more eyes and hands you've got on these various tasks, the better, so enlist the help of your crew and passengers.

That engine that's been burbling and slowly warming should be at operational temperature by now. Check its gauges and ensure that all is within the appropriate range.

ALERT

Littering at sea kills marine animals. Ingested plastic can cause starvation, intestinal injury, and ultimately death. Some birds even mistakenly feed plastic to their young, and turtles have been known to mistake plastic for jellyfish. Please don't litter at sea; the consequences are devastating.

Some slips are like parking bays in that the boat is backed into its spot. In this instance, you'll take what's appropriate from the description that follows and simply edge out slowly. However, other slips are more like cars parked along a street and parallel with the sidewalk. Like parking and exiting in a car, it can be a little trickier in this kind of circumstance than simply pulling away. Follow these instructions, and you'll find it's all very logical.

Unlike a car, boats can move laterally. This is both good and bad news. On the one hand, wind and current can push you in directions you don't want to go. On the other hand, with fenders, lines, and brute strength, you can force the boat in directions you do want to go.

ESSENTIALS

When launching your boat, follow these few simple rules:

- Don't impede others at the launch pad; do your preparations away from the ramp.
- Raise the motor, remove the support bracket, and put in the drain plug.
- Disconnect the trailer wiring and all straps.
- Adjust the equipment.
- Check fluid levels and connect the fuel tank.

Checking the Water Level

In all shallow water maneuvers, a skipper should post lookouts on the deck closest to the direction of movement. In other words, if backing up, place lookouts on the stern; if proceeding forward, place lookouts on the bow.

Ensure that sails either are not hoisted or are allowed to luff. If you're not under engine power, give your lookouts boat hooks, paddles, or poles to enable them to leverage the boat away from obstructions under the surface.

If the water's reasonably clear, the lookouts should watch for any obstructions under the surface, and the boat should move as slowly as possible until the water is deep enough.

If the water is murky, either use electronic depth-sounding equipment, such as depth or fish finder, or use a rope with a weight attached to it. Repeatedly throw the rope out, letting the weight sink to the bottom, and recover it. Be careful not to run over the line and entangle it in the propeller.

These methods are equally important for all types of boats. However, on small boats lift retractable centerboards and rudders out of the way as an extra precaution.

Watching the Wind

Judging wind direction is fairly obvious. You can generally feel which way the wind is blowing. Alternatively, watch for wave ripples and water spray, nearby flags or windsocks, or smoke from a funnel or chimney in the distance.

If you're having trouble figuring out the wind direction, watch the birds. They always know the wind direction and will land and stand facing into the wind.

The best conditions are when the wind or current is gently pushing the vessel away from the shore. Start the motor and let it idle to warm. Cast off all lines except the stern spring line, which you must simultaneously pay some slack. By releasing all lines, the boat will move off the dock ahead of the wind, but the slackened stern spring will come up tight and exaggerate the bow's rotation away from the dock and ideally set you up for getting underway in a single smooth move. The reason you give slack to the stern line is because, unlike the way a car moves, a boat's pivot allows it to rotate and damage itself on the wharf. Once you're clear of the wharf and away from obstructions, recover the fenders, shift the transmission drive into forward gear, and then depart at idling speed.

It's a little more complex when the wind is holding you onto the dock, so you'll need a little more planning, but it's essentially the same maneuver in reverse. This time, cast off all lines except an after bow spring line. The bow spring will keep you from going ahead, yet casting off all other lines allows the stern to pivot out and away from the dock. Having a forward fender in place to protect the bow from the dock is good insurance.

Here comes the really important part. Turn the rudder or outboard motor so that it thrusts against the shore. This causes the stern to be pushed away from the dock. Shift into forward gear. This procedure needs to be done at idle speed and as slowly as possible. The stern will swing away from the dock. Keep your eye on the bow to ensure that it doesn't pivot around and crunch into the wharf. Once you've got a clear way to stern that is free of all obstacles and traffic, cast off the spring line and gently back to wind away from the dock. Once safely away from the dock, engage forward gear and idle away from the dock.

Deciphering the Currents

Currents may be a little more difficult to judge, but by spending a few minutes observing the direction in which flotsam or drifting debris is moving, you can get a reasonable idea of local current direction and speed. Do note that, because currents are greatly affected by local topography and obstructions, you need to consider the entire course and note how the currents in various regions are causing debris to float.

A good indicator for current direction is boats at anchor. They are usually anchored from their bows, making their stern trail down the current with the bow point up the current.

FIGURE 7-13:
Undocking

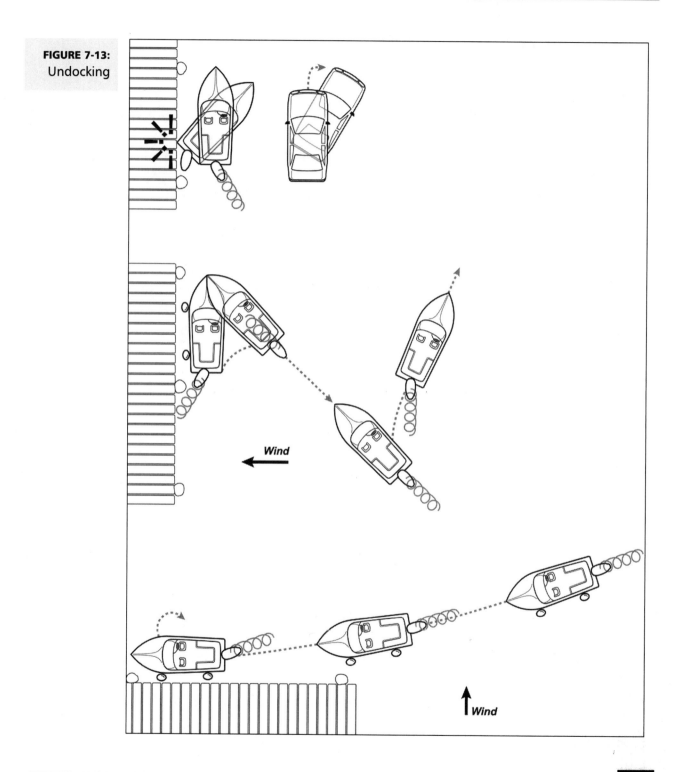

Wind

Wind

Getting Underway

Once you've undocked, immediately recover and stow all lines and fenders to eliminate tripping hazards. Be sure to control your speed in the marina and while leaving the harbor. Stay well alert for other boats, swimmers, or floating and submerged obstacles and debris. Rope, sacking, and plastic bags are a scourge in the harbor. They foul up your propeller and drive shaft and block your water-cooling system's intake. Keep an eye open for them and either have a crew member scoop them up with a boat hook or at the very least avoid them.

Always make sure to turn off all AC breakers onboard and then immediately disconnect the power cord from the dock before coiling. Do not undo the power cord from the boat and carry it off; you may slip and land with a live wire in the water.

CHAPTER 8
Handling Your Boat

O f all the skills, we've found that handling your boat while moving is one of the most difficult to write about because it's really something you learn by actually doing. A tremendous number of hands-on nuances and moment-by-moment observations add polish to the basic principles we list in this chapter.

Safely Maneuvering Your Boat

As the head honcho aboard, you have a tremendous obligation and responsibility toward your crew and all other people or things that your boat might encounter. Lives are quite literally in your hands, and you will be solely accountable for all and any personal or property damage that might occur.

First of all, you'll want to become familiar with the handling characteristics of your boat. Know how it responds to the controls at your fingertips. Understand its turning circle—both to port and starboard—its idling speed, its cruising speed, its top speed, its reverse speed under power, and how quickly you can reverse halt and reverse the direction of your travel. To do so, get out into open water and pick up a reference point, such as a piece of floating debris that would not cause damage in the event you blow it and have a collision.

In addition, diligently study the charts for any area you might visit and pick your course with care, avoiding any risks that might endanger souls or property. In the event of an emergency, the most vital answer you'll have to give rescuers is where you are. Therefore, know your precise location at all times and keep a constant lookout for unexpected dangers that suddenly loom in your vicinity. Use landmarks, navigational aides, and any other means possible to keep a running point of reference as to your progress.

FACTS

Handle your boat responsibly. Never take risks that could endanger you or your crew. Make sure to choose a safe course. Always know where you are. Always watch the weather carefully. Always follow the rules of the road. Know your boat and how it maneuvers in different conditions. Always render assistance to other boaters in distress or danger.

Before you leave the safety of the mooring area, everyone aboard should have checked the fit and condition of his or her lifejacket and stowed it where it can be retrieved in an instant. Also, check the function of all peripheral equipment, such as whistles, lights, and clips. Once you're sailing free but not yet exposed to extreme dangers, ensure that lifelines are properly secured with enough length and play to make them function as they should.

The sea has many moods and can change them without warning. Watch out for changes in wind, weather, and current, as well as the buildup of cloud and mist. Understand how these will affect your course heading, destination arrival time, and ability to maintain a visual picture of your immediate and extended environment.

Beyond abiding by the immediate laws of any given area, such as speed limits and off-limits areas, be courteous and handle your boat defensively. Assume that any other persons potentially in your path really don't know what they're doing and will probably make mistakes, so give them a wide berth and control your speed.

You should also do the following:

- Systematically test all the sails and understand what combinations work best under different circumstances. Also, make sure that your reefing lines are sufficient.
- Purposefully make limited mistakes under controlled conditions to understand where the limits of your boat are and see what degree of compensation and margin for error exists.
- Conduct man-overboard trials and practice retrieval. In doing so, become intimately familiar with your safety and recovery equipment and again make limited errors to develop methods of overcoming potential glitches.
- Drop anchor in a safe area to check whether the anchor equipment and recovery system is in good condition and properly stowed.

In addition, whenever you're handling halyards, you should make sure that both ends of the halyard are in your hands, or that one end is securely attached and the other is in your hand, or that both ends are securely attached to something. If you don't apply these rules, it's likely that one end of the halyard will fly to the top of the mast, which will cause one of the crew to follow it up in order to bring it back down.

Likewise, winch handles can be nasty things to lose or abuse, especially when you factor in their cost. Winch handles left unattended in a winch or loose on deck can suddenly be lurched overboard by a sudden wave or a kick of the foot, or they can snag or trip passersby and cause them to stumble, fall, or tumble overboard. Always ensure that the handle is in your hand, or it's in the winch and in your hand, or it's safely stowed in its proper location.

And here's something else you may not have thought about: When you're at the helm, never sail where you see birds wading, where you see waves building or breaking, or where you see kelp bobbing. Why? It's shallow.

Keeping Station

Station keeping is the ability to hold your position in the water without moving in any direction relative to the land or some other object. It's piloting your vessel *at* a location as opposed *to* a location.

We believe that holding station is fundamental to good seamanship, and to safety, and is the cornerstone to learning to dock. This section might seem

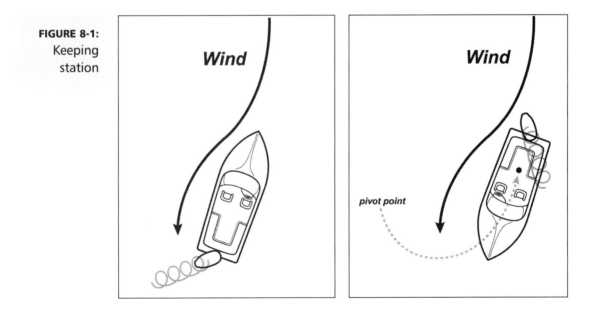

FIGURE 8-1:
Keeping station

extraordinarily long given that it seems like such a simple and insignificant part of sailing, but we believe that it's the best place to start when you want to learn how to control your vessel. Though holding on station is actually a fairly advanced skill when done properly, it's not intimidating or dangerous—just frustrating. It's also the very best way to familiarize yourself with your boat's slow speed-handling characteristics, which becomes crucial when you move on to the docking portion of this section.

Why You Need to Keep Station

You may wonder why it's important to stay in one spot. During your sailing career, any number of situations can and will present themselves that require you to hold station. Commonly, you'll need to wait for someone else to clear a slip or for other boats to get out of your way before you proceed along the next leg through the marina to or from your dock. You may need to stop and talk to someone on shore or another vessel. You may need to hold station as you edge in to embark or disembark passengers and cargo from land or another vessel. You may be involved in a search and rescue, in which case there are many times when the helmsman's job is just to hold still—often this might be in a storm, at night, near reefs and other vessels, and with the victims, the rescuers, and debris in the water and exposed to your propeller and bow.

Even if the conditions are extremely calm, remember that you are still legally considered to be underway when you're keeping station and are therefore responsible for the handling of your boat. Keep a close watch all about you and be prepared to get moving promptly should circumstances change and require you to do so. Bear in mind that a boat that appears to be motionless on a second-by-second scale may still stray quite far off course on a minute-by-minute scale. The rule here is to stay on the helm with the engine running.

Holding station well is a trick that requires quite a bit of experience, but it's one well worth learning. You need good reflexes and a degree of anticipation or instinct for what might happen next so that you can compensate for it before it's on you and overwhelming your every effort to make amends.

How to Keep Station

With just a little breeze or current, keeping station is much more difficult than it seems. To practice, you'll want to find a nonthreatening marker in open water away from other traffic. A small buoy on a light anchor will usually do the trick.

When the conditions are too active to keep station, you can begin to make small circles or figure eights. If conditions deteriorate or you don't have enough room to maneuver even slowly, then you should consider getting the heck out of the area and to safer conditions with all haste.

ALERT

In some cases, fuel conservation may be a high priority. No matter what, though, it's a cost-efficient and environmentally friendly thing to be aware of. Here are a few tips to help you conserve fuel:

- Keep your engine well maintained.
- Make sure that you are using the correct propeller.
- Use an engine that fits your boat.
- Make sure to use the proper mix of oil for your motor.
- Keep the hull clean.

The first major rule is to align the boat bow up into the wind and/or current. Of course, currents and wind don't always cooperate, and you'll be forced to make a compromise that "feels" right. The reason for aligning into the current or wind is that these forces tend to push the boat sideways, making it yaw as it goes broadside before the force. Because boats only have propulsion fore and aft, the only way to control the hull is to keep the main force that is trying to move you coming onto your bow so that you can match it by powering forward into it.

Wind, in particular, will tend to push your bow off to one side or the other. The trouble is, if the force manages to move the bow off center, then you expose the entire side of the hull to the oncoming force, and the situation rapidly deteriorates as the boat begins to move laterally or sideways. So, constantly making the most minute adjustments is vital.

Just imagine that you can view the situation from directly overhead. You're holding station with your bow directly into the wind, and then the wind starts forcing you off to starboard in a clockwise direction. The boat now is not only being pushed astern but also fully to starboard. As you apply forward propulsion and steer to port, at first, the thrust of the propeller's discharge current *also* pushes the boat farther to starboard, exaggerating the problem.

The best thing you can do to keep station is to pay attention and catch any yawing early. With practice, you will be able to hold your boat almost directly into the wind for as long you care to. It may, however, require a lot of concentration until it becomes second nature. You'll also need to remain in gear, occasionally applying forward thrust. The trick now is to balance the tendency of the oncoming force—either the wind or current—to turn your vessel with sufficient power to provide your rudder with traction and ability to turn the boat, yet not apply so much thrust that you make headway. The exercise is, after all, to keep station.

Trying to hold position by alternating between forward and reverse thrusts complicates the matter because steering in reverse adds a whole new layer of complexity to the equation. And, if there is any appreciable wind, the dynamics become almost too complex to explain. This is why we suggest that it is sometimes better to circle back to position once you have come too far off the mark.

An Alternative

There is an alternative to the techniques discussed, and that is to go *stern* to wind. Given the right boat, steering may actually be easier stern to wind. However, in many boats, steering in reverse gear can be a real bear. Smaller boats with outboard engines might find this technique possible. Also, consider that propellers are designed to thrust forward, and so tend to have much less thrust in reverse. This can be something of a disadvantage in rough weather, but it can be most useful in lighter winds when the forward thrust of the boat in forward gear would be too great.

The other advantage to reversing to wind or current is that, when reversing, the propeller thrust pulls the boat into its maneuver rather than pushing it. Thus, the vessel's pivot point moves to aft. What this aft-displaced pivot point does is create a weathervane situation in which the bow tends to find its own equilibrium in the wind. The wind's yawing force will be mitigated to some extent by the same principles that cause a weathervane's longer trailing end to point downwind. It's the difference between balancing a stick vertically on your finger or hanging it down between your fingers.

How you hold station is a matter of preference, but we do suggest that you do your best to master both methods. They both are the foundation for smooth undocking and docking. There is much more to know than can possibly be presented here, so consider purchasing *Boat Docking, Close Quarters Maneuvering for Small Craft,* by Charles T. Low.

Maneuvering at Close Quarters

We sail to be away from it all—away from strangers, land, and the bustle of life. However, there is simply no way around the fact that sailing starts, ends, and often includes threading our way through other boats, obstructions, channels, and natural or legal obstacles. When you plot it all on a timeline, depending on where you live and the type of sailing you do, you'll find that the average sailor is contending with close quarters techniques for a very large percentage of the time. It therefore makes sense to learn the techniques and make it as enjoyable and stress free as possible.

Even if crowded sailing conditions are not an issue in your case, the fundamentals still must be mastered because encountering obstructions and traffic are ultimately inevitable and a single silly but avoidable mistake will spoil your whole day—or worse!

When you're entering a narrow waterway or harbor, try to establish whether any other vessels are making their way through the narrows. Watch for masts that are moving and try to judge their speed and direction.

In reverse gear, the majority of boats tend to crab to port due to the asymmetry of propeller thrust. Those that don't crab to port will crab to starboard. You'll hear sailors talk about the stern "walking." By becoming aware of your boat's tendency, you can put it to good use. When you know you're going to have to use reverse, compensate for the walk with a little extra space between you and obstructions or let the walk help you exaggerate a turn.

A little time on the water will give you the feel of how your boat responds to the various controls. With practice on holding station behind you, you'll be much more comfortable when it comes time to dock.

FACTS

If you're sailing in clear water and would like to determine your distance from the horizon, use the following formula: The distance from the horizon = 1.17 × the square root of the height above the sea in feet.

Navigating Locks

A lock is a section of a waterway, such as a canal, that is closed off with gates. In a lock, vessels in transit are raised or lowered by raising or lowering the water level of that section. Locks are used to move boats between bodies of water that have different levels of elevation. Naturally, you're not going to encounter locks at sea level—unless you're going through the Panama Canal, in which case the difference in water height is due to the two oceans experiencing rising and falling tides that are interrupted by the American continents.

As you approach a lock, you need to contact the lockmaster via VHF radio. The channel the lockmaster monitors may vary from area to area, but there should be a sign posted at the entrance of the lock with specific instructions for how to contact the lockmaster.

Use caution as you approach the lock and pay attention to the traffic signal at the lock entrance. If the signal is red, you should stay well clear and keep an eye out for boats exiting the lock. Once the gates to the lock entrance are fully open and all traffic has vacated the lock, the signal will turn green, indicating that it's safe to enter the lock.

Prior to making your entrance, you need to rig fenders on both sides of your vessel. Although many locks have lines available at predetermined locations, you should have your own lines prepared and ready fore and aft in the event that you need them.

After you enter the lock, the lockmaster will give you specific instructions and may drop lines to you. Once you have secured, you should cut your engine and radar.

QUESTIONS?

Have you ever wondered how you're supposed to know which bank is which?
Here's a little tip for you: When you're sailing down a river, the left bank is the bank to the left of a person looking downstream.

Once all boats are secured in the lock, the lock gate you've just entered is closed, and the gate at the other end of the lock is opened slightly to allow water to either flow in or out of the lock you're in—and so raise or lower your vessel to a new height. As the water level rises (or falls), the crew members manning the lines on the bow and stern will have to take up the slack (or pay out slack) to keep the boat stable and in the correct position. The inrush or outflow of water will cause some turbulence, and you're likely to experience the wash of current shoving the boat. So long as your fenders are in place and secure and your rub rail is not sliding up the side of the lock, the surge will do no harm.

Once at the new level, the exit gates open completely and you can start your engine. After you've cast off the lines, follow the direction of the lockmaster and exit the lock slowly. Be aware of boat traffic waiting to enter the lock from the other side. When you are finally clear and underway, take in and stow the fenders.

Going Through Estuaries

Moon- and sun-induced bumps aside, water always tries to find its natural vertical equilibrium. Naturally, because the water must physically flow in to flood the furthermost areas, it must make its way up from the opening to the sea. This has two effects. If the opening to the sea is narrow and the waterway inland is extensive, the volume of water passing in and out will be great and powerful, making it a dangerous place to navigate or linger.

When measured at the mouth and at the furthermost reaches simultaneously, there can be a significant lag between high and low tide extremes, with the high only reaching inland and emptying to full low long after the adjacent ocean and mouth experience their extreme. Local publications and sources would generally inform you of the specifics of each region.

Trimming Your Boat

Trimming your boat refers to the relative balance of the boat within the water and the consequent shape that it offers the water rushing toward it. To trim a boat, you therefore redistribute this angle by moving ballast or by trimming the sails or adding hydrofoils. Because simple body weight adjustments make a big difference, trimming will both be more noticeable and easily adjustable on smaller boats. Regardless of this fact, the point needs to be made that the greatest resistance your boat comes up against is the water rushing toward it.

ESSENTIALS You're cruising along and suddenly see an appealing spot to beach your boat. What do you do? Approach the shore slowly. Lift the centerboard carefully and gradually as the water becomes shallow. When you touch bottom, let the sheets fly, get out of the boat with the bow line, and haul it to shore. Do also drop the sails.

The water drag that affects the hull is often difficult to detect, but there are ways to find and reduce it. With more weight in the stern, the bow obviously rises as the stern falls, and large swirls will begin to form in your wake. These are not good. They tell you the same thing that leech telltales would tell you—the hull is dragging through the water and the water is not flowing in an even pattern under it. To solve the problem, try to get some weight toward the front or mechanically alter the boat's dynamics so that the stern is allowed to rise.

Also, take a look at your wake. The bigger and more turbulent your wake, the more water you're disturbing—and disturbing water costs precious energy that should be spent in forward motion. An oversized wake may be the result of your hull's shape, your load distribution, or your boat's displacement (mass). Try to do whatever you can to reduce the size of your wake.

Heeling in the Beam

Heeling over to the side is fun, but it's not necessarily the most efficient way to sail. Your quest is to keep the boat as flat as possible—as though it's at rest. You need to keep your keel as deep as possible in order to stop yourself from slipping sideways through the water. Using boats with a removable centerboard, you can demonstrate this quite easily by rigging them similarly and then simply lifting one boat's board halfway out. The one with the deeper keel will certainly be quicker.

Of course, if you consider two extremes, you'll have another clear picture of why you'd want to flatten the boat. With the mast vertical, it presents the largest possible area to the wind. If you were to push the boat right over so that the mast lay parallel with the water, absolutely no wind would be in the sails. It follows that you need as vertical a mast as possible in order to grab a bunch of wind.

Of course, if a gust does strike, the boat will naturally heel. The onus is then on the skipper to spill sufficient wind to bring the mast back to an optimum pitch.

On the other hand, if you hauled down all of your sails, the boat would sit quite nicely on the water's surface, but it wouldn't go to any destination. The balance between boat heeling and maximum efficiency is a delicate one.

Judging the Edge

Keep in mind that wind doesn't always blow evenly with uniform strength, and there will be times when you need to know that a gust is about to hit you. Experienced sailors know precisely the moment that such a squall will hit and are able to take appropriate action at the critical moment. They might tell you it's like voodoo that they can't explain. Though the feeling gives them a critical advantage in both the departments of safety and competitiveness, they're not necessarily holding out on you. It's just that they've been doing it so long that they've forgotten the intricacies.

ALERT

Weather changes don't have to take you by surprise. Watch for these signs of changing weather:

- A sudden change in the wind and drop in temperature
- Rapid vertically rising clouds and other cloud buildup
- A rapid drop in the barometric pressure
- Any weather changes in the west

Those little telltales on your sail will offer you a lot of feedback on precisely what is happening to the wind high above the water's surface. By diligently watching the telltales, you'll see the wind's gust before you feel its response through the boat heeling or surging. Eventually, with hundreds and thousands of hours on the water, you'll barely need to use your eyes anymore; you'll begin to hear the change and sense it a moment before it hits.

In light winds, this is important if you're looking to eke the last ounce of energy out of every wind breath. In heavy weather, sudden gusts can be devastating to life and limb and rip your rigging to pieces.

When you react, keep in mind that you're trying to maintain an even speed through the water. When the gust hits, you'll want to make the most out of it while not running risks. React to the blast's strength by swinging your bow upwind, maintaining that course as long as the blast continues, and then bearing off as the blast diminishes.

In light conditions, you'll maintain the same speed but gain a little extra ground against the wind. In heavy weather, you'll instantly spill the surplus power from the sail while maintaining your speed. In dangerous situations, you can supplement this action by sheeting out and loosing the draft from your sail.

Using Wind and Sails to Steer Your Boat

If you take a look at a sailboard, you'll notice that there's no rudder for steering. Of course, there's a fin, but that serves the same purpose as the keel or centerboard—it's a pivot. In order to turn the boat, you need to use your weight displacement and the power of the wind in your sails. On larger boats, it's a little difficult to significantly shift weight efficiently enough to steer the entire vessel, but the principle of using sail power is a possibility.

When you think about it, your rudder turns the boat by dragging at an awkward angle through the water. Of course, anything dragged through the water costs you precious energy and forward motion. So it follows that the less you can steer by dragging and the more you can steer by applying productive power, the better.

Using the Wind

The more you shift the wind's center of effort ahead of the boat's keel or pivot, the more the boat will want to point downwind. Conversely, the more you slack off on sail power fore and apply sail power aft, the more the boat will pivot and bring its bow up to windward.

The bigger the boat, the more complex constant adjustments become, but it is important to set the sails appropriately so that your average rudder compensation is brought to an absolute minimum.

Sailing Without a Rudder

You may be able to actually sail a small boat without the need of a rudder. If you want to practice, try the following steps. Keep in mind that you should only attempt these steps if you have plenty of sailing experience and are prepared to make mistakes that could capsize you.

1. Pick a day with light-to-moderate wind.
2. Get out into clear and open water with no chance of dinging anything or anyone.
3. Remove the rudder completely.
4. Get the boat moving on a beam reach.

5. To head up, trim the main, ease the jib, and heel the boat to leeward.
6. To bear off, trim the jib, ease the main, and heel the boat to windward.

To see just how successful this technique is, arrange to sail alongside someone with a similar rig who is not using the technique. Besides the competition's making a better sailor of you, you'll have a point of reference to see precisely how to make improvements to your technique.

Tacking

Tacking is the act of changing from one position or direction to another. If you've ever watched auto racing, you've noticed that cornering is where races are won or lost and that the cars that consistently pick the best line into the corner make fewer mistakes and come out of the corner at higher speeds than those who have not set themselves up correctly. You've probably felt these same dynamics at work as you drive your own car around corners. Because tacking is essentially the same maneuver as cornering, similar dynamics are at work. As such, tacking is a vital transition where ground and momentum can either be gained or lost very quickly if your approach is not correct.

Again, tacking is an area in which experience will be your best teacher. Experimenting with making your tacks long and smooth or fast and choppy will give you an idea of the most appropriate decision under each condition and for your vessel.

One of the keys to tacking is to maintain momentum throughout the maneuver. Obviously, because the wind direction will remain constant and your relative sail position will be altering, there will be a period when you are actually decelerating, and you'll need to shift your momentum through the eye of the tack where your boat will momentarily run the risk of being in irons. The less momentum you have coming into the tack, the more you allow your rudder to drag through the water. The longer you remain on an upwind heading, the more risk you'll have of actualizing an in-irons condition.

FIGURE 8-2:
Tacking to
sail upwind

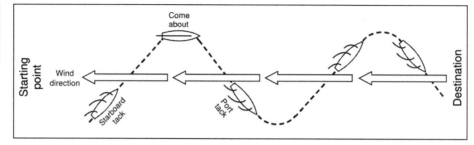

On the other extreme, if you jam your boat through the tack, apart from jarring your crew, turning the swinging boom into a violently swinging weapon, and placing excessive strain on your entire rig, you'll also decelerate very suddenly—and then face the prospect of a delayed acceleration on your new heading.

Going into the tack, you have a given speed. Coming through the tack you decelerate, and coming out onto the other heading you will logically be traveling relatively slower—or practically stalled. Again, as with a cornering car coming through a sharp bend, you'll have to shift gears in order to accelerate back to cruising speed. Sure, you could remain in top gear and eventually get to top speed, but this would hardly be an optimum way of doing so.

Various methods of tacking will suit every vessel, its sail configuration, and circumstance. The only way to be proficient in all of these circumstances is to practice them by placing yourself in each situation. However, do remember to communicate what your intentions are with your crew before executing them, or you may well inadvertently find yourself conducting a search-and-rescue mission to tend to bruised, bumped, and man-overboard situations. Also, do ensure that these maneuvers take place well away from anyone or anything that could pose potential hazards.

Finally, remember that tacking can also be a dangerous technique. As you come about, the windward and leeward sides of the sail suddenly switch. The result is that the sail suddenly fills with wind coming from the opposite side and hundreds or even thousands of pounds of sail-filled power suddenly swings the solid boom through an arc defined by the mast. Because the boom is often at head height, if the skipper fails to warn passengers and crew to keep heads down, the boom will give someone a smack they won't forget in a hurry.

Anchoring

Besides those all-important slumbers in the sun when you leisurely sip your *non*alcoholic beverage or lazily haul hungry fish aboard, you may also need to drop anchor in order to control the boat when hostile circumstances threaten. Consider onshore gales, or engine or steering failure. Under these circumstances you've got to maintain your position and keep your bow up into any oncoming bad weather or waves. Again, it is only practice that can ensure smooth operation under the stress of emergency.

The first consideration is selecting an appropriate anchor for the task at hand. To the uninitiated, it comes as a surprise that all anchors are not made equal. The selection depends on a host of circumstances, but the most important are the size of the boat and the ocean floor's terrain at any given location.

Types of Anchors

Sure, a rock tied to a line would be a better anchor than nothing at all, but the size rock required to hold even a small craft wouldn't be a welcome passenger. Good anchor function has a lot less to do with the weight of the anchor than its shape. The anchor works because it holds onto the terrain. If you wanted to hold all the sand you could fit in your hand, you wouldn't spread your fingers. But to hold many larger stones, you'd spread your fingers as far apart as possible to pile more on. Because the anchor is essentially doing this same job on the bottom of the ocean, it needs to be suited to either rock or sand.

Commonly, anchors consist of a shaft with a movable crosspiece (the stock) at its top end and two curved arms ending in spadelike points (the flukes) at its bottom end. Alternatively, the arms are more bucket-shaped and designed to grab a sandy floor. The three most common anchors you'll encounter are flukes, danforths, and mushrooms.

It's unlikely then that you'll have just one anchor aboard. The more variety you have at your disposal to cover every eventuality, the better off you'll be. Once you've arrived at your chosen destination, try to get an idea of what kind of topography your anchor will be landing on and put down the appropriate design.

Retrieval Systems

Almost as important as having an anchor hold your position is the ability to retrieve it at will. To do so, you'll obviously need to attach the anchor with a sufficiently strong line or chain, or a combination of both. Taken together, the anchor setup, including line and chain, is called ground tackle.

However, anchors sometimes stick fast in rock crevices, and cutting the line is not always the smart option. Specifically, for this reason, most anchors are cunningly designed with a sacrificial break-loose option. When the anchor is jammed and you put enough pressure on it, the sacrificial clasp breaks free, and the leverage of the anchor rope's pull is transferred to a different angle on the anchor unit. Under most conditions, this allows the obstruction to be circumvented and the disabled anchor to be retrieved and then reset to its functional configuration.

Scope

The amount of rope you allow overboard when at anchor is called the scope. The amount of scope depends on water depth and weather conditions. The deeper the water and the more severe the weather becomes, the more scope you allow.

First of all, measure the water depth. Under normal conditions, for normal recreation, you'll allow the scope to be at least five times the depth. However, if you decide to stay overnight, build in that little margin of error and bring the scope up to eight times the depth. Don't forget to add the distance your bow cleat is from the water surface to the depth before making your calculation.

An important observation to make is that the anchor might well drag a distance before it catches and holds fast, so you'll certainly need to build in a margin of error. After you've dropped the anchor, keep an eye on a few markers to establish how long you drift before the anchor sets and you begin to hold your position.

At this stationary position, you need to understand another important concept. Consider the fact that, because the boat can now swing in an arc around the point that the anchor grips, you need a margin of error that allows you a sizable radius so that you can swing around the anchor pivot. Take a good look around and estimate what objects your arc could intersect if the wind or current shifts. Also, if and when you do swing, the boat will pull on the anchor from a different position, and this may loosen the anchor and allow it to slide another distance before it finds a new hold. Don't forget to take this possibility into account.

However, when mooring near other similarly moored boats, understand that the same tide and wind factors will allow them to swing in their own arc. You'll all be doing so in unison, so the relative distances between you should remain the same unless they have more scope or either their anchor or your anchor drags excessively.

Steps to a Smooth Anchoring

These steps are probably obvious to a smart skipper like you, but you'll want to give them a glance anyway.

- Select a venue that will offer you the maximum shelter from current, wind, and boat traffic.
- Don't be shy about asking other boats at anchor how much scope they've allowed, what kind of anchor they dropped (if it isn't plainly obvious what terrain you're over), and how well their anchor is sitting.
- Take a look at whether other boats are anchored bow and stern or only at the bow and then anchor in the same manner.
- Before dropping anchor, ensure that all shackles, fixtures, and fittings are in good condition and within operational specification.
- Neatly lay the total amount of anchor rope you'll need on the deck so it can run smoothly overboard without tangling or snarling objects or people.

- If you don't want to make a chump out of yourself, before you drop anchor, remember to secure the rope at the point you intend it to hold.

- Bring the boat to a position just upwind or upcurrent of the spot you intend the anchor to find its hold, keeping the bow into the wind or current.

- Lower the anchor in a controlled fashion until it touches the ground and the rope begins to slacken. Then, use the motor to gently back away from that position until all of the predetermined rope is overboard. Allow the motor to gently drag the anchor until you feel it has bitten. With someone's hand on the rope, this will be easy to feel as the submerged unit bumps into an obstacle. At this point, don't let the prop foul the rope in the water.

- From time to time, check your bearings and ensure that the anchor hasn't dragged. However, do keep in mind, and make compensation for the fact that your bearings will change as a result of current and wind shifts altering your relative position to the anchor. This is not just your duty, but everyone's aboard, so make them aware of this fact and tell them to communicate with you if they assess any danger at all. (Never show irritation with false alarms; they're a lot less expensive than silent mistakes.)

- When it's time to retrieve the anchor, reverse the procedure and gently use the motor to ride forward and help you recover rope slack. Put the motor into neutral when the rope hangs vertically from the bow. Recleat the line at this point and then gently ride forward once more under motor power. That way, you're using the boat's own force to free the anchor. Apart from saving on blistered hands, it will also save your crew from being dragged overboard or having extremities injured if the rise of the swell pulls their wayward appendages into rigging.

- Once free, bring the engine to neutral and recover the anchor, coiling the line in a neat fashion. With the anchor at the water surface, you can clean it, if necessary. Only stow the line after it has dried.

CHAPTER 9

Docking Your Boat

Docking is to sailing what putting is to golf. There is little point in mastering all of the blue-yonder techniques if you can't finish the day with a deft and safe touch. In this chapter, we cover all of the most important docking tactics in the most common conditions you're likely to encounter.

Practice Pays Off

Ideally, you've practiced docking in private before you attempt it publicly for the first time. We're not getting weird on you, but this is a really important issue. Nobody likes making mistakes, but we all like it a lot less when there's an audience.

And don't think that you won't have an audience. Marinas and docks are favorite haunts for rubberneckers. As you enter the enclosure, you'll feel their eyes on you, watching as you burble by. It will feel as though everyone's watching you. The downside is that they certainly will be if you start crashing into things, so it's a really good idea to get a little practice out of the public eye.

To practice, find a backwater somewhere, a venue or various venues that provide all of the possible tide and wind variables you're likely to encounter. That way, you can make mistakes to your heart's content—in front of your eyes only.

Stowing the Sails

Stowing your sails—technically called mooring your boat—is the first task you'll need to tackle when you're ready to put your boat away. It's a smart idea to have the sails already stowed before you enter the mooring area because sudden gusts and confined spaces are not the best of bedfellows for a yachtsman.

To stow your sails:

1. Loosen the sheets, vang, cunningham, and halyard.
2. Remove the sails by reversing the procedure you used to put them up.
3. Properly fold the sails and stow the lines.
4. Remove the halyards, raise the boom, and coil all other lines that are not the lines you'll be using in the mooring procedure.

Don't overlook routine maintenance. If you see any cracks or bulging at the bottom of load areas, have someone take a closer look. These signs could indicate trouble. To prolong the life of your bungee cords, apply sunblock to them. (Yes, sunblock!) If you would like clean and soft lines, soak them in fabric softener and then rinse and dry them.

Creating a Docking Plan

As if you hadn't guessed, besides being a heck of a lot more fun, sailing's a little more complex than driving a car. It's more like flying a plane, where landings are everything. In this instance, landfalls are vital. But first, there are a few preparations you have to make before you arrive at your final destination.

Before approaching the dock, reduce your speed. Then, you need to consider the conditions under which you will dock and understand which approach you will use. Identify each of the lines you will be using and lay them out so that they're not obstructed and can quickly be employed. Ensure that one end of each docking line is secured to the boat. Next, get the fenders into position.

ESSENTIALS

Whenever you unload your boat, do it away from the ramp. Back your trailer into the water without submerging your tires. Then attach the bow line and shut off the engine prior to raising it. Next, winch the boat and secure it. Don't forget to clean up out of the ramp area and also to allow water to drain from the bilge.

Finally, brief the crew and passengers by giving them specific instructions on how you will make the approach and what you expect of each of them. If conditions are difficult or your crew and passengers are inexperienced, quiz each one of them to make sure that they really understand what they must do and the implications of how to do it and what to do if things go wrong. Then you're ready to dock.

Never connect a dock water supply to the pressure side of the water system on your boat. All it would take is a flexible section to rupture, and you will have a boat that's full of water and headed straight to the bottom.

The Ideal Docking: Port to Shore

Provided that you've got the room to maneuver, the ideal way to bring a boat alongside the dock is to approach at an angle and come alongside with either your port or starboard side up against the dock. This approach allows you to accurately aim the boat for a particular spot, and you are less likely to scrape the dock as you bring the boat in.

FIGURE 9-1(a):
Portside to docking dissected

FIGURE 9-1(b):
Coasting and the power turn to keep up the momentum

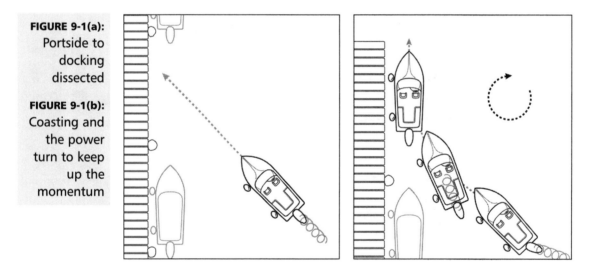

It makes sense that the sharpest turns are more easily made when the boat is going as slow as possible, because it will slip less widely through the turn. Yet to maneuver the turn accurately you need some power. The challenge is to reconcile these conflicting demands (more power for steering ability, less power to slow the boat down) by using power intermittently and in short bursts with enough vigor to successfully maneuver the boat into docking position.

Your Second Choice: Bow to Shore

Now that you're an expert in holding position, the other alternative for a safe, though less elegant, docking procedure is to disembark crew hands onto the harbor wharf and let them manually bring the stern in and tie it off. In some situations, there may be little else you can do than adopt this solution, whereas in others—such as strong offshore winds—it might be just this side of impossible to pull the stern around into the wind to tie it off.

Docking in Difficult Conditions

Sometimes docking is easier to do than at other times. When the conditions are difficult, don't become stubborn, reckless, or hasty about fine technique—especially when you're just learning or conditions are adverse. Take the simplest route you can and the one you are most comfortable with. Remember that you can always return later and redock when conditions are better, or you have more hands on deck, or your fatigue allows you more latitude.

Remember that docking in windy conditions is probably one of the most challenging sailing techniques you'll have to master. The following sections describe just a few of the techniques you can use. As you practice, you'll make variations that suit your personal style, prevailing conditions, and boat handling peculiarities. Close quarter maneuvering and docking are inevitable necessities of sailing. Learn to love them and practice as often as you can.

Docking Stern to Shore

Much as docking bow first is the optimum way for beginners to learn, stern docking offers many advantages when it comes to coping with difficult conditions and minimizing danger to the rudder and propeller from submerged obstacles. Stern docking also makes loading and unloading cargo, passengers, and victuals into the cockpit area so much easier (see **FIGURE 9-2**).

FIGURE 9-2:
Docking
stern to shore

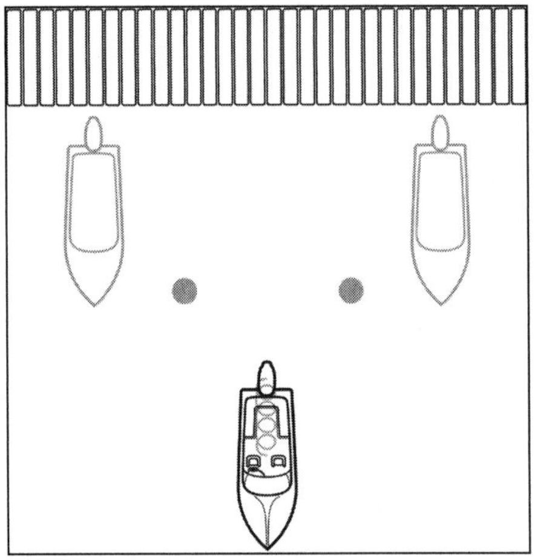

Poor steering and asymmetric propeller thrust are the chief culprits for making the stern-to maneuver so tough. One way to handle the crabbing of asymmetric thrust is sparing the use of the propeller. A short burst or reverse propeller will get the boat moving astern and give sufficient steerage to the rudder as the boat drifts backward. Try it out and see how your boat does. Not every boat reacts well. If you're fitted with an outboard, the fact that the propeller changes its orientation and pulls the boat on a new tack is very handy in reverse.

Another solution is to bring the stern part way in and then walk the boat or use lines to bring the boat into position.

Docking in a Quartering Wind

Docking in calm weather and docking in a quartering wind are two entirely different stories. A quartering wind is a wind that is running onto the dock at an angle off the shore. It's a beast to contend with, and it's nearly impossible to illustrate this in a diagram. Because things tend to happen at a different pace, the hull is crabbing sideways through the water, angles change to compensate for the wind's thrust. Power thrust and rudder angle must be applied in different ratios and for different durations, and margins for error tend to shrink. On paper, we simply can't show that much information without burying you in vector arrows and notations. The best thing we can do is to impart to you some level of appreciation for the design of hulls, the geometry of steering and propulsion forces, and how they combine in a confluence of linear vectors and momentums.

If you take a look at the diagram (**FIGURE 9-3**), you will see that the berth requires you to bring the starboard side of the boat alongside, with a starboard quartering wind pushing you across and onto the neighboring berth that already has a boat moored there. Assuming something of a strong wind, if your approach is wrong, you could quickly hash the job and put yourself in dire straits if you want to back out of the situation without doing damage.

FIGURE 9-3:
Boat
docking in a
quartering
wind

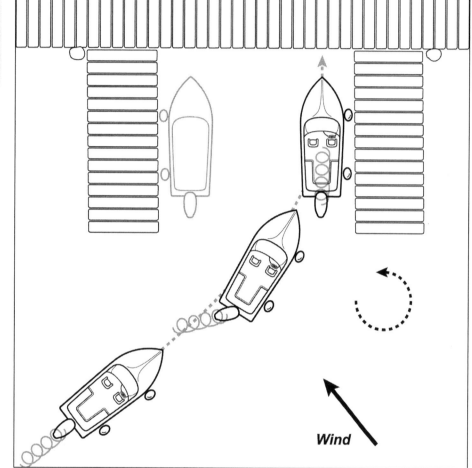

Wind

If the wind is quite strong and/or your boat tends to crab quickly, you'll have very little time to disembark the crew and have them secure lines ashore. Our first piece of advice is to circle around a few times to feel out the situation and prepare your crew with last-minute instructions. This advice is especially true if you're still something of a novice, haven't yet got the feel of your boat in similar conditions, are bringing it into an unfamiliar berth, your crew is inexperienced, or nobody is ashore to help with the mooring. You don't need to rush unless, of course, you're on fire or sinking. This circling about should give you a good idea of how steady or gusty the wind is, how it moves through this part of the harbor, and how your boat will react when you anticipate its wind drift, throttle back, and so lose some degree of steering.

Remember the lessons on momentum and taking firm control of the boat—well, now is the time you'll put them to good use. Be gentle but firm with your commitment to a course.

The idea now is to presteer—to take an appropriate angle of attack a few degrees upwind and let the wind's thrust correct you snugly into position. With the right angle and momentum, you'll be counterbalancing your momentum into the wind with the wind's breaking effect as it pushes you off the dock. No doubt you can visualize how, with a little experience, this is one of those maneuvers that can feel almost poetic as you execute it. Indeed, you can add a little flair by keeping the bow angle quite steep and then just touching off on the throttle to skid the stern in and fast to the land at the last moment.

Finally, it's much more elegant to clumsily manhandle the boat into position than to crash and crunch your way to a halt. Using lots of fenders, you can come alongside the moored boat or dock opposite your berth to your windward side. You can then send crew ashore with long lines to manually haul the boat across the strait and make it fast.

Docking Broadside to the Wind

Bringing the boat alongside when the wind is howling offshore also needs a deft hand. Fortunately, unless there are offshore anchorages or developments, this one at least allows a good margin for error.

To create a more interesting scenario, we've illustrated a diagram that doesn't allow for an easy run in to the mooring. You'd make a wide sweep and then bring the bow up and across the wind. Again, all that skill that you acquired when you practiced holding station that will come into play. It's back to the old challenge of getting sufficient momentum and anticipation to counteract the wind's force while bringing you in at a gentle coast.

FIGURE 9-4:
Docking
broadside to
the wind

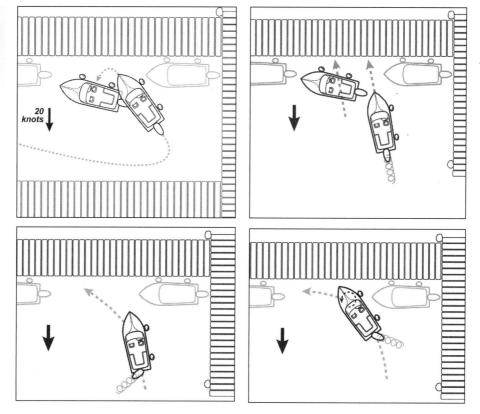

In the diagram (**FIGURE 9-4**), that funny little hook arrow indicates
what will happen if you don't nail the docking on the first run. The
diagrams that follow should help you to get around it.

One option is to bring the boat in much more to one side of the slip
than you would if there were no wind. You do this because you control
the boat by powering into your turn, which will move the boat forward in
the slip. The wide angle allows for this, keeping you in good position.

The preceding figure shows that the stronger the offshore wind, the
more perpendicular your approach to the dock will be, and the longer
you will delay your turn. As you've heard repeatedly, this maneuver
requires positive control of your helm. You'll find that the best approach
will be more radical angles on the rudder and shorter and sharper bursts
of the power. We're not saying that you should be reckless, but that you
need to be firm and smooth as always.

If you learn to master it, momentum is your best ally. Compare this technique to throwing a baseball: You wind up the momentum with your run into the dock and then give a firm thrust as you give wheel to your final turn. The gray arrows, in the diagram, show the momentum that you develop. The idea is to make it persist just long enough to touch the dock broadside.

We do have some trepidation giving advice that you should take charge of the helm with "positive control" and so on, so we hope you treat this advice with the due caution that it entails. It is certainly better to err on the side of caution: Approach the dock with a forthright attitude, but give yourself latitude to bear off or back up for a second approach if you see that you've made a misjudgment. All our insistence for you to be in control is simply to ensure that you are not timid with the maneuvers. If you took our advice and spent some time practicing holding station and coasting out in open water, then this will all come very quickly to you.

As a final note, don't let anyone rush you—not crew, passengers, other boaters, or marina staff. Naturally, you don't want to dither under the thrusting bows of a supertanker—even though the law states that "power gives way to sail"—but you'll likely never be preparing to dock directly from shipping and traffic lanes anyway, so let them wait. Most of all, don't let your ego rush you.

With some practice, you'll find that there is another philosophy that also works. Bring the boat up with its head into the wind and bring it almost to a stop just as it's about to touch land. As you come to a halt, the wind will begin to push the bow around.

A deft touch on the throttle will tend to push you back toward the shore. Let the wind turn you and constantly adjust your angle to the dock with small adjustments on the wheel and throttle. It's not the easiest skill, but it does work.

Once you have a working understanding of how this tactic works, try to blend the two—momentum and finesse. You commit just a little less momentum and gently nudge the boat alongside. It's a trick that comes with hands-on practice. It's also very frustrating because the bow will quickly blow away from the dock and this will be exaggerated if you're too vigorous in trying to push the stern toward the dock.

Docking in Close Quarters

The trick with docking is learning to coast to a halt. A good way to get the hang of it is to drop a light anchor and buoy and use it as a marker. If you can drop a line of three or more buoys, you can treat them as a dockside or wharf and get some really tremendous practice feeling how far away you can throttle back and coast to a halt at the chosen spot.

As you begin the approach, be very aware of the throttle setting and keep your hand on the throttle lever at all times. A calm and orderly approach will generally require minimum speed; even an idle might be too fast. The trouble is that the steering mechanism—normally a rudder—requires water moving over it in order to be effective. The less water that flows by, the less effect it will have on directional control. If the boat is equipped with an outboard motor, the problem is exaggerated because a turn depends on the direction that the propeller is thrusting relative to the boat's orientation, so when there is not thrust from the propeller, steering is almost nonexistent.

The answer is to intermittently use short gentle bursts of throttle to nudge the boat through the water. However, when the engine is in neutral and coasting, your ability to steer might be compromised, so the maneuver requires heightened concentration. The trick is to keep the boat tracking accurately toward a desired mooring point. If you feel that the boat is drifting off course, a little touch on the throttle will generally help you gain control.

Again, unless the boat has an outboard, the forward momentum acting on the rudder will be the primary means of steerage. Water, being a fluid medium, creates a situation in which the less the momentum, the greater the exaggeration of every turn. Once a boat begins to turn in a given direction, it will tend to continue in motion and keep turning in that direction even after the rudder is brought to a new bearing, unless there is sufficient thrust added to the equation (**FIGURE 9-5**).

This tendency can be confounding for novice skippers. The trick is discovering precisely what combination of momentum and rudder turn will give you a desired result. It's all about timing and figuring out what point to begin a turn and when to countersteer to slow the turn.

Another element is the use of reverse gear. If you're coming in too fast, the natural and usually appropriate action to take is to use reverse thrust to stop momentum. Of course, this action will also limit the ability to steer and eventually reverse the direction of steering when the vessel begins to move in the reverse direction.

You can often make a quick course alteration by swinging the wheel hard over to the desired direction and then giving a brief burst on the throttle. Trouble is, if you give too much power, even if you then shut down, that tendency to side-slip will cause the stern to keep side and there could be little you can do in confined spaces to halt the direction.

FIGURE 9-5:
Close quarter
maneuvering

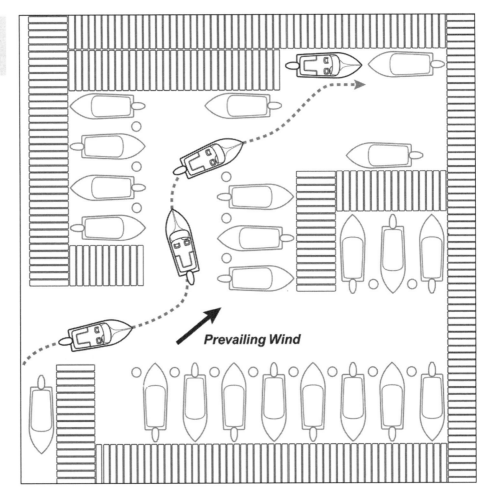

Prevailing Wind

Docking Around an Obstacle

From time to time, you'll encounter an obstacle between you and your tie-off point. Consider a situation where the marina staff asks you to move your boat around another boat and berth just beyond one that is already moored. To bring a level of complexity, imagine that a stiff breeze is blowing offshore. The moment you untie, the boat will be pushed sideways, away from the shore. What you need to do is keep the bow pointing upwind, but this task is a little more difficult than you might first realize.

As if to confound the situation, if you hold the rudder hard over to compensate for the wind's thrust and give too much power to give the rudder some leverage, the propeller's initial thrust will force you farther away from the dock and exaggerate your angle, sometimes making it near impossible to align yourself for docking. If this happens, the best thing you can do is back off into open water and make a new approach.

FIGURE 9-6: Maneuvering around an obstacle in the wind

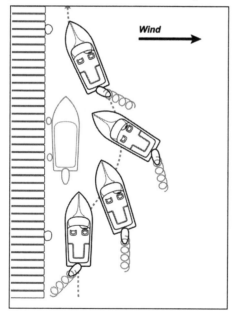

Wind

The trick for getting it right the first time is to be aware of where the bow of the boat is pointing. If you lose control of the bow and try to correct with a sharp turn at slow speeds and in this beam wind, the hull will definitely not track straight through the water, and you'll have a significant challenge wresting control back. As you allow the hull to slip sideways away from the land, you need to be concentrating on getting the boat to turn. There's no time to wait and see what course the boat will take and then react, so get the rudder hard over and give the engine a quick thrust of power. This maneuver requires you to be decisive and take control of the bow immediately.

In tight confines, and with increasingly heavy weather, the margin for error becomes slim, so practice this on your own terms in conditions that you can cope with. Different boats handle differently in different conditions, so it depends on a variety of issues precisely how you'll need to customize this description, such as whether you steer with a rudder or a propeller (an outboard or screw drive), whether you have a deep keel (and what type), and whether yours is a wallowing heavy-displacement hull or a light shallow-draft racer. Nevertheless, the general principles apply fairly well to almost any design of boat.

Most of us are familiar with parking cars, and we know that it's just about impossible for a car to execute a similar maneuver in the way described. With a car, you need to back into the parallel parking bay. Of course, a car has its steering wheels in the front. With a boat, your rudder and steering pivot is in the stern, so it makes sense that any attempt to back into a berth like this with a boat will turn into a fiasco—especially when the wind is up to further complicate matters.

Docking Temporarily

With boats temporarily obstructing your path, it's best to take up a temporary mooring. If there is someone on shore to assist, come alongside and toss him or her a line. If there's no shore assistance, gently bring your bow to the dock and let a crew member go ashore to attach an appropriate line.

Remember to reduce speed well before you approach. Boats don't have brakes, and an emergency stop, even with motors slammed full astern, takes longer than you'd imagine.

Assess the wind direction relative to the dock. If the direction is toward the dock, steer the boat for a point that will place you a couple of feet away, but level with the dock, and the wind will push you snugly home where you can secure the bow, stern, and spring lines.

If the wind is blowing away from the dock, approach the dock at an angle of around 25 degrees and either have a crew member step ashore with the bow line or pass it to a waiting dockhand. Boats with outboard or inboard-outboard engines can then turn the motors toward the dock and power the stern in. Once alongside, the stern and other lines can be secured.

Boats with inboard engines don't have this luxury, and you'll need to use a bow spring to keep the bow from moving forward. Then, using a combination of engine thrust and rudder position, leverage the boat around the restraining line, and the stern will be forced toward the dock where you can secure it. If the boat has two engines, you're in a little more luck because you can use them with opposite thrust and they'll leverage off each another.

When You're Short on Crew

Two of the simplest and most effective techniques when you're short on crew are to:

- Run out a line amidships and tie it ashore; cleating it will be even better if that is possible because it will be only a temporary tie until you get longer lines in place and adjusted.
- Get a spring line in place and use the counterthrust of the propeller and rudder against the dock to hold you suspended against the spring line's resistance.

Although the second spring line option is very effective, it needs a little more practice and time. Try both options in forgiving conditions to see which you're comfortable with.

ESSENTIALS

Want a little help with some boating chores? Try using some household items. To help lubricate the seals, moving parts, and O-rings, pour a shot of cooking oil into your marine toilet. Use Teflon grease to coat your propeller the next time you take it out to polish.

Alternatively a low line with ends attached at the bow and the stern can be used. You can use it in conjunction with power or try to manhandle the boat either ahead or astern from this single point. Get it balanced with the resistance holding the boat parallel to the dock and tie it off or cleat it to the dock as quickly as possible. You'll then tie off with bow and stern lines as normal.

Tying Up Your Boat

The docking procedure isn't over until you've got the boat tied off. In a stiff offshore—or more accurately off-berth—wind, you'll only have a brief window of opportunity to secure a line ashore. An experienced crew will realize that they have to jump to it, but rookies will need a little coaching ahead of time. Ensure that everyone knows the part they'll play, precisely what equipment will be used and where it is, and how to execute the job without delay or hesitation.

FIGURE 9-7:
That secure feeling

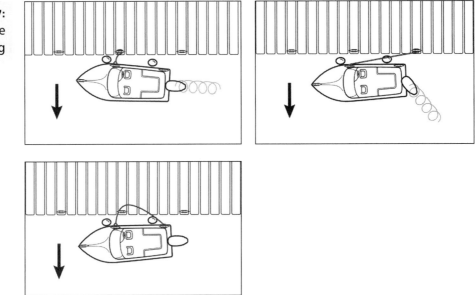

Dealing with Tides

If you're tying in an area that has a large tidal range, permit sufficient play in your lines to allow for tidal variance. Too little slack in a line tied at high tide could either break the line or leave the boat dangling in midair as the water recedes.

By contrast, too much slack at low tides could allow the boat to wander around with a mind of its own when the water floods and there are fathoms of play in the line. On the other hand, if you tie with too little play on the wharf too close to the water line at low tide, when high water returns, the boat could either be pulled under or the line could be hydraulically wrenched into the structure and cause untold damage.

Mooring Anchors

Where dock is at a premium, permanently placed anchors are attached to buoys. Though a little inconvenient for instant and direct access to the boat, moorings are cheaper to maintain and, for larger vessels, less hassle to secure to than a solid quayside.

At day's start, a skeleton crew would usually take a tender to the boat, disengage it and then bring it to the quay where the people, goods, and equipment would be loaded. At day's end, this procedure would then be reversed.

To moor, approach the buoy slowly. You'll find two main types of floats. If there are two buoys, attach to the smaller buoy by scooping it up with a boat hook and attaching it to your bow cleat. If there is only a single large buoy, scoop it up, attach your anchor line to the bottom of this buoy, and then drop the buoy overboard once more and tie your line off with little scope.

Though a relatively simple procedure to hitch up to the mooring, there are some associated dangers, such as overshooting the mark and fouling the prop or a crew member being yanked overboard if the approach is too vigorous.

Once You're Docked

Once you've docked, you'll want to remember certain things. For starters, remember that water movement is tirelessly working away at your boat's securing lines. Whenever you'll be leaving a boat tied to the slip for more than a few days, ensure that you add antichafing gear to whatever surfaces run the risk of being rubbed in the wrong way.

Also, keep in mind that boat fenders are meant to be squashed, squeezed, and crushed. Usually inflated with air, they're tough customers designed to absorb the shocks and attrition of life between a rock and a hard place. Like any other safety equipment, the price you'd expect to pay for them all depends on the replacement value of the boat you're protecting. If you figure that a piece of Styrofoam that washed up will do, then go for it, but we'd suggest a top-grade, commercially available unit designed for the task.

Remember that the larger your boat, the larger the task at hand, and the more extensive and robust the fender needs to be. Usually the minimum number of fenders you'd employ would be three: one off the bow, one amidships, and one off the stern. These points are all obviously at the most extreme parts of your vessel and are likely to come into contact with the dock or any other solid object.

Where docksides are rough or barnacle encrusted, do ensure that a dock board is placed on the outside of the fender to ensure that excessive abrasion or puncturing does not occur.

FIGURE 9-8:
Fenders
for every
occasion

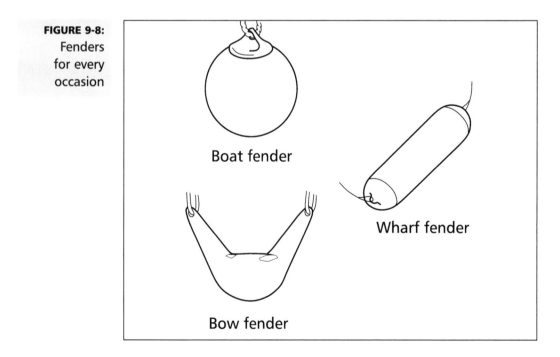

Boat fender

Wharf fender

Bow fender

CHAPTER 10

Weathering the Conditions

When the weather is good, our only advice is enjoy it, but keep your eyes peeled for any signs of a change. It's not simply high wind or stormy seas on the way that you're looking for, but simple fog as well. This chapter also deals with the dangers posed by wind and waves.

Checking the Forecast

In the United States, we're spoiled—we've got twenty-four hours of weather on TV, newspapers, the Internet, local telephone numbers to audio weather-predicting services, as well as WX-1, WX-2, or WX-3 buttons on your VHF. So there's no excuse not to check the weather forecast when you're about to sail.

If you're a weekend warrior and only sail local haunts, you'll be interested in the weather for that specific area, over short periods of time. On the other hand, if you're into cruising, you'll be concerned with the weather projections over a period of days and its behavior in the wider areas. Those sailors who venture out in the latitudes where weather is variable rather than merely seasonal must go beyond this and learn to make their own meteorological maps and forecasts for themselves.

Beyond the ideal weather you're seeking, you're most interested in the foul weather you're trying to avoid. However, the term *foul weather* is subjective and means different things to different people. You might consider even one cloud in the sky and anything over eight knots to be foul. Single-handed sailors in the doldrums think of foul weather as a glass sea with no breeze in sight! One man's meat is another man's poison.

Essentials

You've probably heard the rhyme "Red sky at morning, sailors take warning. Red sky at night, sailor's delight." While many rhymes are quite accurate, never rely on them for your safety. Always listen to the weather reports before setting sail.

Having stated this, there is weather that's just plain nasty to be out in. For example, it might be great to have twenty-five knots in your sails when the water's calm, but if the wind were just fifteen knots and the sea was lumpy with chop, we'd personally call that foul.

In general, when you're gauging the weather, you should look out for:

- **Fronts:** Apart from usually being associated with dips in barometric pressure, fronts are what their name suggests—the leading edge of nasty weather that sweeps across a clear sky bringing bad weather in its wake.

- **Thunderheads:** These anvil-shaped clouds, technically referred to as *cumulonimbus* clouds, show you which way the storm is heading by the direction that the anvil is pointing; once you've spotted these clouds on the horizon, the storm can be over you within an hour. When you see these clouds, get out of the way.

- **Lightning:** Generally accompanying thunderheads, lightning is an electrical charge looking for a place to ground, such as the steering wheel. Lightning can be a very unwelcome visitor that might stretch way out from distant clouds and touch your vessel under clear skies, so get out of the way or at least below deck.

In addition to the weather report you need before embarking on a journey, it's wise to keep constantly updating the information—both from official sources as well as by personal observation.

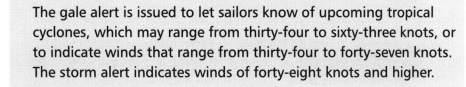

The gale alert is issued to let sailors know of upcoming tropical cyclones, which may range from thirty-four to sixty-three knots, or to indicate winds that range from thirty-four to forty-seven knots. The storm alert indicates winds of forty-eight knots and higher.

Remember that although computers and satellite-originated data have taken a lot of the guesswork out of weather prediction, it is not yet a foolproof science, and Mother Nature still throws plenty of curve balls. As data is built and computer-simulated models become ever more sophisticated, you can expect the prediction of weather to become an ever more precise undertaking. But for now, for the most part, no weather predictor would wager his or her salary on a precise forecast.

Avoiding Surprises

Sailing is about safety, and safety is about preparedness. So, the first rule is knowing what to anticipate. Before planning a trip, not only should you check the forecast, you should make yourself aware of all the conditions you'll be likely to encounter.

Study the nautical charts of the area so that you know where all of the obstructions, traffic, and reefs are located. That way, if you unexpectedly run into heavy weather, you'll be in a better position to develop a master plan to thread your way out of it.

You also need to make sure that you constantly update the weather forecast you acquired before undocking. While asea, you'll want to listen for updates on your VHF radio and react as quickly as possible to changes in the prediction. Of course, a good instinct for bad weather is among the best skills in an skipper's arsenal, but it takes a lot of experience and is generally region specific, so don't expect to export your local instincts to other regions.

If you are navigating in fog, plot your course following the bottom contour and plot dashed lines paralleling it by about fifty to 100 yards on either side to keep you on course.

With the right forewarning and preparation, you should be in good shape to tackle most conditions. Obviously, the best way to handle rough weather is to get to shore immediately and avoid it completely. However, this may not be practical if you are on an extended cruise. In this case, you should prepare yourself, your vessel, and your crew for what is to come.

Depending upon the specifications of your vessel's size, design, and equipment, the local conditions, and the severity of the oncoming weather, your list of precautionary measures and actions will grow.

Preparing for Bad Weather

Try as we might and plan as we might, life and sailing are simply arenas where trouble will strike from time to time. The best way to deal with foul weather will always be to avoid it altogether. Short of a war, we can't think of any other reason you'd have to put to sea if you suspect there is bad weather on the way. Watch the reports and keep your eye on the horizon.

But if you can't make it inland quickly enough, you'll want to take some precautions. If you're well ahead of the storm, you need to shift yourself and your crew into gear. As soon as you've identified that you're on a collision course with the weather and have no way around it, assemble the crew and passengers for a briefing. Be honest, but don't incite panic or fear. Give them an insight into your boat's design in terms of its ability to ride out the weather that you're going to meet. If you really have bad news for them, first meet with your most senior crew to brief them, then bring in the more junior members, and finally break it to the passengers.

Your general list of issues to cover, and the order to cover them, is as follows:

- Call the crew and passengers together to explain the situation in detail. This is not a time for accusations or blame. This is the time for true leadership to emerge. Emotions might begin to run high, but panic can be disastrous, so keep everyone focused on dealing with the situation the way it is—not the way they'd like it to be or the way it could have been.
- Ensure that everyone knows what to do, when to do it, and whom they are taking their orders from when the extreme weather arrives.
- Bring to their attention the facts that keeping bodyweight low, holding on, moving only when necessary, keeping a keen watch on the developing situation, moving predictably without running or overacting, and staying below decks are the best way to reduce the possibility of injury or overboard situations.
- Give every person at least one assignment that will last the duration of the storm. It will keep their minds busy and quell their fears—an idle mind is the devil's workshop.
- If it's possible, alter your course and head for sheltered waters.
- Get out PFDs and other foul-weather gear.
- Insist that all hands are to wear the PFDs henceforth. Don't wait for the storm to be in sight. Do this immediately so that everyone will at

least get used to the fit and have time to solve any problems or challenges that might arise.

- Make sure emergency equipment that you may need is accessible, such as hand pumps, bailers, first-aid kit, sound-signaling device, and so on.
- Determine your position as accurately as you can and plot it on your chart. Remember to note the time, your heading, and your speed.
- Report your position, heading, and details of your preparation to the Coast Guard and other vessels or stations in the area.
- Determine the proximity and movement of the storm regularly and keep everyone apprised of the anticipated time you'll encounter the various stages of the storm.
- Close all portholes and secure all hatches.
- Be sure that bilges are pumped dry ahead of the storm. Besides creating the safety margin of having as much free board—distance between your gunwale or deck and the water—as possible, you want to stop water in your bilge from sloshing back and forth and potentially destabilizing the boat when it begins to roll.
- Secure all loose gear above decks by lashing it down.
- Secure all loose gear below decks by stowing away or, at the very least, covering smaller items with larger ones.
- Keep a vigil on Channel 16 of your VHF radio to get updates and severity forecasts so that you can factor them into your plans and preparations.

If the situation is clearly turning severe, it's now time to break out your abandon-ship procedures and review them. You'll want to ensure that the life raft is ready for deployment, and it contains emergency food and water. Rig jack lines and/or lifelines and require that anyone who must go on deck wear a safety harness. Prepare your sea anchor or drogue. Illuminate your navigation lights and, if possible, change to a full fuel tank. You'll also want to watch carefully for floating debris and other boats.

Get to know your sailing area and find areas that give shelter during hurricanes. As an absolute last resort, if you're stuck in a hurricane and trapped in a bay where you believe that your boat is certain to be wrecked, it is better to purposefully sink it on your own terms. Naturally, your first priority is the safety of lives, but once you've got everyone to safety, scuttle the boat into water that is neither so shallow that waves are breaking but not so deep that it will make recovery too difficult. If possible, get all electronics onto shore.

Avoiding Lightning

Lightning is an upper-air electrical charge with millions of volts looking for a way to the ground—or water, as the case may be. On land, we all know that under a tree is a bad place to be when lightning is possible. So, how much worse is it to be under a beautifully erected metal mast? Not surprisingly, with little competition from the surrounding flat expanse of water, lightning can be a very unwelcome visitor that might stretch way out from distant clouds and touch your vessel under clear skies.

ESSENTIALS | The odds are very small, but the best protection from lightning is to head in to port before a storm hits. If you cannot get off the boat, stay away from any metal fittings and the mast, if it is metal.

The rule here is to get out of the way when thunderclouds are within five miles of you. Because this is sometimes impossible, at least get below decks and stay well away from all metals that may be grounded. Unfortunately, the steering wheel is likely to be one of these no-no articles.

Wherever possible, haul down all vertical units, such as fishing poles and antennas. Then, keep your head down. If your mast does get struck by lightning, provided you're not touching it, the charge should dissipate into the water directly through the grounding.

Encountering Waterspouts

Waterspouts are the nautical versions of tornadoes. In short, you don't want to meet up with them. Taking a direct hit from one of these impressive beauties will tie your rigging in a knot. They certainly won't be hard to spot as their 20- to 100-foot-plus girths spiral down from low-hanging cumulonimbus clouds.

Unfortunately, boaters in the Keys might underestimate the dangers of waterspouts because they're so common. Waterspouts probably occur more frequently in the Florida Keys than anywhere in the world. Waters around the Keys see 400 or 500 waterspouts a year.

Many waterspouts hit the Florida Keys because the weather and geography supply two necessary ingredients. First, the islands and the shallow water around them help heat the air. During the summer, which is waterspout season, the air is extremely humid with temperatures from about 85°F/30°C to around 95°F/35°C. The heat causes the air to rise, and, as it rises, the air's humidity condenses into the tiny water droplets that make up clouds. As water vapor condenses, it releases more heat, making the air rise even faster. Rising air currents are needed for waterspout formation.

The second waterspout ingredient in the Keys seems to be the regular east or northeast trade winds that blow right down the islands. These winds help line up the clouds. Lines of clouds encourage waterspouts. Exactly how is one of the questions researchers are trying to answer.

Waterspouts are likely to form when the clouds are growing upward. In the Keys, waterspouts are most likely to form between 4 to 7 P.M. with a secondary maximum from 11 A.M. to 1 P.M. A few waterspouts form around sunrise.

After the Florida Keys, the next most active U.S. waterspout area is the southeast Florida coast from around Stuart south to Homestead. Tampa Bay has the greatest number of damaging waterspouts, probably because the shores of the bay are so built up. Places around the Gulf of Mexico along with the Atlantic Coast northward to Chesapeake Bay are also likely to see waterspouts.

Waterspouts have been reported on the West Coast from Tatoohs Island, Washington, south to San Diego, California, but they tend to be weak and short-lived. Waterspouts also skip across the Great Lakes and Utah's Great Salt Lake from time to time.

Facing a Wave

If you're unfortunate enough to ever face an unexpected wave about to break and don't have time to run away from it—and if you've seen the wave, it's usually too late—make absolutely sure that you're not broadside to its movement, or it will roll or capsize you. Being stern-on to such a wave is not the ideal angle either.

To prove this, sit and watch people playing along the seashore where waves are crashing. Those who pay no attention to oncoming waves get flattened into the sand. Those who spot a wave about to curl over them and try to run away get nailed almost as hard. However, those with experience face the wave and shove through it with power and the sharpest part of their body—their head.

What you've got to try to do is keep the sharpest part of your boat—namely, your bow—up into the oncoming rush and get your weight back to lift the bow, but not so far back that it can easily roll you over backward. Then, the moment before you're hit, apply forward thrust and simultaneously throw as much weight as you can muster toward the bow as you strike the rushing water.

In a worst-case scenario, as in a prolonged storm where the waves are likely to keep rolling at you for many minutes or hours and you can't afford to take even one on the broadside, you'll need to take some additional precautions. In a similar way that an arrow is just a stick if it doesn't have feathered flights, without a thrust from behind your boat and a steady hand on the tiller, your boat is no more than a cork in a river rapid. In this scenario, even the most experienced skipper would be hard-pressed to keep his or her vessel head up into driving surf for more than a few minutes without making a mistake.

You'll desperately need to get something over the bow that will act like the flights of an arrow—only in reverse. The idea is not to weight the bow down, but to offer the surf the most resistance at the bow and allow the stern to trail toward the line of least resistance. Parachute-like devices are ideal.

Interpreting Weather Proverbs

There is an awful lot of wisdom to some sailing proverbs, so you'll want to learn to heed them well:

> *Red sky in the morning is the sailor's warning.*
> *Red sky in the night is a sailor's delight.*

The message above is clear and needs no further explanation.

> *Although a red sky at night may be a sailor's delight,*
> *Orange or yellow can hurt a fellow.*

Clouds that turn these colors at sundown indicate excessive humidity moving in. Rain is likely, and storms are possible.

> *Mackerel scales and mares' tails make tall ships carry low sails.*

Anytime you see a black line of clouds approaching on the horizon, it's time to scuttle on home with all haste. If your craft is slow and the distance home is great, the only alternative is to batten down the hatches, don your PFDs, rain gear, and life lines, and prepare for the ride of your life.

A low, black bank of clouds stretching from horizon to horizon is a *squall line.* Traveling at up to a mile per minute, goading a gentle breeze into a tempest from one moment to the next, these can be vicious little creeps that spoil your whole day. The nicest place to be when they bite is at home with soup on the boil.

CHAPTER 11
Dealing with Wind

Wind plays an important role in your boating experience. Not only do you need to understand how wind works, but you need to know what to do when the wind isn't working in your favor. As an added bonus, we even cover seasickness—an unfortunate side effect of wind.

Understanding the Wind

When air passes over hot surfaces, it rises rapidly, leaving a vacuum or low pressure in its wake. The earth is made up of many different components—water, desert, rock, vegetation, and so on—that heat at different rates. As a result, the relative rising of heated air, and falling of cooled upper air, creates huge pools of differing air pressures. Because air is in a gaseous form and a gas will always find its natural pressure equilibrium, air movement—or wind—rushes from regions of relatively high pressure to regions of relatively low pressure.

Naturally, the greater the difference in relative pressures between adjacent high and low pressure zones, and the distance or proximity of these extremes to each nother, the more violent the air movement will be and the higher the wind speed will be. As a result, excessive wind delivers some nasty byproducts, such as waves, rain, and storms.

To complicate the matter, because oceans differ in depth and relative origin—some flow from polar regions while others flow from the tropics—they, too, carry an inherent ambient temperature that influences the air above them.

Naming the Winds

We name the winds according to the compass bearing they're blowing *from*. In other words, a westerly wind comes from the west—no prizes for getting that right. However, just to be difficult, we name currents according to the direction they are *traveling to*.

So, if there's a current coming out of the south and a wind that picks up is also blowing from the south, what do we have? We'd have a southerly wind and a north streaming current.

Knowing What the Wind Carries with It

Though wind in itself is one issue a sailor must consider, the amount of moisture and electric charge it carries with it is quite another. Not all winds are made the same and carry similar clouds, rain, and lightning with them. Depending on where in the world you are, you'll need to consider the local conditions before judging whether an anticipated wind is good or bad news.

And, if you think no wind is great news, think about how often you've seen fog during windy conditions. We didn't think so! And, unfortunately, fog can be one of the nastiest experiences for a sailor.

Measuring and Tracking Air Pressure

So, if air pressure is so important, you'd expect we can measure and track its changes, and you'd be right. When you look at a weather map, you'll see swirling lines that trace the edges of increasing or decreasing pressure zones. At their centers, they'll display either an *H* or an *L,* which indicates a high or low pressure zone respectively.

The numbers logged on each of these lines indicate the pressure at sea surface, at a particular time of day, and at a specific location on the earth. Not too many years ago, weather plotters who drew these maps relied on ship readings and weather outposts to report their pressure readings at certain times of day. From there, they'd plot these numbers onto maps and play connect the dots until they had interpolated where the pressure lines most likely ran through areas that they had not received any hard information from.

Assessing the Wind

Pleasure sailors generally seek steady but strong winds and generally temperate climates. Not surprisingly then, most sailing activity takes place in a band on either side of the equator where these two conditions are most prevalent.

Also, because the vast majority of sailors rarely venture too far from land, it's worth noting that wind is generally slowed by the land, and less steady than it might be farther out to sea where there are no obstructions and the air can move freely.

In marinas and harbors, wind conditions might be generally light but gusty, while out a way on the water strength picks up, and the feed becomes a little more constant. So you need to beware of two things: sudden gusts when you're near shore and much more wind than you bargained for once you're out on open water.

To help you assess how much wind is really out there, systems and facilities are in place to provide you with a tool to make the correct judgments. First, weather reports generally will tell you wind direction and speed. And, second, through the Beaufort scale, which uses open sea conditions as its base, you'll be able to equate these rather nebulous details with a very tangible image:

NUMBER	WIND SPEED (KNOTS)	DESCRIPTION	EFFECT ON WATER
0	Less than 1	Calm	Mirror-calm surface
1	1–3	Light air	Scale-like ripples
2	4–6	Light breeze	Wavelets, no breaking
3	7–10	Gentle breeze	Crest begins to break
4	11–16	Moderate breeze	Waves 1½–4 feet, numerous whitecaps
5	17–21	Fresh breeze	Waves 4–8 feet, some spray
6	22–27	Strong wind	Waves 8–13 feet, whitecaps everywhere
7	28–33	Near gale	Waves 13–20 feet, white foam, wave streaks
8	34–40	Gale	Waves increase in length, foam blown off to sea, sea streaks white

NUMBER	WIND SPEED (KNOTS)	DESCRIPTION	EFFECT ON WATER
9	41–47	Strong gale	Waves over 20 feet, limited visibility
10	48–55	Storm	Waves 20–30 feet, sea heavily streaked
11	56–63	Violent storm	Waves to 45 feet, sea nearly white
12	64–71	Hurricane or extremely violent storm	Waves over 45 feet, sea completely white, visibility near zero

Beyond prevailing wind, even on a calm day, you're likely to experience some kind of breeze whenever land and sea meet. Because the land heats more quickly during the day and then cools quicker at night, light breezes tend to blow onshore by day and offshore by night. These localized air movements are usually gentle and of little consequence apart from being useful to smaller craft.

Figuring Out Chop, Swell, and Waves

Out on the water, you'll experience chop, swell, and waves. Chop is small and localized wave motion that tosses a boat about with a high frequency, and swell is its cousin.

The wind is only half of the equation in determining when it's going to be too rough for you and your boat. The other is the fetch, or the distance the wind will blow over unobstructed water. A long fetch can create big waves even on an inland lake with fifteen-knot winds, while a short fetch will prevent much stronger winds from making the water too rough for comfort.

When chop graduates to swell, it is more uniform in direction, form, and slower frequency. It can also be much taller and has a more regular and vertical motion on the boat—as opposed to chop, which tends to oscillate the boat in unpredictable directions around its center of gravity—turning everyone aboard green with seasickness.

When swells turn angry, they graduate into waves. These are the teeth of the sea, and you don't want to be anywhere near them. But in order to stay out of their way and cope with them, you do need to understand them.

As wind blows over a beach or dirt parking lot, the friction at the surface lifts particles. Depending on the strength of the wind and the distance over which it remains in contact with the dusty surface, you'd expect an increasingly proportionate amount of silt to be carried.

In this same way, wind blowing over water has friction with the water surface and even lifts particles that evaporate and rise into clouds or are visible in high winds as spray along the surface. On the other hand, water has different properties than grit. Being a liquid, water allows a wave motion to be set up. The dynamics of wind and water allow the water particle to advance in the direction of wind movement in tumbling circles.

FACTS

Three factors make up a wave: its wind speed, the time the wind has been blowing, and its fetch. The four factors that waves are measured by are their height, length, steepness, and period.

The first sign that swell and waves will eventually result—hours later and miles downwind—is an unevenness in the water surface. This is called chop and is characterized by small, irregularly shaped peaks and valleys of water that may vary from inches to a few feet in height between trough and peak.

The longer and stronger the wind keeps up the friction across the surface, the greater will be the tumbling and advancing energy of the individual molecules, and consequently, the greater will be the resulting wave motion of the entire mass that all the molecules constitute. The distance over which the wind blows and causes the first chop, then swell, is called the fetch of the wind.

When the fetch is sufficiently long the wave motion sorts itself out into a more regular pattern, known as a swell. These swells then march in long lines over the oceans of the world. In addition, if a lake or other body of water is sufficiently large to allow for a decent fetch, waves will ultimately result there, too.

In deep water—that is, water with a depth at least four units deep for every three units of wave amplitude or height—the wave motion or swells move at around fifteen knots. However, when the sea bottom becomes less than four units deep for every three units of wave height, the wave motion is stalled and slowed in the bottom traverse of its oscillation, and the top of the oscillation consequently overtakes it—resulting in the swell breaking into a wave.

Watching Out for Breaking Waves

Swell in itself provides little more than an unpleasant elevator ride up to a broad crest, a swoop down into the following trough, then up and down, repeated hour in and hour out—not the most pleasant experience for the uninitiated.

Wind-Collapsed Waves

If the swell is accompanied by strong wind—as would be the case near the Arctic Circles—the tops of each crest might become unstable and roll over, creating several feet of tumbling and angry surge atop each crest. In some extreme instances this whitewater might even be several feet high and thick. That's not the place to be if you don't know what you're doing and don't have the right equipment.

True Waves

A true breaking wave depends on water depth. If the water depth gently decreases, the break is not too dramatic, and the wave simply crumbles from the top.

On the other hand, if the sea depth suddenly shallows—as is the case with blinder reefs and submerged rocks, the wave is suddenly halted, and the resulting wave pitches over and breaks violently. The common term for such a wave is a *breaker,* and it's characterized by a hollow air-filled chamber that makes a thudding sound.

You don't want to be anywhere near a blind reef when a swell occurs, because there is little warning to such a dangerous and violent occurrence. A cubic yard of water weighs about a ton. Therefore, a three-foot section of a three-foot-high wave traveling at a dozen knots will hit you with a force capable of sweeping the crew into the water, seriously damaging equipment, and even sinking the vessel.

Do remember the lessons on assessing water depth and keep an eye out for any swirls on the surface or lumping swells that might indicate that the swell is becoming a little large to be traveling through the depth of water. Often, these physical changes in the water's surface profile indicate that a reef, sandbar, or rock pinnacle will shortly be the sight of breaking waves, either as a result of dropping tide or rising swell size.

Huge Waves

For truly massive waves to develop, you need steady, strong, and extended wind blowing over a large body of water. For this reason, there's not an awful lot of good surf in the Mediterranean where there simply isn't enough distance and wind speed to impart its kinetic energy to the water. On the other hand, the Pacific is a massive body of water with more than enough wind bands to generate the type of surf we see in Hawaii.

FACTS

You will need your hand-held compass if you lose sight of land or if fog suddenly rolls in. Every compass has an arrow that will default to pointing to magnetic north. Turn to the right and the arrow will continue to point north, but the dial will tell you that you are facing east at 90 degrees.

Once developed, large swells can extend laterally and run on for hundreds or thousands of miles so that a large enough storm system deep in the South Pacific might spawn large swell and waves that will race by California some days later. With the advent of better climatology predictions and satellite application, predicting waves is quickly becoming quite an accurate science.

Another notable region for high surf is the frigid southern oceanic waters. These are constantly thrashed by hurricane force gales that blow for weeks over thousands of miles of open sea. The waves that they build are the infamous terrors our ancestors faced when they rounded Cape Horn on the southern tip of South America, and the Cape of Storms off South Africa. Colossal waves, some dozens of feet tall, were the stuff of nightmares for sailors in past centuries—and thus they remain to this day.

Contrary to intuition, hurricanes do not produce particularly large waves. Rather, they produce storm surge, where a large volume of water is forced ashore and swamps communities and carries surprisingly massive vessels up into the most unlikely land terrains. The reason for this is that hurricanes, though violent, are generally fairly localized storm systems as far as wave development is concerned.

Tsunamis and Tidal Waves

Another violent localized event can trigger monumentally large waves. Quite wrongly termed *tidal waves,* tsunamis are associated with seismic activity and rush away from the epicenter of earthquakes and volcanic eruptions, traveling at enormous speeds that might well approach 500 mph. Surprisingly, a tsunami might actually be rather small out in the open ocean, and one could pass under your boat without you even realizing anything untoward was afoot. However, because of its speed, when the tsunami slams into shallower water, that entire 500 mph wave of energy has to go somewhere, so it goes upward. Without warning, the wave will suck water back from the shore and turn into a tower of water anywhere from perhaps ten feet high up to 100 feet or more. Though that is an awfully large wave with inestimable power, it's also so very rare that it's really not worth worrying about.

Tidal waves, on the other hand, are an unusual rise of water along the seashore. Although you won't want to face tidal waves either, they're at least not a real tsunami.

Handling Bad Wind

Bad wind is not a medical condition. In sailing terms, *bad wind* refers to your sails' experiencing a disruption in the flow of the wind reaching them. If the bad air is being created by other boat sails, you'll obviously not have the same wind power that they will, and you'll be sure to be traveling slower than they will. To remedy this, you'll have to find your way to clear air. But, to do so, your first priority is to establish the exact originator of the bad air. The following pointers will help you in doing so.

Blanketing

Blanketing is what the term implies. When there is a boat to windward, its sail blankets or stops the air from getting to your sail. It is a windless pocket of air, a form of umbra, that will vary in size, shape, and extent, depending on various circumstances such as wind speed, direction, and consistency; sail shape and size; relative position to the wind; and your respective headings.

If you're caught in this intense doldrum, your boat will tend to decelerate until the blanket overtakes you. The wind will then snap into your sails once more, and you'll begin to accelerate once again. But if you don't take evasive action at this point, you'll end up sailing directly back into the blanket.

If possible, without hitting the blanketer, shift to a new tack. If you've got a fast enough vessel and rig, and you're hemmed in by other boats, objects, or course requirement, hang back enough to build enough momentum to push you through the blanket and on to clear air ahead. Naturally, if you don't have sufficient momentum, the best you could hope to do is to cross in the blanketer's wake and attempt to pass on the windward side.

Backwinding

Whereas the blanket is a small but intense area relatively close to the blanketer's rig, the backwind zone is a much larger area that surrounds it. Again, think of the umbra of the sun when the earth experiences an eclipse. Only a small portion of the earth will experience a relatively short-lived period of total darkness, whereas there is a much larger area of shadow.

The same principle is true for wind. Beyond being a large area of lowered wind intensity, it is also an area of turbulence. As if this is not enough, the *back* part of the backwind term derives its name from the wind that turns the corner around the leading edge of the sail. As it rushes into the relative vacuum caused on the leeward side of the sail, it is actually changing the wind's relative direction. Therefore, from your perspective in the zone, you'll be facing more of a headwind, with a consequent loss of power and potential for speed.

Weathering Seasickness

Seasickness is the final nasty that wind and water can serve. If you've ever suffered this ill, the mere mention of the word will probably raise a rash of gooseflesh up your spine. Even writing this section, I'm tormented by serious Pavlovian induced memories of once again being about ten years old and lying sprawled on deck, praying to die while everyone around seems oblivious. This was truly what happened, since many seasoned sailors have little sympathy for landlubbers with no tolerance for the ocean's rocking.

Regardless of whether you're ever afflicted, you're certain to be affected. Whether you're sailing lakes or the open ocean, the fact that you're on the water where there is wind-chop practically guarantees that you'll have to deal with this unpleasantness at some point in your career. Even if you're fortunate enough not to be directly afflicted by this subcategory of motion sickness, at some time or other you'll have crew or passengers who are affected, and you'll need to be involved by at least preparing them for it or assisting them through it.

QUESTIONS?

Are there any nonpharmaceutical measures for seasickness?
Yes! For a nonprescription alternative, you can try the ReliefBand, available at *www.reliefband.com*.

As with any motion sickness, seasickness starts as a disagreement between the information from the eyes and the balance mechanism in the inner ear. The eyes say that the world is not moving, and the balance mechanism says that it is. The brain tries for a while to reconcile the two, and then the stomach gets involved and threatens to jettison its contents if the other two won't agree.

With three organs now in dispute, the brain becomes awfully tired and sets up a yawning routine while trying to close the eyes—presumably to distract the other organs from beginning a trend. Just as everything seems to be finding an equilibrium, the stomach makes good on its promise, and the rest of the body begins to shiver and shake.

Symptoms

Symptoms vary from mild nausea to outright debilitation. On the severe side of the scale, victims will display all the joys of someone with a raging hangover—nausea, dizziness, gastrointestinal afflictions such as vomiting, and slick bowel movements. These symptoms can all be very nasty and can even be dangerous for the sufferer if the dehydration of fluids through the body's elimination is allowed to continue for prolonged periods.

The good news here is that dehydration would be rare because the trip will probably be over before any lasting damage can be done, and the sufferer generally rallies within minutes of coming ashore. On the other hand, if the trip is a little longer, the body will generally adapt to the motion, and the sickness will disappear. Then, when returning to land, some sufferers claim a spell of experiencing landsickness because the ground is no longer moving and their balance mechanism thinks it ought to be—while the eyes disagree!

Scared Sick

We've got a theory that once an individual has been seasick, they're hypnotized that it is likely to happen again. At the mere mention of putting to sea, the stomach appears to have the best memory of all the organs because it will immediately begin doing the twist without needing any disagreement between sight and balance. By the time the latter two do begin, the stomach is so ready that it's positively gleeful to be sick. On the bright side, with perseverance, the body does eventually become immune to the rocking and rolling of nautical life.

Prevention

You can use several techniques and medications to allay the worst of seasickness. By watching the horizon and keeping your eyes out of the boat, sight is brought a little more in synch with balance, but this is not a panacea by any means.

Some swear by certain food combinations the night before and during the event. Others absolutely shun alcohol intake for dozens of hours before putting to sea, while a few crazies reckon—very unwisely and without foundation—that a shot of whiskey can settle the stomach.

Imbibed medications in tablet form have a tendency to create drowsiness, and we have had little success with wrist patches. By contrast, ear patches are, according to our experience, the most successful preventative measure. They're placed behind the ear several hours before setting off and evidently work by tranquilizing one of the major culprits that sets up disagreement—the inner ear balance mechanism. Manufacturers claim that they continue to work for up to three days. Several years ago, they were removed from the market altogether and have now made a reappearance once more. Certainly, at time and place of writing, they can only be procured with a doctor's prescription.

Beyond these ideas, here are some more tips for potential victims:

- Eat and drink moderately the night before a voyage and have normal sleep.
- Eat a light breakfast, such as cereal and fruit. Don't touch anything greasy.
- Stay outdoors. Swinging curtains and sliding crockery supercharges the argument within.
- Keep as close to the boat's center of gravity as possible. If you can reach the closest point to the pivot around which the boat is moving, without going below decks, so much the better.

- Stay as close to the water level and amidships as possible.
- Drink carbonated soda and eat dry crackers.
- Avoid oily and aromatic foods.
- Know that, no matter how bad it might get, it will end back on solid ground.
- Stay home if the weather is bound to be rough.

Because the stomach is one of the primary problems of children, sufferers should try to avoid odors of any kind and keep the freshness of the breeze in their face. Often, cold water splashed onto the face and neck, and, if possible, a swim is an immeasurable help.

CHAPTER 12

Factoring in Tides

In terms of their effect on your happy or distressed sailing, tides aren't in the same league as wind and waves, but they're still important elements of the entire sailing issue. In addition, they can conspire with the waves to create more havoc than you'd otherwise experience.

High and Low Tides

Technically speaking, tides are the periodic vertical rises and falls of oceans that occur with two cycles per day—two high and two low tides. Each extreme is spaced approximately six hours apart.

Tides are created by the gravitational pulls of the moon and the sun, either combining their strengths or canceling each other's strength. Water is literally attracted vertically toward the two forces, leaving us with bumps of water that follow the heavenly bodies through the water. These bumps are experienced as more vertical water and a consequent rise in the tide.

Absolute high tide is reached when the bump of water travels directly through that region of ocean. By contrast, at 90 degrees on the earth's surface to the bumps, water is relatively diminished, and so a trough is formed. This is experienced as a low tide.

FIGURE 12-1(a): Semidiurnal tide: Two high and two low tides every day

FIGURE 12-1(b): Diurnal tide: One high and one low tide every day

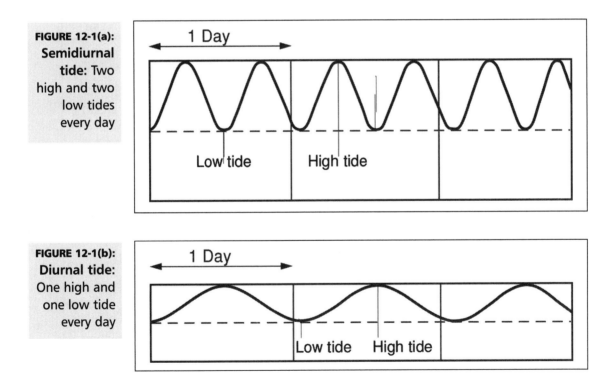

FIGURE 12-1(c):
Mixed tide:
Two high and
two low tides
per day

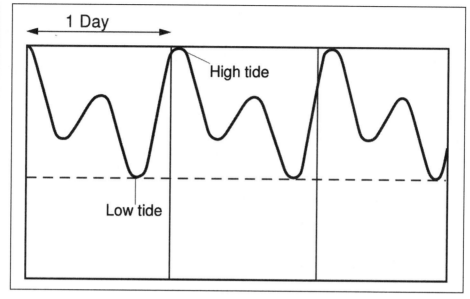

Tidal Ranges

For many reasons, tidal ranges—the difference between maximum and minimum high and low tides—differ considerably from region to region. Some regions might typically only experience just a one-foot range, while the distant extreme might approach 50 feet! That's either 50 feet of water where solid ground was six hours previously, or 50 feet of water where terra firma will be in just six short hours, depending on which way you look at it.

For sailors, small tidal ranges are of little consequence, but large ranges could quite conceivably leave unsuspecting skippers with their vessels literally high and dry. In addition, many of these high-ranging zones are located in bays or enclosures with tight headlands. In order to fill and empty, the heads that open to the ocean experience tremendous surges of inward or outward bound water that flows with the strength of a river. Such enormous movements of water are bound to offer a danger to any boater or swimmer. The whole setup can become like a toilet bowl that flushes out and then fills four times per day.

Fortunately, tidal ranges and periods are about the most predictable of all the sailing phenomena and therefore pose a reduced risk to the mariners. Though the sun's gravitational pull is several-fold that of the moon, it is so very distant from us that its effect on the ocean is relatively minimal. The moon's bump is therefore larger, and the tide is therefore higher.

The Moon's Relationship with Tides

These days, most people are familiar with the fact that we circle the sun, while the moon circles us. The phases of the moon we observe from earth are therefore nothing but changing light and shadow effects from our perspective.

At new moon, from our perspective, the moon is not illuminated because the sun and moon share the same part of the sky. The moon's dark side shows toward us, while the more distant sun's brilliance blots it out. In other words, the angle is 0 degrees, and both gravitational fields pull along the same vector or direction, doubling their strength and the lump of water they draw.

FACTS

The flood current is the water flowing upstream. The ebb current is the water running downstream. Typically, all coasts have two tides per day, and they vary according to the geographics of each area. A small lake or reservoir does not have any tides but may have tricky currents that churn up the water.

At full moon, the opposite is true, and the moon is fully illuminated by the light of the sun, which is now behind us. Because they're at 180 degrees relative to us, they're pulling in opposite directions and their respective high tides are large, while the associated low tides are equally low.

At phases in between moon phases, the sun's and moon's relative angles from our perspective tend to cancel each other out until, at first and last quarter, they form a right angle and both attract their high tides into regions that would otherwise be a low tide.

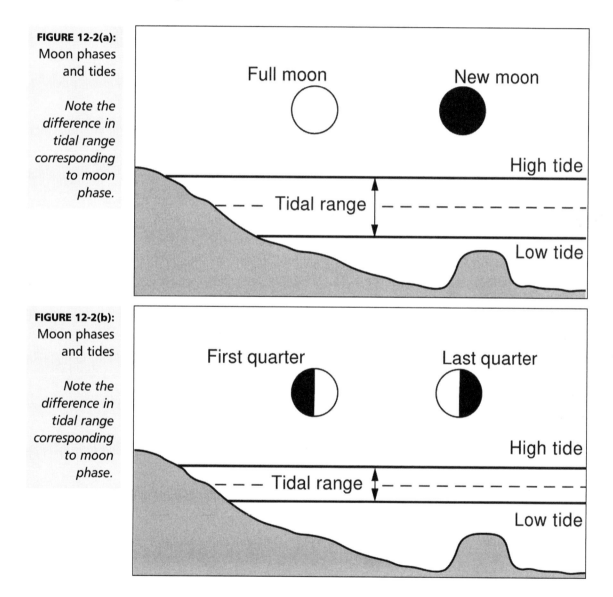

FIGURE 12-2(a):
Moon phases and tides

Note the difference in tidal range corresponding to moon phase.

FIGURE 12-2(b):
Moon phases and tides

Note the difference in tidal range corresponding to moon phase.

The Moon and Gravity

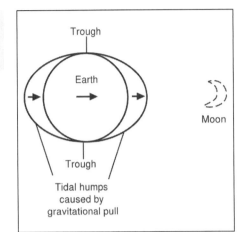

FIGURE 12-3:

Moon gravity causes tides

Trough

Earth

Moon

Trough

Tidal humps
caused by
gravitational pull

The moon is the strongest factor affecting tides via gravitational pull. Gravity causes the water of the oceans to bulge slightly toward the attracting bodies. The strongest tides are on new and full moons when the sun and moon are aligned. The weakest tides are at the moon's quarter periods, when the moon is at a 90-degree angle to the line of pull of the sun. Because of the progression of the moon phases, today's high tide at noon will become a low tide at about noon seven days from now, and a high tide very close to noon once again fourteen days from now. The moon rotates around the earth not every twenty-four hours, but every twenty-four hours and fifty minutes. Thus, the tidal periods are fifty minutes later on each of our earth days.

Tidal Names

For safety's sake, the extremes of tidal ranges that result from the heavenly conspiracy phenomena need to be labeled.

- Spring tides are tides around new and full moons. They are the highest highs and lowest lows.
- Neap tides are the least tidal range variance within the cycle. These are the tides associated with first and last quarters of the moon.

Tides do display some variation from summer to winter, but, in sailing terms, this is generally not significant.

Wind-Driven Tides

As with hurricanes, wind can move water, so it does have the effect of canceling or exaggerating the natural tidal flow. Because wind occurrence and direction is unpredictable, its effect creates something of a limited wildcard to the tidal zone saga.

The predicted tides are based on the pull of the moon, sun, and earth, but they can't take into account the effect of winds. Winds can even create tides in fresh water.

Sea Level and Water Depth

With all this water height variation, it's interesting to note that altitude, as calculated against sea level, takes a mean average between high and low tides as the reference point.

Boaters rarely speak of sea level, but rather of sea surface, sea bottom, boat's draft (how much water it draws—how deeply in the water it sits and how much water depth needs to exist for it to pass safely), or sea depth. These related concepts are all important and together are termed *controlling depth*. Controlling depth is the maximum draft of a vessel that can pass over a given spot in a channel at mean low tide. For example, a vessel with a five-foot draft will go aground in a channel with a controlling depth of 4'11" at mean low tide.

Larger keelboats may require upward of five feet of controlling depth to keep their keel from grinding into the bottom. Knowledge of tide heights is thus critical for inshore navigation, especially for keelboats.

Tide Tables to the Rescue

All over the word, marine authorities have long histories of tides and their ranges and continue to plot and predict their every move. In the United States, the National Ocean Service plots and forecasts tidal height and current data. They also collate this information for locations around the world and make it available.

As long as you mainly sail in your own region, you'll begin to note the rhythm of the ebbs and flows, neaps and springs. To take the guesswork out of it, most bait shops, marinas, and other interested parties give away handy tidal charts that list local tides. But when you venture far from home and cannot get local tables, the full-sized tables offer you the wonderful experience of converting data to arrive at conclusions for your region of interest.

FACTS

Did you know that the figurative term *seven seas* means all the waters of the earth? That all the so-called *oceans* are really only parts of the one vast ocean that covers the face of the earth, the "world ocean"? And that the Pacific Ocean is about 63,800,000 square miles in area and is the largest ocean on earth?

Happily, computers are taking the torture out of the conversion process. Electronic tide charts such as TideMaster can take over the thankless task of pencil and calculator and predict tides well into the future to help with those all important forays you're planning a year from now.

How to Treat the Tides

Like everything else on the water, you should treat tides with the utmost respect. Sure, they're generally slow and lazy, but they can also sneak up and cause the inattentive sailor plenty of anguish and discomfort.

If you must venture into shallow water, check out when high tide will be and then ride in very cautiously on the rising tide about halfway to full. To be on the safe side, check when the tide peaks and be sure to vacate the area into deeper water—not halfway to low tide, but a little earlier, such as at only one third of the way to low tide. For example, if full high is at noon, begin your approach at 9 A.M., and shift on out of the area by 2 P.M. If you do happen to run aground at 11 A.M., you'll still have an additional hour of flooding tide to refloat your little catastrophe.

Oh, yes, the threats tides pose are not just from below—on a full tide, overhead obstructions become a very real danger. Apart from feeling a proper nitwit for demasting your vessel on a bridge, it could also cost you a pretty penny. Remember that the abbreviation *BC* applies to Bridge Clearance and indicates the vertical height between water surface and overhead obstructions.

CHAPTER 13

Running Aground

Cynics say that there are only three kinds of skippers: those who have run aground, those who will run aground, and those who have but won't admit it. We think that's a little harsh, but it does demonstrate why every boater needs to know what to do if the unfortunate event ever happens.

Knowing How to React

Despite all the equipment, charts, warnings and other efforts to stay off shoals, beaches, or rocks, groundings do happen. What you do in the next few moments can make a tremendous difference.

Instead of blindly reacting with a knee-jerk response, take a moment to assess the situation. The first order of business is to see whether the hull has been compromised. Do you see any sign of taking on water? If you're holed in the hull, you'll need to take immediate action. If you suspect a high probability of a rock bottom, it becomes especially vital that you don't attempt to refloat the craft immediately. The very rocks you are beached on might be the only thing keeping your boat afloat!

Unless you're absolutely certain that you're on a narrow sand shoal with deep water directly ahead, do not attempt to power over the obstacle, or you'll most likely just run harder aground. Likewise, don't immediately attempt to back off of the obstruction by putting the boat into reverse and powering away. You're definitely in shallow water, so attempts to back up might result in your propellers stirring up mud and vegetation that will be sucked into the water intake and cause your engines to overheat. You might also destroy your propeller and drive shaft if you hit a submerged object.

ESSENTIALS

To give yourself confidence in emergencies, make sure to practice the crew-overboard maneuver. You'll also want to practice anchoring, capsizing, and righting in calm shallow water, as well as heaving to in a breeze.

If the damage is considerable, set out an anchor or two to keep your boat in place for the time being. Even if you don't need any immediate assistance, you should radio the Coast Guard, other local authority, or other boats and advise them of your situation and your intended actions.

Of course, if you're in any form of wave or surge zone—such as a beach, reef, or strait of a river—your immediate concern is how bad the situation is likely to be within the next few moments. At around a ton per cubic yard, moving water is extraordinarily powerful and blindly uncompromising. If the surge is strong or larger sets of waves are threatening, you'll need to take action very quickly because the choice to stay put on the obstruction might not be yours. Worse yet, water action might begin to break the hull apart.

If you're holed, you need to immediately establish where and how severe the damage is. Every case will have its own cure, but it's fairly certain that you'll need to make emergency repairs and brace the holed area before taking the boat off the ground.

The severity of the immediate and imminent situation, the structure of your vessel, the experience of your crew and passengers, and other prevailing conditions will dictate what you do next. If you're aground in a relatively small and shallow draft vessel, it may be possible to use a boat hook or similar object to pole yourself away from the obstruction.

FACTS

Flotsam refers to the parts of a wrecked vessel that float on the sea. Jetsam are items that are purposely thrown overboard to help the goods from perishing if the vessel goes down or to lighten the vessel to stop it from going down.

If you have a dinghy or other craft aboard, launch it and take soundings all around the boat. A simple weight on a string or oar should do just fine. If your investigations prove that the situation is dire or likely to become dire, it's a good idea to confirm this to the Coast Guard and others on the VHF radio and execute appropriate distress signals.

If you're not in imminent danger and believe that you can proceed without creating or encountering more danger, start to assess your next steps: How did you get here and is there a clear path to retreat along? If not, where does deeper water lie? What is the tide doing?

If you're sailing in areas where the possibility of grounding is high, consider becoming a member of a commercial towing organization. Your local authority, Coast Guard office, or marina should be able to point you in the right direction.

Floating Off on a Rising Tide

If the tide is coming in, then you'll have progressively better water depth under your keel to float yourself free. Even if you might free yourself sooner if another vessel pulled you off, letting the tide float you off is far less stressful on your hull and your crew.

What is important at this point is to establish the direction of the water's flow around your hull. You need to set out an anchor or even two angled in the direction of the wind and waves to prevent the rising tide from carrying you farther up on the shoal.

Freeing Yourself When the Tide Is Falling

If the tide is falling, then the situation will progressively worsen, and you must accelerate efforts to extract yourself. First, assess how much farther the tide is likely to fall and what it will do in the immediate vicinity of your vessel when it does. As wave action and surge tend to increase, the shallower the water becomes. If you anticipate that it will become increasingly difficult to refloat, then you need to move really fast.

Depending on your hull design below the water line, you could be in for a difficult time as it begins to heel ever farther over to one side. If you see that you're not going to get the hull refloated immediately and it's clear that the outgoing tide will exacerbate the situation, then you need to consider cushioning and supporting the hull.

ALERT

To check for gas leaks, you can use dish soap bubbles on propane fittings. It's nice to have a strobe light and whistle on every life vest. You'll also want to make sure that all cleats and pad eyes have the correct size backing plates.

If you're high and dry, have signaled for help, have completed all the evasive action, hull bracing, and cushioning you can, then you might as well make good of the situation until help or the tide returns. Use the opportunity to inspect your hull, shore it up, and even give it a clean!

FACTS

To find the eye of a hurricane in the Northern Hemisphere, face the wind and, with your right hand, point 112 degrees to your right. In the Southern Hemisphere, face the wind with your left hand and point 112 degrees to your left.

Getting Free When You're Barely Aground

If you're only superficially aground, you may be able to get off without assistance. First, determine where deeper water and an escape path lie; it may not be the direction from which you came.

Next, try to reduce draft—the amount of water you need to float—by getting weight out of the vessel. Liquid is extremely heavy, so if you can spare it, empty your water tanks. Move your heaviest gear and ballast, including passengers, to the dingy and ferry them to safety.

On a sailboat, you've typically got a deep keel and a high mast. Without bringing too much stress to bear on the rig or capsizing the entire vessel, it's worth running a halyard out to one side and either attaching it to an anchor or another boat. Apply gentle force; the lateral roll of the boat might tip the boat and keel sufficiently to effectively reduce the draft.

Using the Wind to Heel the Boat

Another technique is to use the wind to heel the boat. You'll use the jib sail for this and what you've got to be certain of is that you don't set it in such a way that it provides motion in the wrong direction. You need to set the sail across the wind so all the energy goes into heeling the boat. With the draft effectively reduced by heeling, you can try to power off the bar.

Taking a Tow

If you have another vessel standing by to help, see whether they can pull you off in the most appropriate direction. Ensure that the rescue boat doesn't strand herself in the same shallows you're wallowing in! Don't take a chance—the rescue boat should run an anchor from the direction she's approaching from in order to keep her clear so that she can pull herself free if required. Only tie the towline off on deck fittings that can withstand the tremendous strain of the pull.

While attempting the pull, evacuate all hands and only approach the line if it is critical to do so. Keep low and try to ensure that a sturdy physical barrier is between the rope under strain and humans. Rope stretch stores vast amounts of energy. If the line parts or the fitting to which it is attached pulls free, it will whip like a slingshot. Serious injury and death are very possible for anyone caught in the resulting whiplash.

FIGURE 13-1:
Towing

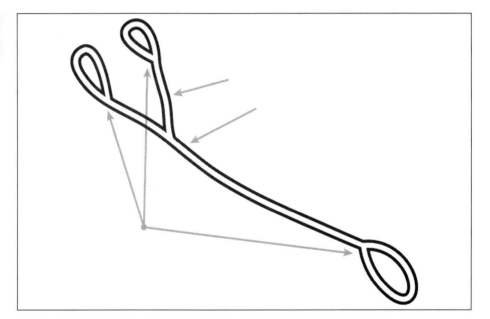

Causing as Much Wake as Possible

If there is no way to execute a tow, another possible remedy is for the rescue boat to cause as much wake as possible in the immediate vicinity—avoiding the shallows, of course. The idea is that the waves that form might be sufficient to lift your boat free. This is a long shot and can only be attempted when you're certain that the bottom is soft enough not to damage your hull if you bounce. Sand bottoms would probably not do you much damage.

In case of steering failure or a situation that forces you not to adhere to the rules of the road, use two red lights in a vertical line, which means that the vessel is not under command.

Winching Yourself Off

If you believe that you can move the boat either forward or astern off the obstruction, then you can use a technique called kedging off. Lay an anchor in the direction in which you want to move and use one of your winches to apply force on the line. The more scope, or distance from the boat, that you can achieve on the line, the better. Use a dinghy or a bundle of PFDs to carry the anchor as far away as practical.

Remember that boat-sized anchors and dinghies make bad sailing companions. When you use a dinghy to run the anchor out, tie the anchor to the dinghy's bow cleat and leave it hanging in the water. It will make for slow headway and delicate maneuvering, but it provides for an easy uncleat when you're over the drop zone.

CHAPTER 14

Knowing the Regulations

These days, all boating is regulated to one degree or another. Before you put your boat in the water, find out which governing authorities potentially could have jurisdiction over you, your boat, and your actions by contacting your local Coast Guard or any other marine authority. This chapter takes a look at some of the organizations that might impact your day.

Port Authorities

The American Association of Port Authorities includes the major port authorities in the United States, Canada, Latin America, and the Caribbean. In addition, it also represents a host of associate members, firms, and individuals who govern coastal waters and ports.

In order to obtain an updated list of regulations and information, please contact the American Association of Port Authorities at 1010 Duke Street, Alexandria, Virginia 22314–3589; phone: ✆ (703) 684-5700; fax: ✍ (703) 684-6321; e-mail: ✉ *info@aapa-ports.org*.

National and International Regulations

You can contact the following organizations to get a current list of their area of authority, regulations, and other recommendations.

- The Federal Maritime Commission was established in 1961 as an independent government agency, responsible for regulating shipping in the foreign trades of the United States. The Commission's five members are appointed by the president with the advice and consent of the Senate. The contact information is FMC Headquarters, 800 North Capitol Street, N.W., Washington, D.C. 20573.
- You can also contact the International Maritime Organization at 4 Albert Embankment, London SE1 7SR; phone: ✆ 0171-735 7611; fax: ✍ 0171 587 3210; telex: 23588.

FACTS

The United States Sailing Association is the national governing body of sailing and has a membership organization of 25,000 sailing groups. Members receive discounts on sailing travel, publications, videos, and other products. To find out more about your local organization, call ✆ (401) 849-5200 or write to USSA, Box 209, Newport, RI 02840.

U.S. Coast Guard

The U.S. Coast Guard provides boating safety, consumer, and Coast Guard policy information to the boating public Monday through Friday, 8 A.M. to 4 P.M. EST. Its infoline is ☎ (800) 368-5647.

You can rely on the Coast Guard to undertake the following specific duties at this number:

- Provide a wide range of Coast Guard program and safety information through the use of knowledgeable, courteous customer service representatives.
- Direct you to a customer service representative within five seconds of receipt of your call.
- Provide immediate access to subject matter experts when your question requires a technical response.
- Provide immediate access to a supervisor if requested.
- Take reports of possible boat defects from you.
- Respond to your requests for printed matter within twenty-four hours.
- Provide information on specific subjects twenty-four hours a day via a menu of recorded messages.
- Handle boat registration at a national level.

FIGURE 14-1:
Loran

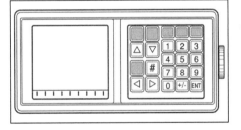

The Coast Guard also provides search-and-rescue services on demand twenty-four hours a day, seven days a week, throughout the United States maritime region. It immediately answers all telephone calls requesting assistance twenty-four hours a day, seven days a week, and monitors Channel 16, the VHF-FM National Distress System twenty-four hours a day, seven days a week.

It also offers navigational aids, such as the Loran navigation signal, the Differential Global Positioning System (GPS) navigation signal, the Omega navigation signal, and navigational systems of short-range aids and buoys for U.S coastal and harbor navigation, with individual aids. For more on the Coast Guard's duties, go to ✍*www.cglalb.com/license.htm* or ✍*www.uscg.mil.*

Skipper Licenses

To qualify for a skipper's license, you need to establish precisely what tuition you will require, where you can get it, and how to sign up for the appropriate examination. You can do so by contacting any of the following organizations:

- Local sailing and yacht clubs
- The American Red Cross
- Community groups (including city and state funded programs)
- Sailing and racing organizations and associations
- U.S. Navy bases (for active duty or retired military personnel and their families, plus some government workers)
- Sailboat rental and charter companies
- Sailing schools

All of these organizations should be quite easy to find by contacting any local, state, or national chapter or by looking in the phone book.

SSENTIALS

COLREGS is the agreement on how boats should conduct themselves in international waters. This is the abbreviation for the International Regulations for Prevention of Collision at Sea. Please always abide by all rules of the sea.

Insurance

We'll put it quite simply: If you can't afford the insurance on your vessel, seriously consider selling it and buying a vessel you can afford to insure.

The water is unpredictable, and damage to vessels really does occur. Insurance assessors will take the condition of your boat, your general age and experience, the waters you sail, and any specific coverage that you request, into account.

If you're not going to have coverage over your vessel, at the very least take out third-party coverage. That way, you're protected in cases of injury or death.

FACTS

Stern lights are only visible when you are behind a boat. These lights help identify the vessel. One of the light combinations is yellow over yellow, which refers to the lights of a tug pushing a barge, but this only applies to the inland rules. Yellow over white are the lights of a tug towing astern.

Float Plans

You don't have to write out a float plan, but you should. This simple written log records your intentions for those ashore. At the very least, you need to tell someone where you are going.

When you create your float plan, include your intended destination and schedule. In addition, include the skipper's name and phone number. This way, in case there's a mixup and you end up at home while the rest of the world is out looking for you, potential rescuers can make a simple call and short-circuit the whole song and dance routine.

QUESTIONS?

What is a non-technical method of determining a boat's speed? To determine your speed, measure the distance between an arbitrary point that you choose from the bow and then another from the stern. Drop a chip in the water at the bow. Time how long it takes to travel pass the stern. Then divide the distance in feet by the time in seconds and multiply by 0.6 to equal the speed in knots.

Your float plan should also include a description of your boat, including its color, design, size, and registration numbers. Also include any emergency contacts, as well as your next of kin, and other emergency numbers, such as the Coast Guard, sheriff's office, lifeguards, and marine patrol.

It's best to lodge this information with harbor authorities, but if this is impossible or impractical, at least leave it with a responsible adult ashore. Then don't forget to contact that person once you return so that they don't call out the cavalry on a false alarm.

Carrying Capacities

Next to alcohol abuse, one of the most foolish things a skipper can do is overload a vessel. Many authorities place upper limits on a boat's carrying capacity. Find out whether any apply to your boat in the areas that you intend to sail.

Alcohol is the cause of one-third of all boating fatalities. The penalties are severe if you're found to be under the influence. Fines can go up to $5,000 and include mandatory substance abuse counseling, imprisonment of up to one year, and nonpaid public service work.

But regulations and live bodies aside, any cargo aboard—including fuel, equipment, or shipped water or rainwater in the holds—adds to the boat's displacement or load. Besides reducing freeboard, or distance from the gunwales to the water's surface, it can change a boat's center of gravity and cause innumerable problems when the boat moves in any direction or on the roll of the swell.

Speeding

Of course, in sailing terms, speeding would apply mainly to tenders. Nevertheless, it is necessary to point out once more just how hard the water becomes at speed. When you start getting up over ten knots, you can consider that you're entering the realm of "dangerous speed."

Drinking and Boating

Boating and alcohol don't mix—period. Like driving, it's a sad fact that the majority of boating fatalities involve alcohol. Besides being minimalist with the stuff for crew and passengers, take the designated driver rule with you when you leave your car and board the boat. Skippers always stay sober.

Legal limits vary from state to state, but all have BWI (boating while intoxicated) laws that limit your blood/alcohol range to anywhere between .05 to .08. Penalties may include a fine of $5,000, imprisonment of up to twelve months, community service, and substance abuse counseling. If a fatality is linked to alcohol, prison time can jump to five years.

FACTS

Nine out of ten deaths at sea are due to drowning, and about half of the deaths at sea are alcohol-related. More than 1,000 people die in boating accidents every year.

Boater's hypnosis occurs after four hours of exposure to powerboat noise, sun, glare, vibration, wind, and motion and causes similar symptoms of being legally drunk; alcohol intensifies these symptoms.

CHAPTER 15

Understanding Sailing Etiquette

Though etiquette applies to the interpersonal niceties onboard and relative respects shown to and between skippers, crews, and accomplished individuals, this chapter is really an extension of sailing rules. The little courtesies that are voluntarily extended make sailing that much safer and that much more enjoyable.

The Ten Commandments

Sailing etiquette is really just a collection of the conformities and norms that will make you a nice individual to be around and your boat and crew a welcome fellow of the waterways. In short, when we as a community cease volunteering to offer etiquette, much of it will probably have to be forced on us by legislation.

Experience shows that the sailors who typically display the best etiquette are those who've been involved in the sport for many years. On the other end of the scale are newcomers. Perhaps it's just that nobody's explained the easy and difficult way of doing this. Or perhaps the big outlay on equipment they've just made clouds their perception of how important and invincible they are within the greater scheme. Invariably, they're not doing anyone any favors.

FACTS

A power-driven vessel needs to keep out of the way of a vessel that is broken down, has restricted maneuverability, is transferring supplies to another vessel, is sailing under sail only, is propelled by paddles or oars, or is fishing.

Decades ago, the sailing fraternity was so small that there was virtually no need for even a single rule and no need to have Big Brother breathing down your neck, ensuring that you comply. Today, the very freedoms we turn to sailing for are slowly being eroded. And this situation is only likely to tighten as the boating zones clog with ever more upstarts who haven't passed on the traditions of the ages.

Because we're writing these unwritten rules down, we'll just stop beating about the bush and call them what they are—they're RULES.

Thou shalt:

- Never disobey posted rules—even though you may not be observed and could get away with it.
- Not perform in a dumb way or in any silly manner while on the helm or getting gas.

- Never make waves for other vessels, especially in harbors and places of rest.
- Not anchor in a trafficked place or foolhardy manner.
- Never release thy offal or other foreign matter overboard.
- Not maketh a nasty din.
- Not speak like a vagabond in an improper manner to other boaters or on the radio machine.
- Never allow thine upper decks and hull to look like a den of iniquity or other place of ill-repute—this includes thy manner of dress.
- Not misunderstand or fail to respond to flag or other signals.
- Never hang out thy dirty laundry—in literal, visible, or audio terms—equally.
- Not be a boor, twit, or other unsociable animal in any other ways.

Oops, that was eleven, but who's counting?

Right of Way

One courtesy is that power should give way, but does that rule always apply? Under the bows of a supertanker, you'll certainly suspend this rule, but that's not etiquette—that's survival. The question is, if you can easily give way while the powered vessel would be compromised in some way, what do you do?

Personally, we think, what the heck—give way and tip your hat. The gesture will be appreciated and duplicated down the line—until the time comes that you receive the same fine gesture.

Perhaps this is one area that you can't see ever being legislated. On the other hand, if people were more courteous, then the local lake down the road from us wouldn't have to be segregated with sailors here, skiers there, and paddlers somewhere else. In short, we'd all have a wider range to enjoy.

An all-around white light must indicate the direction if your fishing gear extends over 492 feet (150 meters) from the boat. You can remember this by thinking that the lights have stopped over a white fish.

Clothing at the Yacht Club

Besides reserving a little modesty while on deck and among other craft, the issue of club dress isn't to force everyone into bow ties and jackets, though these might just lend a touch of elegance to the occasional event. The point can be much more practically made.

Don't traipse through the club while dripping wet or sit on chairs with a less than dry rump. It's not fair for those who follow you. It's not particularly kind to other members for you to break from swabbing the bilge and then sit down to Sunday lunch in all your aromatic finery. And it's not fair to bring your scantily clad and ill-behaved hordes into the club for a drink when you know retired corps are holding their annual convention.

The Skipper Sets the Tone

Whether you agree or not, while on the water, the big boss holds sway down to some of the most rudimentary issues others might believe are silly. The rule here is that all others should ask if they are in doubt. This goes for which equipment can be used or handled and when; where and how goods should be stowed; if, where, and when smoking is allowed; whether glass is allowed aboard; or even if the helmsman can be spoken to at different times.

It might seem petty, and if so, nobody is obligated to sail under that skipper ever again. The point is that it comes down to different strokes for different folks—providing the skipper agrees.

When You're a Visitor

Though tradition dictates that visitors offer to bring a gift or to pay for fuel, the Coast Guard has already ruled that this transaction fits the parameters of "carrying passengers for hire." Because, by the purest definitions, the skipper would then be required to have the appropriate licensing requirements in order for operating a "chartered fee" business, it is therefore a sensitive issue that the individuals need to discuss between themselves.

Guests need to understand that sailing is fraught with chores. They need to be prepared to give reasonable assistance.

Though the boat might have sufficient safety equipment and foul weather gear for the regular complement and some guests, wherever they reasonably can, guests should be prepared to bring their own personal equipment. In addition, when a guest has special needs such as foods or medication, he or she is certainly expected to provide them.

ESSENTIALS

If you decide that you'd like to bring a gift for a sailor, consider a docking line; charts; books; gadgets like stocking stuffers, wind gauges, pocket knives, fids, sail twine, flashlights, and so on; photos; GPS; radios; binoculars; cushions; or warm and dry clothing.

The guest's attitude should certainly be open to learning the elementary aspects of sailing, courtesy, and safety. Beyond this, food preparation and general cleanup will probably be on the roster, and guests need to be prepared to muck-in.

Lastly, everybody—skipper, crew, and guest alike—has a fiduciary responsibility to be at the departure point, on time, every time.

The Great Outdoors

Sailing offers notoriously ferocious sunburns. All aboard should cover for one another by providing whatever sun protection they can, which may be hats, creams, clothing, or sunglasses.

To have a pleasant sailing experience, it's vital to dress appropriately to the conditions. Light colors do the best job of reflecting light and keeping the individual cool. On the other hand, dark colors and rainproof gear does the best job keeping the cold, wet, and wind out. Modern fabrics such as Gore-Tex are a godsend to the sailor.

Heat loss through the skull can be extremely high at sea. Ensure that everyone has headwear for both sun and cold. Also, don't forget gloves if there's any chance of cold. The wind-chill factor out at sea can be surprisingly severe.

What you get is precisely what you pay for. Apparel at sea needs to be more than a fashion statement; it needs to be practical, too. Ensure that you've got good quality foul-weather gear.

Eating on Board

There's nothing like the wind and water to build up an appetite. Petite birdlike creatures can unexpectedly transform into calorie-guzzling gannets within a few hours.

The food you bring aboard is more correctly called victuals in the nautical sense. Whatever you're planning to bring along as grub, just make sure that there's plenty of it because there are not a lot of places you can pick up a quick snack if you do run out.

Some larger boats are outfitted with wonderful galleys, but it's generally best to bring ready-prepared meals that can easily be warmed or tossed together in no time.

The larger boats might also have barbecues out over the stern. When you do fire up the barbecue, ensure that you're on a single-bow anchor so that the smoke and embers can blow away to sea and not into the sails. On a note of etiquette, do also ensure that you're not upwind of other vessels whose day your enjoyment will destroy.

Precooked chicken will take a lot less time to be done on the coals. Use the self-starting type of charcoal because it's clean, fast, safe, and easy to use. Line the bottom of the grill with foil to stop grease from dripping onto any part of the boat. This way, you can simply discard the foil after use, leaving the grill easy to clean.

QUESTIONS?

How do you keep food fresh on a boat?
We have a few inside tips for you. Start by removing plastic wrappings. In addition, store your potatoes and tomatoes in a dark place.

Make no mistake, with exercise in the wind, you'll need to drink an awful lot, so bring far more water than you need. It's not the world's most expensive commodity, so don't skimp.

On cruises longer than a day or two, the time will come when most civilized beings will begin to think about scraping the scum from their bodies. Even though, by definition, boats sail on water, it is not always the water people want to wash in, so storage tanks need to be provided for this purpose. On the other hand, water weighs and takes up valuable stowage space, so it is therefore not an endless resource for trippers. Sound conservation methods and rationing systems are a reality, and everyone aboard needs to be keenly aware not to use more than their allotment.

ALERT

You've probably heard the saying "Green over White, Trawling Tonight." It simply means that the vessel is trawling, which is quite different from fishing. Another way to help you remember this is that when you see the green over white, think of a piece of green seaweed from the bottom of the ocean.

At Anchor

Wherever there's a favorable or charming spot to anchor, you can be pretty sure that neighboring vessels will not be long or far away. The first to an anchorage has the seniority. Provided that the anchor does not drag, the vessel that anchors second is obligated to reset the anchor in the event that there is any interference between vessels.

It is clear then that whichever boats drag anchor should have the good grace to admit to this fact and not embroil themselves in arguments with their fellows. There is, of course, the element of ego and power-play at stake, but this human peculiarity aside, resetting an anchor is really not such a tough task that it's worth bad blood.

At the Dock

Docking rates are a little like hotel rates in that they alter by season and by day of week. It's not a good idea to try discussing rates over the open airwaves.

As you approach a dock, you can by all means have the fenders secured and ready, but keep them on the inside of your guardrail and only toss them overboard during your final approach. To travel with fenders hanging out over the sides of your vessel would be a little like stripping down to your underwear in your car and then checking your mailbox before arriving home through the front door—it's cheesy and it's not good etiquette at all.

ESSENTIALS

Always be considerate to your fellow boaters. Make sure to turn off your VHF radio, instruments, and all outside lights. There is nothing worse than having to listen to noise when you're out on the water trying to enjoy nature.

Whether alongside or at anchor, do respect other boaters by not using your generator early in the morning or late at night. Sound can travel an awful long way over the water, so this really is a no-no.

CHAPTER 16

Playing It Safe

When the unexpected happens, you need to be prepared. Taking a few precautions before you sail can help you avoid potentially dangerous situations. At the very least, you'll know how to react in an emergency situation, which will help minimize injury and damage to individuals as well as boats.

Take a Safety Course

No matter how well you maintain your boat and equipment or how well you know the waterways, be sure to take a boat safety course. To find one, ask around at your local club or marina. Besides getting very good information and hints from your local marina or boating store(s), you can also find the date and location for the Coast Guard Auxiliary's upcoming Boating Skills and Seamanship Course. These can be invaluable.

In addition, be certain to ensure that those who regularly accompany you onto the water undertake the course. In fact, take the course with them, even if it means repeating it several times. You may be surprised what you don't know or have forgotten.

FACTS

By congressional charter, the American Red Cross is responsible for preventing and relieving suffering and accidents. The American Red Cross provides courses, standards, and materials in first aid, swimming, CPR, lifeguarding, lifesaving, kayaking, canoeing, and boating safely.

Stock a First-Aid Kit

Every boat needs a basic first-aid kit. At a minimum, the first-aid kit should contain the following items:

- A basic first-aid manual
- Antiseptic ointment
- Rubbing alcohol
- An assortment of bandages, gauze pads, and tape
- Tweezers
- Sunburn lotion
- Aspirin and other over-the-counter pain medications
- Diarrhea treatments
- Eye drops, such as Visine
- Plastic gloves
- Antiseptic soap

Conduct a Semiannual Safety Check

At least twice a year, you'll want to ensure that all emergency equipment is maintained in proper working order. This equipment includes bilge pumps, fire extinguishers, and leak-stopping and shoring equipment tools and materials.

PFDs

Check your PFDs for wear or abrasion, weak or torn seams, secure straps, and buckles. If your PFDs are equipped with inflation devices, check to be sure that the cartridges are secure and charged.

ALERT

To test your PFD, jump into a pool and make sure that the straps, zips, and ties are properly fastened. If correctly fastened, the PFD should stay in place and not ride up over your chin. Also make sure that your mouth is well above the water when you relax. Your PFD may act differently in heavy seas.

Fire Extinguishers

Make sure that you have the required number and types of fire extinguishers and that everyone on board knows how to use them. They should be easily accessible. One should be reachable from the helm or cockpit. You'll also want to make sure that any serviceable units have been tagged by a licensed facility.

Fuel System

Check your fuel system to make sure that it's properly grounded at the filter, tank, deck, and pump and that it's free from rust or contamination. Watch out for any leaks from the tank, hose, or fittings. You'll also want to make sure that the fuel tank is secured and look for a fuel shut-off valve on the tank and at the engine. Your engine compartment and engine should be clean and free of oily rags or flammable materials. You'll also want to have a blower switch at a remote location and make sure that your fuel system is protected from siphoning.

Safety Equipment

Check up on your safety equipment. Check to see whether the rails or lifelines are in good condition. Make sure that the stanchions or pulpit is securely mounted. Ensure that all hardware is tight and sealed at the deck. Double-check that grab rails are secure and free of corrosion or snags and that nonskid surfaces are free from accumulated dirt or excess wear.

Ground Tackle

You'll want to make sure that you have at least two anchors on board and that your anchor and rope are adequate for your boat and bottom conditions. Check that the tackle is properly secured. Take a peek at the length of chain at anchor and the thimble on the rope and safety-wired shackles. Don't forget to check the chafing gear, which you'll need for extended stays or storm conditions. Make sure that the anchor is stowed for quick accessibility.

Stoves

Your stoves should be labeled and designated for marine use and properly ventilated to remove carbon monoxide from the cabin. If the stove is built-in, make sure that it's properly insulated and free from combustible materials, CNG, and LPG (propane). You'll want to have retainers or rails for your pots and pans while you're underway.

The tank should have a tightly secured shut-off valve. Have proper labeling and cautions in place at the tank location and also make sure that it's stored in a separate compartment from the vessel's interior and engine room. The compartment should also be ventilated overboard and below the level of the tank base. Hoses, lines, and fittings should be approved and inspected.

SSENTIALS   Mast lights are shown to identify vessels more precisely and are in addition to the running lights. A sailboat does not have a mast light. Powerboats do have a white masthead light.

Electrical System

When it comes to your electrical system, use wiring that has been approved for marine applications. The system should be neatly bundled and secured and protected against chafing and strain. You should have adequate flex between the bulkhead and engine connections, and it should be clear of the exhaust system and bilge. The system should also be protected by circuit breakers or fuses and have grounds to zincs if required. Lastly, check to see whether the wire terminals and connections are sealed to prevent corrosion.

Bilge Pumps

You need to know that your pumps will adequately remove water in an emergency. You'll also want a manual backup, just in case. Bilges should be clean and free to circulate. You should check your bilges frequently and not rely on automatic pumps.

Corrosion Prevention

You want your through-hulls, props, shafts, bearings, rudder fittings, and exposed fastenings to be free of nondestructive corrosion. Zincs are adequate to provide protection. To prevent corrosion, check that your through-hulls are properly bonded. Also inspect the steering cables, engine control linkage and cables, engine mounts, and gear case for corrosion. These items should also be properly lubricated or painted to prevent undue corrosion.

Through-Hulls

Strainers, intakes, and exhaust or discharge fittings should be free from restrictions, such as barnacles, marine growth, or debris. You should also inspect your sea valves for smooth operation. Handles should be attached to valves for quick closure, and your hoses should be in good condition and free from cracking. You'll also want to double hose-clamps below the water line and have an antisiphon valve fitted to the marine toilet. Also make sure that you have through-hull plugs near fittings or attached to the hose in case of an emergency.

Batteries

Batteries should be well secured and stored in noncorrosive, liquid-tight, ventilated containers. Fit nonconductive covers over the posts.

Watch the Weather

If there is one macrofactor over which the sailor has no control, but is still entirely at the mercy of, it's the weather. One of the most important parts of becoming an expert sailor is learning how to understand weather and harness its power, while protecting yourself, your crew, and your vessel from its many dangers.

FACTS

Whether or not you're the superstitious type, you may be interested in these common sailing superstitions:

- Never say *thirteen, egg, rabbit,* or *pig* on any ship.
- If you turn a boat counterclockwise, it is said that you are turning toward the devil.
- To bring yourself luck, put coins under your mast.
- Flowers on board represent a wreath for a doomed crew.

Clearly, no matter how sophisticated humans become, we cannot change the weather to our preference. The best you can do is to understand the basic climatological theory of weather patterns and learn how to interpret and use them to your advantage. Before venturing asea, you should make sure you've done the following:

- Watch the local weather and tides and plan passages to avoid heavy weather.
- Have a well-found yacht: structurally sound and well provisioned and outfitted with proper operating, maintenance, safety and emergency gear and systems.
- Prepare your crew for every weather eventuality and practice emergency procedures.
- Keep your priorities in order: safety, comfort, and then speed.

Fuel Your Boat Safely

Fueling your boat is one of the most dangerous times because it's when exposure between the two enemies—sparks and fumes—is the greatest. As a result, it's best that fueling procedures be executed with a minimum of crew on hand and absolutely no passengers to get in the way or light a cigarette! The rules are:

- Turn all electronics and appliances off.
- Secure all cabins, doors, and hatches and close windows.
- Turn engines and motors off and remove keys from ignitions.
- Ensure that the tank and nozzle are grounded so that no static charges will create a spark.
- Always check all hose connections and securing clamps for snug fit and possible damage.

During the procedure, keep a watchful eye on the procedure, what every person in the immediate area is doing, and for any trace of fuel leakage or spillage in the immediate vicinity—including the surrounding water and bilge. These may be the first signs of a leakage that might turn explosive.

Handling a Spill

If you're vigilant and unlucky enough to encounter fuel floating on the water or spilled into the bilges on deck, immediately stop the filling procedure and remove the filling hose from the boat.

If there's fuel or any water in the bilge, immediately cut the automatic bilge pump. If you don't do this and the pump activates, there is a high likelihood of an explosion. If the spill is into the bilge, as quickly as possible, cover the afflicted area with flame retardant foam. If no foam is available, mix up a soap and water bucket and scoop the soap onto the fuel to reduce the danger.

Carefully siphon the fuel and water mixture out of the area with an all-plastic bilge pump so that you don't cause sparks and get it into a container designed to carry fuels. If a fire occurs, execute the emergency fire drill covered later in this chapter.

Running Out of Gas

Running out of gas, while usually not life threatening, is certainly no fun. Fuel gauges are notoriously inaccurate, and the safest course is to top off the fuel tank every morning before you head out. Face it, out in the blue yonder, it takes a very special kind of person to jog to the nearest gas station.

The amount of fuel you need to carry depends on a variety of factors, but the most important one is "enough fuel to ensure a good margin of safety for your trip."

Use common sense in planning and monitoring every trip. The old rule warns that you should use no more than one-third of the fuel in your tank to reach the destination, which should translate to at least the same one-third to get back, and a reserve third for emergency backup.

Sailing boats are not designed to be either particularly fuel-efficient or provide great performance; they are designed to sail! However, because most sailing boats are displacement rather than planing hulls, you will be pleased to know that they'll give you much better economy than similarly sized motor launches.

To give you an idea of what to expect, and depending on the actual rigs and engine type of the two vessels in question, two 35-foot vessels of different type would achieve approximately the following results with the same fuel:

BOAT	DISTANCE	FUEL AMOUNT	CRUISING SPEED
Sailing boat	300 miles	50 gallons	7 knots
Power cruiser	300 miles	450 gallons	40 knots

It's an interesting comparison and one that will give you a smug feeling whenever you see the glitz-patrol streaking by on the plume of their wake. More than just burning fuel quickly, planing hulls are limited in the amount of fuel they can carry, because their ability to plane is restricted by the weight that they carry. This means that, excluding their ability to sail ahead of the wind without spending a penny on fuel, their fuel range is much shorter.

FACTS

To help keep the interior of your boat mildew free, add a bit of Mildicide powder to the rinse water after washing the interior of your boat. If you do have mildew on your walls, pour three tablespoons of nonchlorine bleach into a spray bottle with water and spray on the mildew and wipe clean.

Prevent and Control Fires

Fire aboard ship is one of the most terrifying experiences a person can have. When at sea, the boat is your entire world. It's the thread upon which your life and the lives of all your crew and passengers depend. No matter how large your boat, it's a very small world with nowhere to hide if the flames run out of control. When a fire occurs, no matter how small it may be, even the largest boat suddenly seems terribly small, and the fire terrifyingly close by.

On land, you can call 911 and make it someone else's problem; professionals will be there in no time to deal with it. You can stand well back and turn your garden hose on it or retreat to a safer distance and wring your hands helplessly. If it really becomes bad, to save life and limb, you can evacuate the area and let the flames burn themselves out. But at sea, there's nowhere to go. You've got to fight the fire and simultaneously prepare to evacuate to a lifeboat. You've got to contend with noxious fumes, a variety of techniques to deal with different materials that are burning, and the potential for explosion of highly flammable materials. And you've got to do it all quickly and efficiently.

To avoid most boat fires, dispose of oily rags or place them in covered containers, clean bilges often, store propane fuel in secure areas, maintain proper gear stowage, and make sure that short-tie cables are correctly connected.

It would seem that, with an endless reservoir of water in every direction to draw on as a fire-fighting agent, fighting a fire at sea would be among the easiest fires a person could face. Yet nothing could be further from the truth. Not all fires are equal, and at sea, this fact is exaggerated. When they burn, different classes of material require different extinguishing agents to quell them.

Preparing for a Fire

Reading this section on fire-fighting is just the first step in safety. Fighting a fire is not something that you can go out and casually practice on weekends. If you don't seek out and subject yourself to professional training in a real-life practice scenario, the very first fire you'll ever face will be the real one on a real boat, with no real help.

So, unless you're supremely confident that you can read the instructions on the various extinguishers you buy, figure out which ones to use and when, and then execute those instructions from memory at one of the most terrifying moments in your life, get some practical professional training.

One of the finest gifts you can give yourself, your crew, and all the passengers you'll ever carry is to undertake and become certified through a basic course in nautical know-how and basic boating safety. See *www.boatsafe.com/nauticalknowhow/boating/index.htm* for details.

Fighting an Onboard Fire

Find the fire's location and establish its size, fueling constituents, likely growth speed, and growth pattern. Take it all in with a single glance and don't waste time on the details. Immediately inform the crew of these details. They should immediately sound the general alarm, broadcast a distress call to the Coast Guard and other vessels, and activate the appropriate fire-fighting equipment and techniques.

Then take the following steps to restrict the fire:

1. Shut off the air supply to the fire by closing ports and hatches.
2. Shut off electrical circuits in the general area.
3. Shut off gas or liquid fuel supplies and ventilation.
4. Position the vessel to minimize any wind effects on the fire.
5. Confine the fire, if possible.
6. Ensure that all hands and passengers are evacuated from the area before activating fixed extinguishing systems or chemical agents.

Extinguishing Fires

The principle of extinguishing any fire is to remove one of the three fire elements that conspire to form a destructive orgy: fuel, heat energy, and oxygen. Simple as this combination sounds, it's not quite so easy to do in practice.

Whereas an agent like water is excellent at extinguishing wood-fueled fires, when water comes into contact with burning oil, it only spreads the blaze. When water makes contact with an electrical fire, catastrophic short-circuiting can be more dangerous than the original flames.

We doubt that there is any manmade environment other than sailing that assembles a more diverse group of potentially lethal materials into a confined space, each of which requires different treatment.

Matching the Extinguisher to the Fire

In order to successfully extinguish any fire, you need to use the most suitable type of extinguishing agent—one that will do the job in the least amount of time, cause the least amount of damage, and result in the least danger to crew members. To make the job of selecting the appropriate agent easier, standardized classifications of fire types have been established. These fall into classes that are lettered *A* through *D*. These classifications group fires that involve materials that have similar burning properties and that require similar extinguishing treatment and agents.

ESSENTIALS Your best weapon against fire is a good knowledge of the following classes of fire you're likely to encounter and the burning characteristics of materials of each.

Unfortunately, fire doesn't make it all that simple. Most fuels are found in combinations. For example, electricity cannot burn in isolation; it burns in combination with other materials, so electrical fires always involve some solid fuel. This fact expands the fire-fighting problem to no fewer than seven classes of fire.

Class A Fires

Class A fires are fires of common combustible solids, such as wood, paper, and plastic. These fires can be extinguished with water that has a temperature below 212°F/100°C. All of these elements require much higher temperatures in order to burn. Water instantly cools the substance, and the chain reaction of heat, fuel, and oxygen is broken.

Water is ideal because it is cheap, plentiful, and doesn't cause more damage to the wooden, paper, or plastic object. You can also use foam and certain dry chemicals. These agents smother the flames by removing oxygen from the combustion triangle.

Class B Fires

When it comes to Class B fires, throwing or spraying water onto burning flammable liquids such as oil, grease, gas and other substances will be disastrous. These substances rapidly give off large amounts of highly flammable vapors. More important, being liquid and lighter than water, these substances float on water. If you make the mistake of applying water to burning oils or gases that are still burning furiously, they will instantly splash away from the water and then flow back on top of the water. Where you possibly had a contained oil fire, the burning oil now hitches a ride to wherever the water below it flows, and you've got a disaster on your hands.

The answer is a smothering agent. Dry chemicals, foam, and carbon dioxide (CO_2) are the ideal. However, if the fire is getting its fuel from an open valve or broken fuel line, your first task is to shut down the source of the fuel. Simply removing the fuel may stop the fire. At the very least, it will make it easier to deal with.

If you're dealing with gas, the first thing you must do is shut down the source of the gas before attempting to extinguish it. This is vitally important because attempts to extinguish the fire while more fuel is rushing in can create an explosive situation that is far more treacherous than the fire itself. The only exception to this rule is when a life is in danger or when the fire must be extinguished in order to reach the gas supply shutoff.

Combination Class A and B Fires

If the fire is a combination of solid fuels and flammable gases or liquids, it's a combination Class A and B fire. Your first choice to smother it is a foam agent.

If no foam is available, you can use a fog of water. Note that a fog of water is not a stream of water or a thrown bucket of water. The water must be applied in a very fine mist, not a rain. If the water applied has the ability to splash, then you'll only spread the fire. Both foam and water fog have some cooling effect on the fire, but you're relying on them to smother the flames.

If the fire is in an enclosed space, carbon dioxide can be effective. If you use carbon dioxide in open spaces, it will dissipate too quickly to have any effect. The very important caution we must give is that carbon dioxide is extremely dangerous because it robs the air of oxygen and can therefore suffocate any humans or animals within the enclosed space—and this includes the person fighting the fire as well.

Class C Fires

Electrical fires can be extremely nasty. The first and most important rule is to ensure that the power source is removed and that no more electricity is flowing. Regardless of whether this is possible or not, never use agents that are conductive to electricity, such as water in any form, to extinguish the flames.

You fight an electrical fire with nonconductive agents such as carbon dioxide, Halon, and dry chemicals. It is important to note that dry chemicals may ruin electronic equipment, so their use may become more expensive than the fire itself.

Combination Class A and C Fires

Treat a combination of A and C fires as a C fire. Eliminate the flow of electricity to the circuit and avoid all forms of water, foam, and other conductive materials. Apply nonconductive agents such as carbon dioxide, Halon, and dry chemicals.

Combination Class B and C Fires

Again, treat this type of fire with utmost care. Remove the flow of fuel and energy where possible and use nonconductive agents. Carbon dioxide, Halon, and dry chemicals will work.

Combination Class D Fires

These particularly nasty fires involve combustible metals such as sodium, and potassium, and their alloys, magnesium, zinc, titanium, and aluminum. They burn at extremely high temperatures with a brilliant and intense flame.

Combustible metal fires can be smothered and controlled with special dry powder agents. These agents are not to be confused with dry chemicals, which are used on the other fires already discussed. Dry powders are used exclusively to extinguish combustible metals.

Water must never be used. Indeed, even in their regular solid state, sodium and potassium are extremely reactive and explosive with water.

Contact with water will make the molten metal of Class D fires splatter and inflict serious burns on anything it touches, as well as promote the chemical chain reaction that sustains the fire.

Regrouping after the Fire

After you've extinguished the fire, you need to conduct a roll call to account for all hands. Then secure the area and set up a fire watch to keep vigil for flare-ups. If you used water to extinguish the fire, immediately begin bilge pumping and mopping operations to rid the hull and companionways of all water.

Abandoning Ship

If you can't extinguish the fire despite your best efforts, you must consider abandoning the ship. Notify the Coast Guard and all other vessels for assistance. Then take the following steps:

1. Deploy the life raft with one crew member aboard.
2. If time allows, load your provisions onto the raft.
3. Have your remaining crew board the raft, followed by the skipper.
4. Deploy your flares and stand by on your hand-held VHF.

Always make sure to neatly flemish or coil any excess line onboard and also on the dock. This isn't just because it looks neater, but because it will prevent an accident from occurring and causing someone to trip and fall.

Respond Quickly to a Person Overboard

Depending on the circumstances and waters you are sailing, losing someone overboard can seem anything from hilariously funny to life-threateningly dire. As a rule, though, this is not a subject that should ever be treated lightly. Even if you're sailing at midday through the balmy shallows of some safe tropical haven, and cousin Joe—who is a great swimmer—has just made a total twit of himself by tripping over his own feet and landing in the drink, hold back the laughter till you've got him safely aboard.

In the unfortunate event of losing a member overboard, immediately take action. If you're in a trafficked area or racing, sound and display the appropriate alarm signals.

How to React

The first person who sees someone going overboard (spotter) must shout "crew overboard" or some reasonable variant of this. They should also yell whether to starboard or port and point to the spot or person in the water. For the duration of the recovery procedure, the spotter must continue to point to the person and never relax this directional signal. All crew not otherwise engaged in bringing the boat about should take up the cry and be prepared to take over pointing duties if they see the victim in case the spotter loses sight of the victim.

In order to push the stern and propeller away from the person in the water, the helmsman must immediately swing the boat in the direction the person fell and shift the engine to neutral and stop the boat. If Joe fell over the port side, swing hard to port.

FACTS

If someone falls overboard, the time you have to act varies dramatically according to the water temperature. This chart shows the relation between water temperature, the time it would take to feel exhaustion, and the expected time of survival.

Water Temperature (F)	Exhaustion	Expected Time of Survival
32.5°	<15 minutes	<15–45 minutes
32.5°–40.0°	15–30 minutes	30–90 minutes
40°–50°	30–60 minutes	1–3 hours
50°–60°	1–2 hours	1–6 hours
60°–70°	2–7 hours	2–40 hours
70°–80°	3–12 hours	3–Indefinitely

Immediately throw a lifesaving device to the victim. Unless absolutely necessary, nobody else should enter the water. If someone enters the water, he or she must be wearing a PFD.

The helmsman must keep the victim in view as he or she carefully brings the boat about. Approaching into the wind or current, carefully navigate back to the victim. Cut the engine as you draw up to the victim. Attach a line to the victim with all haste and ensure that he or she gets a PFD on before attempting to reboard. If it's a small vessel, ensure that weight is evenly distributed as the victim comes aboard.

When You're the One Overboard

When overboard, you can implement several techniques while waiting to be picked up. Whatever you do, do not panic. This is easier said than done, but it's also vital. Panicked thrashing in water is counterproductive.

When clothing becomes wet, it sinks. However, it also provides a degree of insulation against cold and offers something for rescuers to grab hold of and pull you aboard. Therefore, you should keep your clothes on.

With a PFD

FIGURE 16-1: Proper position to float with a PFD

Roll to your back, cross your arms over your chest to conserve heat and energy, and lay as motionless as you can, keeping your head and face out of the water, if possible. If the water is rough, extend your arms and hold them in a crucifix position. Allow your legs to rise as high as possible.

Alternatively, to raise your head and chest higher out of the water, allow your legs and torso to sink to the vertical orientation.

Floating Without Flotation Assistance

Unless you're a good swimmer or have practiced survival floating, you could be in deep trouble. To employ survival floating, hang vertically, feet down, extend your arms, and let your head drop backward so that your face is toward the sky. Push down on the water with your arms, and you should rise enough to take a deep breath. Relax your limbs. As long as you hold the air in your lungs, you won't sink more than an inch or two. When you need another breath, push down once more, and you should rise once again to repeat the exercise.

QUESTIONS?

Have you ever wondered why life jackets are orange?
There's a reason for this. Because orange isn't a color common in nature, it stands out and is easier to see when someone has fallen overboard.

Treading Water

Treading water is a lot more energy-sapping than simply floating. But it'll allow you more access to the air and it'll be much more effective in heavy conditions.

The procedure requires two movements. Your legs need to kick with a scissors motion, as in the leg movement for a breaststroke kick. Meanwhile, your arms need to rotate on the horizontal plane, with the palms of your hands held downward and tilting to form a planing surface that pushes you upward with each stroke.

CHAPTER 17

Using Distress Signals

Vessels of all nationalities have used distress signals for centuries. A system of flags, flares, audio warnings, and other visual or audio signaling methods has been built up over time until it's now widely used and universally understood by seafarers around the globe.

Notifying Authorities: Your Legal Requirements

Much as we might advocate safety and you might respond by doing all you can to be responsible and never make a mistake, accidents do nevertheless happen. With the right training, you should be well prepared to handle most situations and protect life, limb, and property—in that order, of course.

This brings us to certain legal requirements regarding your obligation to notify the authorities of any accidents or unsafe situations. The question is, where do you draw the line between being over-reactive and filing petty occurrences and failing to submit formal situation reports that are legislated requirements?

ALERT

There are four conditions that will require someone to fill out a boating report for an accident:

- Someone has died due to the accident.
- Someone is injured.
- Damage occurs to or by a vessel and other property.
- A passenger disappears.

Here's the scoop. Boating Accident Reports are required to be filed within:

- Forty-eight hours of the occurrence or within twenty-four hours if a person dies.
- Forty-eight hours if a person is injured and medical treatment beyond first aid is required.
- Ten days if only the vessel and/or property is a complete loss or receives damage exceeding $500. (Many states have set a limit less than $500, so contact your local state boating authority to determine the amount.)

- As soon as possible, but not more than twenty-four hours after any person on board a vessel disappears (under circumstances indicating death, injury, or possibly leading to death or injury).

If you'd like more detailed information regarding the forms that pertain to your situation and where and how to submit them, call the Coast Guard's toll-free Customer Information line at ✆ (800) 366-5647.

Using Radio Distress Signals

The trouble with distress is that it so often strikes when we're not in visual contact with assistance. Indeed, it's as though nature and circumstance have conspired to cause the worst distress to occur during violent storms when we're cut off from the outside world by wild seas, driving rain, and other interference. Alternatively, when minor distresses occur beyond the physical horizon of rescuers, they potentially become lethal.

The good news for the modern sailor is that radio is your bridge to the outside world and assistance. Radio penetrates the blackest night and carries volumes of information that our waterborne ancestors could only dream of. Thousands, and perhaps millions, of lives have been saved during the course of the last century due to this simple invention.

These days, two-way radio communication has become so inexpensive that there really is no excuse for a skipper not to have an appropriately powerful rig on board and in good order. The particularly good aspect of radio as a safety device is that it provides instant response in two directions. This means that you can begin reporting a situation as it unfolds and convey a steady stream of mounting or diminishing proportions that your potential rescuers can react appropriately to. In the first instance, rescuers can respond appropriately to your circumstances, perhaps initially giving you instructions on how to solve your problem, and finally scrambling or calling others to your assistance or homing in on your signal if you cannot give then an accurate fix.

Around the globe, channels have been set aside for the exclusive purpose of being listening posts. The idea is to keep these channels free of mundane dialogue and open for anyone in distress who needs a rapid response from a Samaritan. The comforting thought is that networks of Samaritans keep a twenty-four-hour vigil on Channel 16, so that you can rest easy that your radio will crackle to your assistance within moments of putting the call out.

Your radio doesn't work like a telephone, however; you can't just pick it up and call someone whenever and however you want. Instead, you need to follow some simple guidelines:

- Use Channel 16 for distress and hailing only.
- Keep communications on Channel 16 as short as possible.
- In order to avoid interfering with other broadcasts already in progress, listen before transmitting.
- Use minimum transmission power whenever possible.

Obey Radio Regulations

The following details have been summarized from "The Office of Boating Safety—U.S. Coast Guard."

Carrying a Radio

Though we advise that all vessels—especially at sea—carry a marine VHF radio, the regulations state that "most recreational vessels under 20 meters/65.6 feet in length do not have to carry a marine radio."

However, they are explicit and clear that "any vessel that carries a marine radio must follow the rules of the Federal Communications Commission (FCC)."

Obtaining a Radio License

The FCC does not require operators of recreational vessels to carry a radio or to have an individual license to operate VHF marine radios (with or without digital selective calling capability), EPIRBs, or any type of radar. Operators must, however, follow the procedures and courtesies that are required of licensed operators specified in the FCC rules. You may use the name or registration number of your vessel to identify your ship station.

QUESTIONS?

Have you ever wondered what SOS means?
The most widely believed meaning of SOS is that it signifies "Save Our Ship."

Users of a VHF marine radio equipped with digital selective calling will need to obtain a maritime mobile service identity (MMSI) number from the FCC. It is unlawful to use digital selective calling without obtaining this identity.

Vessels that are required to be licensed include the following:

- Vessels that use MF/HF single side-band radio, satellite communications, or telegraphy
- Power-driven vessels over 20 meters\66 feet in length
- Vessels used for commercial purposes including:
  - Vessels documented for commercial use, including commercial fishing vessels.
  - CG-inspected vessels carrying more than six passengers.
  - Towboats more than 7.8 meters/25.74 feet in length.
  - Vessels of more than 100 tons certified to carry at least one passenger.
  - Cargo ships over 300 tons.
  - Any vessel, including a recreational vessel, on an international voyage.

Maintaining a Radio Listening Watch

Vessels not required to carry a marine radio (such as recreational vessels less than 20 meters/66 feet in length), but that voluntarily carry a radio must maintain a watch on Channel 16 (156.800 MHz) whenever the radio is operating and not being used to communicate. Such vessels may alternatively maintain a watch on VHF Channel 9 (156.450 MHz), the boater calling channel.

U.S. vessels required to carry a VHF marine radio, such as commercial fishing vessels, must maintain a watch on Channel 16 while underway whenever the radio is not being used for exchanging communications.

Avoiding False Distress Alerts

It is unlawful to intentionally transmit a false distress alert, or to unintentionally transmit a false distress alert without taking steps to cancel that alert.

Hoaxes can cost lives. It's the old "Cry Wolf" syndrome. Morals and ethics aside, hoaxes can also be very expensive. Every hoax, including fake Mayday calls, is subject to prosecution as a Class D felony under Title 14, Section 85 of the U.S. Code, and liable for a $5,000 fine plus all costs the Coast Guard incurs as a result of the individual's action.

Because issuing a false distress alert is such a serious offense, the Coast Guard and Federal Communications Commission will work vigorously and use whatever means necessary to identify and prosecute any offenders.

Knowing the VHF Marine Radio Channels

The following table contains a partial listing of channels recreational boaters should be familiar with.

FACTS

If you are within five miles of the U.S. shoreline, cellular phones work very well when it comes to keeping in touch. However, if you are going to be traveling farther than that, try the Globalstar satellite telephone service. It offers voice calling, one phone for both cellular and satellite calls, short messaging services, facsimile, global roaming, and data transmission.

CHANNEL	MESSAGE/USE	DESCRIPTION
06	Intership safety	Used for ship-to-ship safety messages and search messages and ship and aircraft of the Coast Guard
09	Boater calling	Established as a supplementary calling channel for noncommercial vessels (recreational boaters) in order to relieve congestion on VHF Channel 16. The Coast Guard announces urgent marine information broadcasts and storm warnings on Channel 9 in the First Coast Guard District (waters off the coast of northern New Jersey, New York, and New England) and USCG Group Grand Haven, Milwaukee, and Sault Ste. Marie (Lake Michigan). For that reason, we strongly urge boaters to use Channel 9 in these waters. Use of Channel 9 in other waters is optional, and we recommend boaters keep turned to and use Channel 16 in those waters unless otherwise notified by the Coast Guard.
13,67	Navigation safety (also known as Bridge-to-Bridge channel)	Ships greater than 20 meters in length maintain a listening watch on this channel in American waters. This channel is available to all ships. Messages must be about ship navigation, such as passing or meeting other ships. You must keep your messages short. Your power output must not be more than one watt. This is also the main working channel at most locks and drawbridges. Channel 67 is for lower Mississippi River only.
16	International distress, safety, and calling	Use this channel to get the attention of another station (calling) or in emergencies. Ships required to carry a radio maintain a listening watch on this channel. USCG and most coast stations also maintain a listening watch on this channel.
21A, 23A, 83A	U.S. Coast Guard only	
22A	Coast Guard liaison and maritime safety information broadcastswarnings.	Announcements of urgent marine information broadcasts and storms (broadcasts announced on Channel 16).
24, 25, 26, 27, 28, 84, 85, 86, 87	Public correspondence (marine operator)	Use these channels to call the marine operator at a public station. By contacting a public coast station, you can make and receive calls from telephones onshore. Except for distress calls, public coast stations usually charge for this service.
70	Digital selective calling	Use this channel for distress and safety calling and for general purpose calling using only digital selective calling (DSC) techniques. Voice communications not allowed.

Note: The U.S. Coast Guard will not be equipped to respond to DSC distress calls on Channel 70 until 2006. In the meantime, use Channel 16.

For a complete listing of VHF channels and frequencies visit the USCG Navigation Center Web site at ✍ *www.navcen.uscg.mil.*

Understanding Radio Protocol

To make a non-emergency call, such as hailing the marina or calling another vessel, you need to make contact on Channel 9 or 16 in the following way:

1. Speak the recipient's name three times; then follow with these words, spoken once. For example, "This is <*insert your name*>."
2. If you have a station license, include your call sign, vessel name, and boat registration number, spoken once.
3. Complete your call by saying, "Over."
4. Wait for the station called to reply.
5. As soon as you've made contact, clear the channel (9 or 16) for others, so suggest going to an alternate working channel to resume your conversation. Name your channel of preference and wait for acknowledgement.
6. Switch to the new channel and repeat the procedure of hailing and wait for a response. You may now continue with your purpose for making contact

Here's an example:

- *Calling station:* "*Wadyawant, Wadyawant, Wadyawant,* this is the sloop *So-Sue-Me,* VBH3904, Over." (Note: You should use the phonetic alphabet to convey the letters VBH, as in Victor, Bravo, Hotel, and overpronounce the numbers 3904 as in, tree, nin_er, zero, fow_er.)
- *Responding station:* "*So-Sue-Me, So-Sue-Me, So-Sue-Me,* this is the motor vessel *Wadyawant,* XAB4579, Over."
- *Calling station:* "Let's go over to Channel 68, switch now and listen."
- *Responding station:* "Switching to Channel 68, over."

Both parties would then immediately switch to Channel 68. The vessel *So-Sue-Me* would then make contact using the same call procedure.

Following a response from *Wadyawant,* normal business can be conducted in concise, to the point, and efficient language with no explicative or foul language ever transmitted.

Using the Phonetic Alphabet

You need to know the phonetic alphabet so you can make a radio call correctly. Here it is:

A – ALPHA	H – HOTEL	O – OSCAR	V – VICTOR
B – BRAVO	I – INDIA	P – PAPA	W – WHISKEY
C – CHARLIE	J – JULIETT	Q – QUEBEC	X – X-RAY
D – DELTA	K – KILO	R – ROMEO	Y – YANKEE
E – ECHO	L – LIMA	S – SIERRA	Z – ZULU
F – FOXTROT	M – MIKE	T – TANGO	
G – GOLF	N – NOVEMBER	U – UNIFORM	

Making Non-Emergency Calls for Help

Minor problems can quickly become serious situations on the water, and with a radio onboard, you're in a position to seek help before it becomes an emergency. However, the Coast Guard is a search-and-rescue authority for all maritime emergencies and is therefore primarily set up for emergency distress calls in which distress is defined as a situation in which you or your boat are threatened by grave or imminent danger requiring assistance.

If you're not in full distress and unlikely to be, then your call might be answered by commercial firms that are monitoring Channel 16. You can choose to accept their assistance, but it will generally cost you a fee. If you were to agree to the assistance of a commercial firm and then refuse their service when then they arrive, you are legally obligated to pay the callout fee, if not the entire negotiated rate.

FACTS

The Coast Guard Auxiliary was created by an act of Congress in 1939 for the promotion of safe boating in the United States. The Volunteer Civilian Arm of the United State Coast Guard, the Auxiliary performs nonprofit services, including examining recreational boats for safety, teaching public boating courses, patrolling navigable and state waterways, and assisting in search and rescue. Call ☎ (800) 368-5647.

The Coast Guard Auxiliary will normally provide what on-the-spot assistance it can and then tow you to the nearest location where you can arrange for a commercial operator to carry out repairs or tow you to port.

It's wise to be familiar with the terms of assistance that be might expected from you. In order to charge a fee for assistance, the party offering assistance must be a bona fide towing salvager licensed by the Coast Guard. It's appropriate to ask whether the party is licensed.

In addition, you'll want to find out whether the company has the necessary equipment to take you in tow or provide other assistance. Ask about the sort of insurance coverage they carry in case you and your vessel are damaged or injured while under tow. Finally, find out how competent the crew is to handle the situation within the context of the prevailing weather and sea conditions.

Making a Distress Call

The radio telephone distress call consists of the distress signal Mayday spoken three times, the words "This is," and the call sign (or vessel registration number or name if no call sign is assigned) of the mobile station in distress, spoken three times.

ESSENTIALS

For more information on distress calls, contact the FCC toll-free number at ☎ (888) CALL-FCC or go to the Web sites ✍ *www.fcc.gov/wtb* or *www.navcen.uscg.mil/marcomms*.

Actually, though Mayday is the most widely known of the calls, there are actually three levels of priority communications: distress, urgent, and safety, identified by Mayday, Pan-pan, and Securite. No matter what signal you use, don't transmit a panicked message; it can confuse a rescue effort. Learn the proper procedures and try to stay calm. Then use the acceptable distress signals.

Mayday

A Mayday call denotes an emergency involving imminent danger to life or vessel. If you hear one and a shore station fails to respond to the call, you should attempt to relay the message and render any assistance. An example Mayday message could be:

- "Mayday, Mayday, Mayday. This is *King Quest,* a 45-foot red sloop. I am six miles off the Charlotte Channel of Dick Island. We have been holed and taking on water rapidly and anticipate sinking within ten minutes. There are six people onboard. Over."
- Cease transmission and listen for a response. Repeat every few minutes or as needed. If you can get no response on the distress Channel 16, briefly try other channels and then return to 16.

Pan-Pan

A Pan-pan call is an urgent message to indicate that a vessel is in trouble, but is not in immediate danger.

An example Pan-pan message might be *"Pan-pan, Pan-pan, Pan-pan.* This is *King Quest,* a 45-foot red sloop. I am six miles off the Charlotte Channel of Dick Island. We have been holed and are taking on some water. There are six people onboard. Over."

Securite

Securite messages are generally prefixes to navigational safety messages, such as weather reports, or navigation hazard updates.

An example Securite message could be "Securite, Securite, Securite, all ships, all ships, all ships. This is Honolulu Radio, Honolulu Radio,

Honolulu Radio for a renewal of a gale advisory please switch to Channel VHF 67. Out."

Hearing a Radio Distress Call

If you hear either a Mayday or a Pan-pan message, make written notes. In all probability, a Coast Guard or shore station will respond, and they may call for all vessels in the vicinity to respond for assistance.

If you hear no response, take on the call and relay the message on the stricken vessel's behalf. Chances are that you will either be successful or at the very least provide the stricken vessel's crew with confidence that their call is being heard. If you receive no response to your call, then the rescue effort becomes your responsibility. You are obligated to lend all assistance that you safely and legally can.

Issuing a Visual Distress Signal

The following extract, from Annex IV of the Coast Guard's Navigation Rules publication, is a list that covers many of the visual (and auditory) distress signals that can be used to attract attention:

* Red flares
* A square flag with a ball or anything resembling a ball suspended above or below it, hoisted above the deck on the mast
* Flames on a vessel
* Orange smoke
* A person slowly and continuously raising and lowering his arms outstretched to each side
* A high intensity white light flashing at fifty to seventy times a minute (in inland waters only)
* A gun fired in one-minute intervals (use extreme caution when firing weapons, especially if they are armed with any form of projectile that leaves the unit)
* A continuous sounding of a fog-signaling apparatus

Recreational vessels are required to carry Coast Guard–approved three-day and three-night visual distress signals. Powered vessels under sixteen feet and open sailing vessels under twenty-six feet without motors are exceptions, unless they are operated at night on coastal waters. Coastal waters are defined as the territorial sea (ocean), the Great Lakes, bays or sounds that empty into the ocean or Great Lakes, and rivers that are wider than two miles across at their mouths and upstream to the point at which the river narrows to two miles.

At time of writing, the anticipated life of a pyrotechnic device—a burning or explosive device—is considered to be forty-two months from its date of manufacture. Any device exceeding this period should be properly disposed of and replaced. Disposal must be subject to the hazardous waste regulations for your county and state, at the very least. Your local authorities will be able to give you specific instructions. Do keep a log of all such expiration dates and commit them to a calendar in order to alert yourself with ample warning.

Firing a Flare

The utmost care must be conducted whenever you handle or use pyrotechnic devices. The dazzling brightness and smoke that they emit is the result of intense heat that will cause severe burns to flesh, hair, clothing, or any other materials that they are brought into contact with. Smoke inhalation and eye exposure must be avoided at all times. Only consider using such a device if the manufacturer's instructions are properly attached to it and clearly understandable.

Apart from the mechanics of using pyrotechnics, be aware that they are finite in that they are exhaustible. Once you've fired off a flare or ignited a device, it cannot be reused. Under circumstances of panic, judgment can be impaired, and the natural reaction is to attract attention as quickly as possible. However, you must take charge of your emotions and ensure that all of the flares are not used in quick succession, or you'll be left with no means of signaling a search party or casual passerby if your first attempts fail.

When you're using flares, make sure that you always read the instructions and note the expiration date. Only use the flares in an emergency situation. When firing, always hold lighted flares downwind and never point them at anyone. Flares should be stored in an easily accessible watertight container.

If there is no person or vessel in sight, fire a single flare vertically or set a smoke flare. Then wait for a visual response of any kind. If there is no response, scan the horizon or appropriate locations for any sign of a vessel or activity.

As soon as you believe that there is an observer, release another flare. When you have your visual response, stand by to signal again; your rescuers might need another fix on you as they close in on your position. When you judge that they have or are likely to deviate from a direct path to your rescue, signal once again. When they are quite close, fire a final signal so that they cannot miss you. Coast Guard search vessels often use their law enforcement blue light to encourage you to signal. If you see them signaling, respond by setting off a flare.

Responding to a Flare

When you see a flare, you are obligated to react to it. The first thing you need to do is make all haste to the location to provide assistance. In doing so, be very aware of the circumstances of the situation. If the vessel has grounded or is exposed to wave action, it will make little sense for you to blunder in to lend assistance, only to put yourself into the same position.

As soon as you can, call the facts of the case to the attention of all listening parties through Channel 16. The Coast Guard and any other rescuers will need all the detail that you can provide. However, the most important pieces of information include your current position and current heading. Latitude and longitude are ideal, but if you can't provide that, any other locating information will be useful. Also supply your magnetic bearing to the source of the flare.

If the Coast Guard can get another simultaneous bearing and position from another vessel that has sighted the flare, they'll be able to accurately pinpoint its source and not endanger life and limb while they race around looking for it.

If you are the only source reporting the flare, rescuers might need to get an idea of what angle the flare rose from the horizon from your perspective. If you are asked to provide this angle, hold your hand out in front of you and make a fist, lining up the bottom of your fist with the horizon. Each of your fingers is equal to approximately two degrees of elevation off the horizon, so all you need to tell them is how many fingers the flare rose above the horizon and they can figure it out.

Another piece of information you can give is the relative speed at which the flare rose and then fell. If the flare rose and fell at equal speed, then it is of the meteor flare type. If it rose quickly and then descended slowly, it is a parachute flare. This assessment tells them how high the flare actually rose from the point it was fired. And, by comparing its actual elevation from source to the number of degrees—your fingers—from your position, they can get a more accurate fix on where to begin the search.

Remembering to Stay in Touch

Once you've made a call to the Coast Guard or any other party who is coming to your rescue, it's only good manners and sense to give them an update of the unfolding circumstance. There's no need to give them a blow-by-blow running commentary of events, but do let them know if another party promises to help and then update them on the progress of that party to your location.

On the other hand, if the situation begins to deteriorate along the lines of the following short list, report the status immediately:

- A storm or deteriorating weather conditions seems imminent or likely.
- You begin taking on water.
- A medical emergency develops.
- Your last reported position changes significantly.

CHAPTER 18

Acquiring the
Racing Mindset

Perhaps the greatest competition you could ever have is simply with nature. Milking the wind for every ounce of push, while remaining on the living side of safety, is what the sport of sailing is all about. Under this definition, there's not a sailor afloat who can afford to skip this chapter.

Have the Attitude

As with any other human endeavor, in the long run, the paramount issue in any winning formula has to be the crew and skipper's attitude. It is the one ingredient that will ultimately make for a champion. It is the element that keeps you reinvesting in equipment and technique and keeps you focused on a long-term goal to be the best—regardless of short-term defeats.

Learn from Mistakes

There isn't a champion who hasn't made major blunders and who doesn't make lesser errors during every event he or she participates in. The difference is that the champion never quits. Though he or she might agonize over the mishap for months, out on the course, the champion forgets about what has happened and concentrates her energy on what is going to happen.

There is certainly enough information and theory available that, if applied, would ensure that no skipper or crew ever makes a mistake. At the risk of laboring a point—that is, the entire point of racing—we race to establish who will make the least mistakes. The person or crew who makes the least errors is called a winner, but they're only a winner until the next event. Every time an event comes up again, the "losers" get to prove that they've learned from their mistakes.

FACTS

Before unfurling the sails, run through this short safety inspection:

- Conduct an inventory of equipment and spares. Always use a checklist—not your memory.
- Check the rigging. Go aloft yourself or send the most experienced of the crew up.
- Stow personal belongings to ensure they're not underfoot.

Remaining proactive under stressful conditions makes the difference between champions and regular folk. Aggressively learn from your mistakes. The more senses you can involve in this learning process, the better. Immediately after an event, record the mistakes. Explore what led up to them, how the mistake could have been avoided, and how your reaction could have rectified or improved the situation. By writing it down, you have now involved additional senses that just thinking about the situation wouldn't have. By seeing it on paper, you'll become your own best and most constructive critic, rather than simply being mad at yourself or someone else.

Event after event, as you build your dossier of errors, you'll begin to see a trend develop. Perhaps you're having trouble on a particular tack or you lose ground coming about. Besides putting in more time practicing these maneuvers, as you find yourself leading up to a similar circumstance in other races, you will know to lift your level of concentration to a new high.

Concentrate on the Present

At the start of any event, all you know is all you know, and all the equipment you have is all the equipment you have. That might seem like a bit of an obvious statement, but read it again—s-l-o-w-l-y. The currency you pay for your victories in is concentration.

It is no great leap of faith to see that, good fortune aside, the only difference you can make to the outcome of an event—but more particularly to attaining the limits of your own ability—is by spending the currency of your concentration wisely. And, like all currency, those who invest wisely receive handsome returns.

Therefore, spending your valuable concentration on events that have occurred up to any particular point in a race yields no dividends. The only issue that matters is what is currently happening around you and how you can influence that moment's circumstance to alter what will happen.

Practice

Because sailing is both a science and an art, practice is the most vital element of improvement. As hinted, what you need to do is focus on your weakest areas—remember, over the long term, the winner is the person who makes the fewest mistakes.

Without a coach to look over your shoulder, it's also important that you have a written list of areas needing improvement. Prioritize these areas to ensure that you don't become sidetracked practicing what is fun when it is practicing what is frustrating that will make the only difference to your results.

ALERT

Most fatal accidents occur when people fall overboard or the boat capsizes and the boaters are not wearing PFDs. On the other hand, most nonfatal accidents are caused by collisions with objects in the water or with other boats. Remember that overloading a boat can increase the possibility of swamping the boat and exposing passengers to risk.

Don't attempt to crowd the entire repertoire into every practice session. Pick just two or three of your worst shortcomings that would fit neatly into a complementary routine and concentrate on those until the end of the session. Unless you're going for Olympic gold, if you've got a two-hour session to work with, set aside the last half-hour for playing and doing all the things you and your crew really enjoy. If you devote the entire session to a grinding routine of just polishing the negatives, you'll begin finding reasons you shouldn't repeat the experience, or your crew will mutiny—whichever comes first.

What follows is a sample list of priorities that you might practice:

- *Tacks:* Practice the ideal approach and concentrate on powering through the transition.
- *Beating:* Learn to feel the wind and the effects steering through the sail rather than the rudder have on overall performance.

- *Close quarter sailing:* Practice with a buddy, alternating position and practice techniques for sailing through each other's blanket and backwinds.
- *Clean starts:* Learn to bring your boat up to a precise predetermined position and heading at an allotted moment in time. To do so, learn to stall your boat as well as pour on a sudden boost.
- *Mark roundings:* Pick a spot or object—preferably a buoy—and bring yourself in on an imaginary course and practice tacking through varying degrees of severity of angle.

Of course, you should conduct these maneuvers out of the way of traffic and beyond the limits of physical confines. Whenever possible, try to practice with other boats as a competitive gauge.

Listen to Constructive Criticism

Learn to discern the difference between constructive and destructive criticism. Destructive criticism is a comment aimed only to strip you of your confidence and has no merit or advice attached to it. By contrast, constructive criticism usually comes from well-meaning individuals who have noted some aspect of your conduct that could be improved. You'll probably want to listen.

When faced with criticism, choose to act rather than react. One of the toughest things to do when someone points out your shortcoming is to say "Thank you" and really mean it. Sure, there are an awful lot of people in this world who only wish you were taller so that their criticism of you could raise their self-esteem higher, but by reacting negatively to their undermining comments, you'll only deliver them a victory.

FACTS

The following formula will help you figure out how many gallons of bottom paint you will need for one coat: Your boat's length × .85 × Beam divided by the square feet covered per gallon listed on the paint can.

It's far better to react positively to criticism. Instead of rising to the challenge by arguing or stalking off in a huff, ask your critic how you might improve your position. If he's seen a problem, the least he can do is offer a solution. At the very least, if his intent was to anger you, you'll frustrate his plan by not rising to the bait.

In private, you can try out the remarks or research them a little further to test them for validity. And, who knows? Perhaps he's inadvertently delivering you a pearl of wisdom with which you can defeat him next time you're out on the water. Success is, after all, the best revenge.

Choose a Mentor

Pick a mentor, someone who consistently achieves better results than you, and sit in her wake, mimicking everything she does. Try to understand why she's doing what she does. If you just can't figure it out, bring it up in conversation—it's a little like that birds-'n-the-bees talk with your kids. Once you're advanced enough to have figured out what they're doing, most sailors will tell you why they're doing it.

Save the Tactics for Later

When you enter your first few races, accept that you're probably not in contention to even place. Therefore, until you're at least acquainted with competition and sailing in a fleet, it's better advice to keep your focus on staying out of harm's way and simply concentrating on sailing to the best of your abilities. For a beginner, basics are far more important than tactics. Only after you're able to get the most performance out of your equipment does the competitive environment become an issue.

To put it in perspective; when you learn to drive, you first learn to just survive the traffic and get to your destination without a ding. As your skills develop, you become a better tactician who can eventually pick a good line into a corner and hold a conversation about philosophy all at the same time.

Likewise, when you're first exposed to a racing environment, you should spend 80 percent of your time focused on your speed and 20 percent focused on your position. As sailing and competition becomes second nature, the bias will naturally shift until you'll just feel the optimum edge of performance and can devote all of your attention to strategy and tactics.

Welcome the Handicap System

Face it, when it comes to racing, not all boat designs are born equal. To open a race up and give every design class a chance of winning, a system of handicapping has been developed to place various classes on a level playing field.

Perhaps this seems a little unfair to the purist who reasons that, if an individual specializes in winning races by investing in superior design, why should a lesser vessel take honors?

Fortunately, this answer is simple: The specialized vessel and crew will still win on pure time and receive the accolades that go with victory, but the little guy is also given a chance to test skill against skill with equipment results a side issue.

ESSENTIALS

> Nautical miles are used on coastal and ocean waters, and statute miles are used for inland areas. When you convert from statute to nautical miles, a factor of 1.15 is used. A statute mile is 5,280 feet in length, while a nautical mile is 6,076.11549 . . . feet long.

In effect then, handicapping allows for two or more winners to emerge from one event. In addition to taking honors for winning on time, there's nothing to stop a racing purist from sweeping to victory in several categories. Besides long-haul racing, many clubs that don't have sufficient vessels in one class to create worthwhile competition will institute a handicap system.

THE EVERYTHING SAILING BOOK

Various systems might be instituted as well. The most common is to review each boat and issue it a number that will serve as a factor or yardstick that will be multiplied against its time. You end up with a tabulated comparative outcome of adjusted finishing position. Beyond handicapping boats, individual skippers and crews might also have a handicap applied that is based on past performance (or lack thereof).

Be a Good Sport

Competitors are governed by rules that they are bound to follow. The fundamental founding principle of these rules is good sportsmanship. But in this day and age of loutish sports professionals assaulting opponents, spectators, and officials alike, what on earth is good sportsmanship?

Authorities reduce this nebulous concept to a simple enough formula. When a competitor has broken a rule, they are either penalized or must retire.

The specific rules that govern racing will obviously alter from class to class and event to event. Suffice it to say that you need to familiarize yourself with the rules as they would apply to you on any given racing occasion.

The Racing Rules of Sailing includes two main sections. The first, Parts 1–7, cover rules that affect all competitors. The second section covers rules that are only applicable to certain race categories. These rules, revised every four years by the International Sailing Federation (ISAF), the international governing body, were revised in 2001. To see a copy of the rules, go to ISAF's Web site at ✍ *www.sailing.org.*

Because sailing is so very technical and fraught with intricate rules that require interpretation, a system of lodging protests and counterprotests has been established.

CHAPTER 19

Competing in Your First Race

C ompetitive sailing is an entire subject in itself, and we can't explore
every possible angle that may
apply to the type of boat or type of races
that you might be interested in. However,
in this chapter, we do our best to introduce you to the basics involved in racing.

Know Your Course

As you've certainly gathered by now, sailing is about as diverse as a sport could be in terms of classes and courses. However, regardless of the size of the boat and the length of the course, one factor remains an obvious constant: All events are conducted over a predetermined course that is laid out and published. The best advantage that any competitor could therefore gain would be to thoroughly know the course before the race is staged.

If the race is being held in your backyard, so to speak, then this is not a problem. You'd know all the tricks and characteristics of the particular area. However, if it's in some far-flung region from your perspective, somewhere that it would be impossible to prescout, then at least familiarize yourself with charts and literature on the area. Try to come to grips with typical weather and wind patterns for that season and understand all of the other issues that might play a factor like safe havens or average boat traffic.

FACTS

Here are a couple of tips you probably wish someone had told you sooner:

- Increase the propeller's pitch by one inch, and it will reduce the rpm by fifty to a hundred.
- Make your wetsuit slide on easier by putting plastic bags on your feet first.

Often, a championship is not just won on a single course, but on a competitor's performance over a series of races. To achieve victory in this situation would obviously require that you devote quite a bit of time to research. On this note, don't become complacent in this endeavor. All other factors being equal, there is little that can be done to consistently beat the sailor who has a home-ground advantage—even if it's only an advantage because you are more familiar with the course than others in the same championship.

Plan Your Start

Getting a good start is no accident; it is the result of practice and planning. The advice that follows is particularly tailored to racing in fleets where there is an armada milling about, jostling for position and excitedly anticipating the cue that will set them on their way.

The larger the fleet, and the shorter the course you are starting, the more critical your start will be. Consider how much bad wind lies downwind of all those sails. You don't want to be anywhere near that zone, and you do want to have a clear run up to the first mark. At the start, you want to be on the right tack approaching the line and have good speed. If you miss your mark, you could find yourself way back with an awful lot of obstacles to overcome even before you can begin to maneuver.

Your best alternative is to formulate a plan and have every member of the crew keyed into it and knowing the role they must play to make it work. Keep in mind, though, that it's one thing to formulate a plan, and quite another to stick to it in the heat of the final moment's excitement. This is especially vital if your crew is new and they are anticipating execution of the plan you strategized. Even if the gap you've seen appears to be a good one, invariably any gains you might make by taking it will be lost when the teamwork comes to pieces and the crew start to doubt your promised word.

Time Your Start

The elements of timing as they present themselves on the start line are being at a given position, and traveling on the right heading, at maximum speed, at a precise moment in time. As a beginner, this task can almost be overwhelming. The steps that follow should help you keep a cool head.

Pick or drop a buoy in the water and then set yourself precise moments in time—say, every five or ten minutes on the clock. Approaching the buoy from different angles and under differing wind conditions, try to place yourself exactly thirty seconds from the buoy at full speed. Then cover that distance and pass the buoy—your imaginary start line—precisely on the allotted five- or ten-minute moment you've selected as your practice start time.

What you're seeking is how far back the thirty-second mark really is under various conditions of wind and approach. Once you're mastering the exercise, introduce more elements of realism: Link up with other boats that want to hone their skills. In the best 007 tradition, sequence your watches, drop two buoys in a configuration similar to the one you'd expect to find at an actual race's start line, and hold a competition to see who is consistently the best judge of speed and distance.

Master Your Race-Day Start

On race day, mill in the nearby vicinity, just upwind of the location you'd like to cross the line. With about ninety seconds to the start gun, try to put yourself on a course that will deliver you to your desired location at the gun. With thirty seconds to go, be absolutely sure that you won't prematurely cross the line. In most instances, it is far better to err on the side of being fifteen seconds late to the line than one second early and overshooting it. With ten seconds to go, you should be under full power and moving at full speed.

As a beginner, your primary objectives are to cross the line after the gun and without hitting anyone. Of course, the vast majority of competitors will have the same idea as you. If you're aiming for the optimum start position, you'll have stiff competition, so, for your first few races, opt for a lesser position or hang a little farther back and fall in behind the lead boats.

QUESTIONS?

Why are boats referred to as she?
Although women were considered to bring bad luck at sea, the word *ship* in the Romance languages is always in the feminine and English-speaking sailors have continued the tradition. Others suggest that a sailor considers his ship second only to his mother and therefore calls a ship "she."

Having stressed that you should be on your approach run with just seconds to go, if you see other boats bearing down on you, it is much better to get out of the way—even if it means that you must come about and then tack back in behind them. Make sure that you are not on a course to being trapped and squeezed between other participants and the committee boat.

It is indeed fine to be late, but only with speed. Hitting the line under full speed is more important than crossing the line at the moment the gun goes. Far too many competitors concentrate more on being right at the line for the start, forsaking speed in order to achieve this. Even if you hit the line a few seconds after them, they still won't be moving all that fast, and you can shoot ahead.

Competition is like a game of chess. At first, you must learn the rules and moves of each piece and how these affect the whole. Once you've grasped that concept you're ready to begin implementing set-play or game plans. Similarly, once you've amassed some experience handling the boat and have a couple of races under your belt, you can begin to consider more tactical starts.

Making the Wind Your Ally

Out on the water, get a feel for the wind and apply the knowledge that you have to get an idea of the ideal position to be in when the start gun fires. The elements that are important at this point are as follows:

- Which side of the line should you be on?
- Which side of the course will offer you the best tactical advantage?
- What tack will set you on this ideal heading to place you on course?
- On this heading, under full power, how many boat lengths of speed are you making every fifteen seconds? This will give you an idea of the distance you need to be away from the line with thirty seconds to go.

These are decisions you can make some time before the final two-minute mark. Leading in to the final minutes, constantly reassess which other boats appear to have a similar plan and consider which of them might be on an intersecting or collision course with your chosen bearing; then make the necessary adjustment to your tack.

As soon as possible, bring your boat up onto the line and go head to the wind. This will give you the opportunity to establish whether either the pin end or committee-boat end is farther ahead. This is particularly important on short courses. Of course, taking the wind and course into consideration, why not pick the closer end? At the least, it will give you a head start.

Choosing Your Tack

The rule you will follow is to establish a tack that will bring your boat to the mark on the straightest possible course. This rule is equally applicable on the other legs of the course. Naturally, the longer the race, the more variance in wind speed and direction you'll be subjected to. This is why your first races really need to be pretty short affairs; in terms of course and time on the water, it is exhausting.

While assessing your best tack, take into consideration that the port tack must give way to boats on a starboard tack. In other words, if you can, try to put yourself on the starboard side of all other vessels. They'll have to give way to you. Likewise, if boats appear on your starboard side, you'll have to give way to them.

Knowing Where the Wind Comes From

In sailing, the side that the wind is coming from is the side of the course that you'll want to be on. This is a decision you can make about thirty minutes before the start. Simply look directly into the wind, and that's precisely where you want to place yourself.

However, bear in mind that the wind direction and strength might alter and continue to vary right up to the start. So constantly make a point of reassessing the wind's direction relative to the start line.

It's one thing to see where you want to be and quite another thing to maneuver your way to that spot through a fleet of milling craft. The best solution here is to be early to the course and take care of all these preliminary decisions as soon as possible.

Going Slowly

As boats converge on a start line, a lot of bad air is created, and following craft run the real risk of collision with those ahead that have lost power in the doldrums. At this point, you'll need to take evasive action if you wish to avoid disaster or a full tack to place you back on course.

As in golf, where powerful drives are only half the game while delicate putts make up the balance, sailing is not all about power and speed at all costs. There are times, like the moments leading up to a start gun, when going slow is the name of the game. To do this on demand while retaining the control to switch on the power at a moment's notice is a real skill that has to be practiced diligently.

FACTS

Ninety percent of oceans are more than two miles deep. More than 70 percent of the total surface of the earth is covered by the sea. The estimated volume of the Earth's oceans is 308,400,000 cubic miles.

The following sections describe several methods you can use. Some might be more appropriate for smaller craft, but they're worth noting, if only for curiosity's sake. To turn these maneuvers into tactics you can implement on demand, you'll need to practice them often and master them. During practice sessions, get a firm understanding of how much you can slow your boat and how quickly you can do so. In addition, also get to know how quickly you can reverse the procedure and be underway again at a moment's notice.

Beam Reach

On a beam reach, head the boat into the wind and let the sail go as much as you need to. On smaller boats, you can also shift your weight to stern and create more drag around the transom, which will provide you with even more braking effect.

Broad Reach

On a broad reach, where you can't effectively position yourself to luff the sails, overtrim them instead. It is not as effective a maneuver, but it will certainly provide you with a fair degree of slowing.

Close Reach or Close Haul

The trick for slowing on these two tacks is not going to be too easy to perform in larger boats. The idea is to turn the sail into a brake by shoving it to leeward beyond the point that it naturally wants to reach. Though this will provide you with a quick method of slowing, it will make the boat a little more difficult to control.

You might consider practicing this technique with other boats. Take it in turns to play follow the leader and then keep a close watch on the boats ahead. When they begin to execute the maneuver, do the same all down the line.

Rudder Drag

Remember that the rudder can create enormous drag? On this occasion, you can use it to your advantage, but do beware of being overexuberant because you might encroach on another boat's lines and make yourself very unpopular.

Make really big rudder movements and, beyond the significant drag you'll be creating below the water line, you'll also effectively be putting more distance between yourself and the start line. Be sure to make these movements as expansively and as often as circumstances dictate.

Achieving the Right Air and the Right Speed

On the start line, it's often difficult to feel that you're in bad air. If you're unfortunate enough to land in this position right off the mark, you could be seriously hampered, as you'll have little momentum to break through the doldrum pocket.

The idea is to become increasingly observant of the fleet building around you and position yourself so that you won't place yourself in such a position. If necessary, move away from everyone else and then, with a few seconds to go, bear off a few degrees to build speed.

Try Backward Sailing

Boats under sail are like bicycles in that they don't like to go backward and they perform horribly when they do, but it is something that can be done when necessary. In fact, you can have a lot of fun practicing this handy skill, and it will be vital if you see you're about to overshoot the line or if you want a boat behind you to pass quickly. Naturally, this is also a skill that might come in handy in a number of situations other than competition.

Bring the boat into the wind, and wait for it to stop with the sail luffing. Shove the boom into the wind and countersteer on the rudder. The boat should begin to move backward. Remember that, in reverse, the rudder will continue to act precisely the opposite to the way it usually works in the forward direction.

Halt Your Boat

Halting is not somewhere between slowing down and reversing; it's a whole new skill in itself. The idea is to control your position, neither gaining nor losing ground—or water, in this instance. Maintaining absolute control over your boat is the name of the game, and you do this by fine-tuning your equipment against the force of the wind.

Bring your vessel almost to wind and maintain the position. You'll notice that the operative word is *almost*. If you bring the boat completely to wind, you'll certainly halt, but then the wind will begin to shove you in the direction of its travel, and you'll be moving again. Besides, you'll be in irons and have no capacity to steer.

Practice Sailing in a Pack

For the beginner, driving is not too difficult on flat and open terrain, but a move onto the highway lends an entirely new meaning to the word *pressure*. In the same way, the only way to become familiar with, and successful, sailing in a pack is to practice sailing in a pack. You'll obviously have to get a bunch of buddies together who'll cooperate, but it will be an effort that can sure pay dividends.

In one exercise, have everyone take a turn as the lead boat, with the other boats as tightly in tow as possible. The lead boat then goes through all of the maneuvers that it normally would in its buildup to the start, and the other boats try to maintain their relative tightly formed positions.

It's going to take a lot of skill and concentration to get this exercise right and keep it consistent. However, on race day, you'll also have to add anticipation to this taxing mix of emotions and efforts, so it's well worth the effort of becoming familiar with whatever you can ahead of time and being a lot more prepared on the big day. Your crew will also need all of the practice they can get.

Avoid intense sun exposure by watching out for water and sand, which reflect UV light straight back at you. Make sure to always wear a wide-brimmed hat, long sleeves, sunglasses (polarized, with protection against UVA and UVB radiation), and sunscreen to avoid sunburn.

If you can't get anyone who'll practice with you, the next best thing is to practice where there is either a lot of flotsam, such as weeds, floating about or in an area where there are other obstructions that would test your ability to tack, slow, jibe, and accelerate. So much the better if you can pick an area with a good flow of current!

Engage in Match Racing

To this point, the advice given has been chiefly concerned with racing in fleets. However, racing can also take place as a one-on-one event, and, as you would have guessed, there is a slight variation you might want to employ in your technique.

Your objective here is to gain the right-of-way advantage over your opponent's boat. To do so, you fall into your opponent's wake and maneuver so that he or she cannot do anything but sail directly ahead.

If the boat heads up tack, you alter course and head up as well. You can both maintain this course for as long as you like, but your opponent cannot tack with you in his or her lee, and you would therefore be dictating his or her line.

If your opponent starts to bear off and jibe, you'd bear to his or her lee. With you in that position, the rules dictate that your opponent must stop and resume his or her heading.

If your opponent is cunning, he or she will have a bunch of sneaky moves to cause you to break your hold. At this point, your well-drilled ability to slow your craft very quickly will be your most important skill.

Rounding Marks

If you want a fair idea of what rounding marks feels like, just imagine a highway without painted lanes that makes a sharp curve and everybody in the bunch wants to be the first out at the far side of the corner. It's at this point that sections or entire events are won and lost. Sometimes there might be a dozen boats heading up to a rounding mark, all essentially in a tied position. By the far side of the mark, the distance between the first and last boat might well have been stretched to twenty-five or more boat lengths.

Laylines

A layline is the closest line you can take close-hauled and still make it around the mark. You'll certainly want to avoid laylines until the windward leg is over and then aim not to reach them until you're about a dozen boat-lengths away. If you don't observe this rule, the boats that tack in front of you will feed you bad air right up to the mark. Without tacking, you'll then be stuck. In addition, if boats are to your lee and you get a sudden lift, the leeward boats will get the good wind they're looking for and will make the mark before you, causing you to cover more distance than you needed to.

Windward Mark

With a small fleet, rounding the windward mark, though exciting, is rarely eventful. What you're aiming to do is to power into the turn about a boat-length above the layline and then bear off on your approach. As you round into the following leg, loosen the sail with an even fashion and ensure that the telltales flow and don't luff.

If you find yourself below the layline, tack once to bring yourself above it. If you've got enough momentum, you might want to risk momentarily running into the wind and hope you can coast around the mark, immediately bearing off into a smooth acceleration.

Reach Mark

This is another usually uneventful mark, what you're looking to do is avoid close competition in this area of the course. If you do have other boats close to you, to ensure you get good air, it is sometimes a good idea to head up for a short period immediately after the mark. By doing so, you'll also be in a good position to approach the leeward mark.

Leeward Mark

This is the big challenge where those with a deep understanding of racing rules and handling experience receive great dividends. It's a critical juncture where a lot of separation between vessels might occur when boats are bunched and aggressions run high.

Before the race, study the rules as they apply, and you'll probably find that those on the outside are forced to allow extra room—a situation that could cost them dearly and deliver a distinct advantage to those on the inside.

Because this is such a critical section, try to practice it as often as you can and with as many willing skippers as you can muster. All you'll need then is a single buoy, and you can play to your heart's delight. To lend a bit of spice, see whether you can wager for a "best of" series with the winner notching up the most number of first roundings. Remember to call your practice finish line a good few boat-lengths' distance to allow for differing styles that might yield faster exits.

Wide Approach

With boats close behind, you may feel as though you need to keep a tight line to the mark in order to stop them squeezing through. However, this can often be a bad move on your part.

No boat that we know of can hug a mark without having to go wide at some point. Therefore, if you hold to the tightest line coming into the turn, you'll be pushed wide on the exit and not set yourself up for an ideal line on to the next mark. On the other hand, if you run wide coming into the mark, the boats coming up will realize that if they try to squeeze in too early, they run the risk of fouling you, and they'll probably resist the temptation.

Again, it is only practice that will probably convince you that this is true, and it is only practice that will polish your technique so that you don't foul it up under the heat of competition.

Try practicing as follows. Pick a mark and approach it along a port broad reach. Point your bow one boat-width from the mark as you overlap the mark. At this point, head up until you're on a close-haul course. Keep repeating this exercise until you find the optimum in efficiency.

Running and Reaching

Because on this leg the boats are pretty quick, positions will tend to be held with fewer changes in relative position than you'd expect in the beat legs. With this in mind, your aim here is to secure your position and set yourself up for rounding the leeward mark. Providing that you don't make mistakes, although the boats giving chase may close the gap, it's unlikely they'll manage to pass. Even if you are overtaken, if you put yourself into the mark on the right course, you'll have a great opportunity to reestablish dominance.

As always, try to ensure that no other competitor places you in a bad wind situation or forces you to make any significant course alterations. These situations might force you to sail additional distances and cost you time.

Depending upon design, boats tend to be a little less stable on downwind runs, and there is therefore an associated risk of mistakes and mishaps. This is doubly true when executing a jibe, as the wind will suddenly change its orientation relative to the sail, and the boat might react in several nasty ways such as pushing you way off course, running up into the wind, capsizing, or slamming you into other boats.

ALERT

Boating accident reports need to be filed within forty-eight hours if a person is injured beyond first aid; within forty-eight hours if a person dies within one day of the accident; and within ten days if there is only damage to the vessel or property.

When wind speed is moderate to heavy, it's important to ensure that the boat has plenty of speed. The closer you can get the boat's speed to match the wind's speed, the less apparent wind will be rushing by from behind, pouring additional power into your sail and making the entire maneuver you undertake so much riskier. If you've got reservations about committing to the jibe, get the boat going as fast as you can and then try to pick a moment when the wind lulls for just a moment.

The other important trick here is to treat rudder movement with the utmost respect and not make large or violent movements. Keep your course straight as the boom swings through the center of the boat. On smaller boats, balance your weight evenly so that you can throw your weight appropriately if it becomes necessary.

On a run or reach, you'll certainly want to know if there are gusts coming up from behind. You're looking for more areas of gusts and trying to steer into them whenever possible.

In the Home Stretch

As far as finishing position goes, any part of the finish line is as good as any other, so pick the side closest to your position. If it's a short race and your finish line was the same line you started from, you'll probably find that the ideal finish point is exactly opposite to the ideal start point.

ALERT

Compared to any other type of boat at sea, the motorboat is known to produce the most injuries overall. The most common injuries seen from motorboat accidents are broken bones, contusions, and lacerations.

Pick your point and hold your course. Often, it's tempting to tack at this point, but that can cost precious seconds. Put yourself on a run that will allow you to dash for the line at maximum speed and try not to use too much rudder on the way in to victory.

As you're coming in on your victory streak, if competitors are on your tail, try to keep them in your wake. On the other hand, if some dirty rotten scoundrel has somehow managed to sneak by, don't just follow in their wake and give them an easy victory. Make them work for it. Take a risk—at this point, you've got nothing to lose.

APPENDIX A

Online Resources and Addresses

We could probably bury you in hundreds of pages of Internet addresses that have to do with sailing. Instead, what follows is a brief alphabetical listing of some interesting sites you might like to visit.

- American Sailing Association:
  www.asa.com

- Basic Racing Manual:
  www.uiowa.edu/~sail/skills/racing_basics

- Beaufort Wind Scale:
  http://hyperg.sftw.umac.mo/robert/sailing/beaufort

- Current surface chart:
  *http://lumahai.soest.hawaii.edu/gifs/models/AVN/
  pac_AVNslp-000.gif*

- Drug control in the sport of sailing:
  http://sailing.org/iyru/drugcontrol

- East Pacific satellite image:
  *http://wxp.atms.purdue.edu/maps/satellite/
  sat_ir_west.gif*

- Eastern North Pacific storm tracks:
  www.hawaii.edu/News/localweather/nep.latest.gif

- Federation Internationale Numismatique Olympique:
  www.fino.org

- First International Conference
  on Maritime Terminology:
  www.refer.fr/termisti/nauterm/nauten.htm

- Forty-eight-hour forecast surface chart:
  *http://lumahai.soest.hawaii.edu/gifs/models/AVN/
  pac_AVNslp-048.gif*

- Guide to weather maps and services:
  *http://covis.atmos.uiuc.edu/guide/wmaps/html/
  weather.home.html*

- International Sailing Federation:
  http://sailing.org

- Latitude 38:
  www.latitude38.com

- Maritime and Admiralty Law:
  http://members.aol.com/dangelaw.admir.html

- Match Racing Manual:
  *www.worldchat.com/public/ghayward/
  match_racing_online*

- National Data Buoy Center:
  www.ndbc.noaa.gov

- NOAA Weatherfax Data:
  http://weather.noaa.gov/fax/ptreyes.shtml

- Oceanweather, Inc.: *www.oceanweather.com*

- Sailing World\Cruising World: *www.sailingworld.com*

- Sea surface temperature:
  (U.S. Navy): *www.fnoc.navy.mil/otis/otis_glbl_sst.gif*

- Twenty-four-hour forecast surface chart:
  *http://lumahai.soest.hawaii.edu/gifs/models/AVN/
  pac_AVNslp-024.gif*

- United States Sailing Association:
  www.olyc.com/ussailing

- U.S. Coast Guard: *www.cglalb.com/license.htm*
  or *www.uscg.mil*

- U.S. Navy Fleet Numerical Meterology and
  Oceanography Center weather maps:
  www.fnmoc.navy.mil

- U.S. Sailing's Review of Regatta Scoring Programs:
  www.ussailing.org/race/main.html
  or
  www.ussailing.org/race/scoring/scor_index.html

- Western North Pacific storm tracks:
  www.hawaii.edu/News/localweather/nwp.latest.gif

- Western Pacific satellite image:
  http://lumahai.soest.hawaii.edu/gifs/gmsIRlast.gif

- Worldwide tropical storms:
  www.solar.ifa.hawaii.edu/tropical/tropical.html

- Worldwide tropical weather (WeatherNet):
  http://cirrus.sprl.umich.edu/wxnet/tropical.html

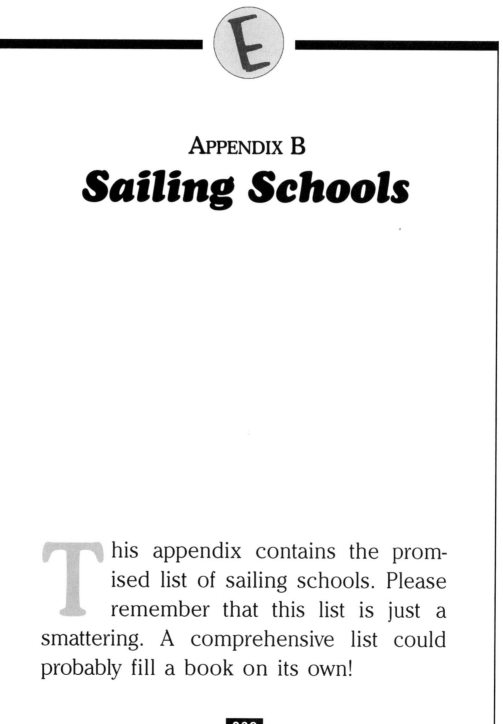

APPENDIX B

Sailing Schools

This appendix contains the promised list of sailing schools. Please remember that this list is just a smattering. A comprehensive list could probably fill a book on its own!

Schools in the Northeastern United States

Connecticut

⚐ Bud's North O'Newport Sailing
Somers, CT
Phone: (860) 763-1980

⚐ Coastline Yacht Club
Noank, CT
Phone: (860) 536-2689
Fax: (860) 572-0778

⚐ Sail the Sounds
Mystic, CT
Phone: (860) 536-5486
www.sailthesounds.com

⚐ Yachting Services of Mystic
West Mystic, CT
Phone: (800) 536-9980
Fax: (860) 536-8411
www.ysmystic.com

Maine

⚐ Bay Island Yacht Charters
Rockland, ME
Phone: (207) 596-7550
Fax: (207) 594-0407
www.sailme.com

⚐ Sawyer's Sailing School
Auburn, ME
Phone: (800) 372-8465, (207) 783-6882
www.sawyerssailingschool.com

Maryland

⚐ Chesapeake Sailing School
Annapolis, MD
Phone: (410) 269-1594
Fax: (410) 268-1049
www.sailingclasses.com

⚐ Getaway Sailing Ltd.
Baltimore, MD
Phone: (410) 342-3110
Fax: (410) 342-5421

⚐ Havre de Grace Sailing School
Havre de Grace, MD
Phone: (410) 939-2869

⚐ The Maryland School of
Sailing & Seamanship
Rock Hall, MD
Phone: (410) 639-7030
Fax: (410) 639-7038
www.mdschool.com

⚐ Upper Bay Sailing School
Worton, MD
Phone: (888) 302-SAIL
www.upperbaysailing.com

Massachusetts

⚐ Boston Harbor Sailing Club
Boston, MA
Phone: (617) 345-9202
www.by-the-sea.com/bhsclub

⚐ Boston Sailing Center
Boston, MA
Phone: (617) 227-4198
Fax: (617) 227-5644
www.bostonsailingcenter.com

New Jersey

⚐ Down Easterly Sailing Adventures
Beach Haven Park, NJ
Phone: (609) 492-2822

⚐ Nelson Sailing Center
Island Heights, NJ
Phone: (908) 270-0022
www.nelsonsailingcenter.com

⚐ New Jersey Sailing School
Pt. Pleasant, NJ
Phone: (732) 295-3450
Fax: (732) 295-3331
www.njplaza.com/sail

⚐ Newport Sailing School & Cruising
Jersey City, NJ
Phone: (201) 626-3210
Fax: (732) 530-1567
www.newportsail.com

⚐ Philadelphia Sailing School
Riverside, NJ
Phone: (609) 461-3992
Fax: (609) 461-9415

New York

⚐ Croton Sailing School
Croton-on-Hudson, NY
Phone: (914) 271-6868, (800) 859-SAIL
Fax: (518) 672-5046
www.crotonsailing.com

⚐ Great Hudson Sailing Center Inc.
Kingston, NY
Phone: (914) 429-1557
www.greathudsonsailing.com

⚐ Manhattan Sailing School
New York, NY
Phone: (212) 786-0400
Fax: (212) 786-3318
www.sailmanhattan.com

⚐ New York Sailing Center & Yacht Club
City Island, NY
Phone: (718) 885-0335
www.startsailing.com

⚐ New York Sailing School
New Rochelle, NY
Phone: (914) 235-6052
Fax: (914) 633-6429
www.nyss.com

⚐ Oyster Bay Sailing School
Oyster Bay, NY
Phone: (516) 624-7900
Fax: (516) 922-4502
www.oysterbaysailing.com

⚐ Polish Sailing Club, Inc.
Brooklyn, NY
Phone: (718) 854-0100, (718) 339-1817

⚐ Port Liberte/North Cove Sailing
New York, NY
Phone: (800) 532-5552
www.sailnyc.com

⚐ Sag Harbor Sailing School, Inc.
Sag Harbor, NY
Phone: (516) 725-5100
Fax: (516) 725-8760
www.yachtworld.com/sagharbor

⚐ Sigsbee Sailing
Port Washington, NY
Phone: (516) 767-0971, (516) 944-6894
Fax: (516) 767-0945

⚓ South Bay Sailing School
Holtsville, NY
Phone: (516) 289-0077

⚓ Yachting Operation Services
Hendersen Harbor, NY
Phone: (315) 938-5494
Fax: (315) 938-5536
www.sailwithyos.com

Pennsylvania

⚓ Liberty Sailing of Philadelphia
Philadelphia, PA
Phone: (215) 923-SAIL
Fax: (215) 393-7559
www.libertynet.org/~sailing

⚓ Midlantic Sailing School
Philadelphia, PA
Phone: (215) 574-1758
Fax: (215) 592-4677
www.midsail.com

Vermont

⚓ NE Quadrant/International Sailing School
Colchester, VT
Phone: (802) 864-9065
Fax: (802) 863-4016
www.harborwatch.com/iss

Schools in the Southeastern United States

Georgia

⚓ Dunbar Sails Inc.
St. Simons Island, GA
Phone: (912) 638-8573
Fax: (912) 638-6905

⚓ Kingdom Yachts Sailing Club
Cumming, GA
Phone: (770) 887-7966
www.andrews.com/kysc

⚓ Lanier Sailing Academy
Bufford, GA
Phone: (770) 945-8810, (800) 684-9463
Fax: (770) 945-4507
www.mindspring.com/~laniersail

⚓ Windsong Sailing Academy
Lilburn, GA
Phone: (404) 256-6700
www.windsongsail.com

Florida

⚓ Adventure Sailing Cruises
Panama City, FL
Phone: (904) 233-5499

⚓ Ahoy Marine & Charters
Ft. Lauderdale, FL
Phone: (954) 564-0199
Fax: (305) 563-8828
www.ahoycharters.com

⚓ Blue Water Sailing School
Ft. Lauderdale, FL
Phone: (954) 763-8464, (800) 255-1840
Fax: (954) 768-0695
www.bwss.com

⚓ The Catamaran Company
Miami Beach, FL
Phone: (800) 262-0308, (305) 538-9446
Fax: (305) 538-1556
www.catamaranco.com

⚓ Chapman School of Seamanship
Stuart, FL
Phone: (561) 283-8130
Fax: (561) 283-2019
www.chapman.org

⚓ Diamond 99 Marina
Melbourne, FL
Phone: (407) 254-1490, (407) 259-6573

⚓ Florida Sailing Club
Palm City, FL
Phone: (305) 361-3611

⚓ Florida Sailing Cruising School
North Ft. Myers, FL
Phone: (941) 656-1339
Fax: (813) 656-2628

⚓ Florida Yacht Charters
Miami Beach, FL
Phone: (800) 537-0050, (305) 532-8600
Fax: (305) 672-2039
http://floridayacht.com

⚓ Ft. Myers Yacht Charters
Cape Coral, FL
Phone: (813) 540-8050
Fax: (941) 549-4901

⚓ Go Native Yacht Charters
Plantation, FL
Phone: (800) 359-9808, (954) 791-4692
www.gnyc.com

⚓ Gulf Wind Yachting Inc.
Naples, FL
Phone: (813) 775-7435

⚓ International Sailing Center
Key Largo, FL
Phone: (305) 451-3287
Fax: (305) 453-0255

⚓ International Sailing School
Punta Gorda, FL
Phone: (941) 639-7492, (800) 824-5040
Fax: (941) 639-0085
www.IntlSailSch.com

⚓ Island Sailing
Ft Lauderdale, FL
Phone: (305) 525-5956

⚓ Island Yachting Center Inc.
Palmetto, FL
Phone: (941) 729-4511
Fax: (941) 722-7677

⚓ Little Palm Island Sailing School
Little Torch Key, FL
Phone: (305) 872-1226

⚓ The Sailing Academy, Inc.
Indian Rocks Beach, FL
Phone: (813) 593-8374

⚓ Sailing School at Sandestin
Destin, FL
Phone: (850) 650-4412
www.saildestin.com

⚓ Sailing South
Destin, FL
Phone: (904) 654-1518

⚓ Southeast Yachting School & Charter
Ft. Lauderdale, FL
Phone: (954) 523-BOAT

⚓ St. Augustine Sailing
St. Augustine, FL
Phone: (800) 683-SAIL (904) 829-0648

⚓ Tropical Diversion
Hollywood, FL
Phone: (954) 921-1044

⚓ Vacation Yachts, Inc.
Ft. Myers, FL
Phone: (941) 437-2800
Fax: (904) 469-8116

⚓ Vinoy Charters & Sailing School
St. Petersburg, FL
Phone: (800) 879-2244

⚓ Windward Sailing School, Inc.
Fernandina Beach, FL
Phone: (904) 261-9125
www.windwardsailing.com

North Carolina

⚓ Broadreach
Raleigh, NC
Phone: (919) 833-1907
Fax: (919) 833-1979

⚓ Down Easterly Sailing Adventure
Oriental, NC
Phone: (919) 249-1650

⚓ North Beach Sailing Inc.
Duck, NC
Phone: (919) 261-6262

⚓ Water Ways
Wilmington, NC
Phone: (910) 256-4282
Fax: (910) 256-9330
http://waterways.wilmington.net

Schools in the Central United States

Virginia

⚓ Lake Sailing Academy
Huddleston, VA
Phone: (888) SAIL-SML
http://pages.prodigy.net/sail.sml

⚓ Norton's Yacht Sales Inc.
Deltaville, VA
Phone: (804) 776-9211
Fax: (804) 776-9044
www.nortonyachts.com

⚓ Trident Charters
Norfolk, VA
Phone: (757) 588-2022
Fax: (757) 427-0249

Arkansas

⚓ Sailing Charters of Arkansas
Paron, AR
Phone: (501) 594-5424
www.maxpages.com/sailingcharter

Illinois

⚓ Fairwind Sail Charters, Inc.
Chicago, IL
Phone: (312) 427-1525
Fax: (312) 567-0366
http://SailWithMe.com/Lessons.html

Kentucky

⚓ Lighthouse Landing Sailing School
Grand Rivers, KY
Phone: (502) 362-8201
www.lighthouselanding.com

Louisiana

⚓ Murray Yacht Sales Inc.
New Orleans, LA
Phone: (504) 283-2507
www.murrayyachtsales.com

⚓ Ship to Shore Co.
Lake Charles, LA
Phone: (318) 474-0730

Michigan

⚓ Bay Breeze Yacht Charters
Traverse City, MI
Phone: (616) 941-0535
Fax: (616) 941-9548

⚓ Lake St. Clair School of Sailing
St. Clair Shores, MI
Phone: (810) 772-5475
Fax: (810) 776-4267

⚓ Torresen Marine Inc.
Muskegon, MI
Phone: (616) 759-8596
www.torresen.com

Mississippi

⚓ Southern Cross Sailing
Long Beach, MS
Phone: (601) 863-6880
www.scsailing.com

Missouri

⚓ Sailing Charters & Academy
Branson, MO
Phone: (417) 739-5555
Fax: (417) 324-3071

⚓ St. Louis Sailing Center
Bridgeton, MO
Phone: (314) 298-0411
Fax: (314) 298-7194

Ohio

⚓ Adventure Plus Yacht Charters
Sandusky, OH
Phone: (419) 625-5000
Fax: (419) 625-4428
www.visitohio.com/adventureplus

⚓ Great Lakes Sailing Academy
Lorain, OH
Phone: (440) 239-9379

⚓ North Coast Sailing School
Cleveland, OH
Phone: (216) 861-6250

⚓ Ohio Sailing Club
Vermilion, OH
Phone: (216) 967-0260, (216) 967-2309
Fax: (216) 967-0297

Oklahoma

⚓ Britt Sails
Oologah, OK
Phone: (918) 712-7245, (918) 443-2859

⚓ Redbud Sailing School
Claremore, OK
Phone: (918) 341-5190
Fax: (918) 341-9166

Tennessee

⚓ Sail Tennessee
Jefferson City, TN
Phone: (423) 475-4009

Texas

⚓ Bay Charter, Inc.
Kemah, TX
Phone: (281) 334-3597
Fax: (281) 474-7420
www.baycharter.com

⚓ Cedar Mills Marina
Gordonville, TX
Phone: (903) 523-4222
Fax: (903) 523-4077
www.cedarmills.com

⚓ Corpus Christi Sailing Center, Inc.
Corpus Christi, TX
Phone: (512) 881-8503
Fax: (512) 881-8504
www.constant.com/sailing

⚓ Dallas/Ft. Worth Sailing School
Grape Vine, TX
Phone: (817) 481-4099

⚓ Magellan Sailing Center, Inc.
Dallas, TX
Phone: (214) 827-8990
www.TheSailboat.com

⚓ Nautica Boat Club
Denison, TX
Phone: (903) 463-7245
Fax: (903) 463-3294

⚓ North Texas Sailing School
Rockwall, TX
Phone: (972) 771-2002
Fax: (972) 771-6029

⚓ Sailing Center on Joe Pool Lake
Fort Worth, TX
Phone: (817) 921-0343
Fax: (817) 921-4040
www.flash.net/~jplsail

⚓ Southwest Sailing Academy
Amarillo, TX
Phone: (806) 351-0188

Wisconsin

⚓ Fox River Marina Inc.
Oshkosh, WI
Phone: (920) 236-4220
Fax: (920) 236-4226

Schools in the Western United States

California

⚓ Blue Dolphin Sailing Club
Balboa Island, CA
Phone: (714) 644-2525
www.bluedolphinsc.com

⚓ California Sailing Academy
Marina Del Rey, CA
Phone: (310) 821-3433
Fax: (310) 821-4141
www.insidewla.com/csa

⚓ Club Nautique
Alameda, CA
Phone: (510) 865-4700
Fax: (510) 865-3851

⚓ Club Nautique
Sausalito, CA
Phone: (415) 332-8001

⚓ Harbor Island Yacht Club
San Diego, CA
Phone: (619) 291-7245
Fax: (619) 296-2482

⚓ Harbor Sailboats
San Diego, CA
Phone: (619) 291-9568, (800) 854-6625
Fax: (619) 291-1473
www.harborsailboats.com

⚓ Live & Learn School of Sailing
Sonora, CA
Phone: (209) 533-4437

⚓ Marina Sailing Channel Island
Oxnard, CA
Phone: (805) 985-5219, (805) 985-3629

⚓ Marina Sailing Long Beach
Long Beach, CA
Phone: (310) 432-4672
Fax: (310) 432-0369
www.marinasailing.com

⚓ Marina Sailing MDR
Marina Del Rey, CA
Phone: (310) 822-6617
Fax: (310) 823-5568

⚓ Marina Sailing NP
Newport Beach, CA
Phone: (714) 673-7763
Fax: (714) 673-7763

⚓ Marina Sailing of San Diego
San Diego, CA
Phone: (619) 221-8286
Fax: (619) 221-8263

⚓ Martin's ASA Sailing School
of Sacramento Folsom
Sacramento, CA
Phone: (916) 369-7700
www.lovetosail.com

⚓ Modern Sailing Academy
Sausalito, CA
Phone: (415) 331-6266
Fax: (415) 331-7065
www.modernsailing.com

⚓ Oceanside Sailing Club & School
Vista, CA
Phone: (619) 722-2518

⚓ Offshore Island Sailing Club
Oxnard, CA
Phone: (805) 985-3600
Fax: (805) 985-3350

⚓ Pacific Sailing
Marina Del Rey, CA
Phone: (310) 823-4064, (619) 345-6722

⚓ Pacific Sailing, Ventura
Oxnard, CA
Phone: (805) 658-6508

⚓ Pacific Yachting School
Santa Cruz, CA
Phone: (408) 423-7245
Fax: (408) 423-4260

⚓ Safe Passage Sailing Center
Foster City, CA
Phone: (415) 715-0252

⚓ Sailing Center of Morro Bay
Morro Bay, CA
Phone: (805) 772-6446
Fax: (805) 772-6818

⚓ Sailing Center of Santa Barbara
Santa Barbara, CA
Phone: (805) 962-2826, (805) 569-2847
Fax: (805) 966-7435
www.sbsailctr.com

⚓ Sailing Solution
San Diego, CA
Phone: (619) 225-8225, (619) 225-8225

⚓ Sailing Ventures
South Lake Tahoe, CA
Phone: (530) 542-1691
www.sailtahoe.com

⚓ San Diego Sailing Academy
San Diego, CA
Phone: (619) 299-9247, (800) 441-8672
Fax: (619) 296-3389
www.sdsa.com

⚓ San Diego Sailing Club & School
San Diego, CA
Phone: (619) 298-6623
Fax: (619) 298-6625

⚓ Sea Mist Skippers of M.D.R.
Marina Del Rey, CA
Phone: (310) 398-8830
Fax: (310) 391-8110
www.seamist-skippers.com/mdr

⚓ Seaforth Boat Rentals
San Diego, CA
(619) 223-1681

⚓ Spinnaker Sailing School
Redwood City, CA
Phone: (415) 363-1390
Fax: (415) 363-0725

⚓ Spinnaker Sailing School
San Francisco, CA
Phone: (415) 543-7333
Fax: (415) 543-7405
www.baysail.com/spinnaker

⚓ Tradewinds Sailing Center
Pt. Richmond, CA
Phone: (510) 232-7999
Fax: (510) 232-8188
www.sfsailing.com/tradewinds/try.html

Colorado

⚓ The Anchorage
Lyons, CO
Phone: (970) 823-6601

⚓ Dillon Marina
Dillon, CO
Phone: (970) 468-5100

⚓ Victoria Sailing School
Morrison, CO
Phone: (303) 697-7433, (303) 898-8498
www.victoriasailingschool.com

Idaho

⚓ The Sail Loft
Bayview, ID
Phone: (208) 683-7245

Nevada

⚓ Sailing Ventures
Zephyr Cove, NV
Phone: (702) 884-4144
Fax: (916) 542-1691
www.sailtahoe.com

Oregon

⚓ Bubba Louie's West Winds Sailing
Hood River, OR
Phone: (541) 386-4222, (800) 880-0861
www.bubbalouie.com

⚓ Island Sailing Club
Portland, OR
Phone: (503) 285-7765
Fax: (503) 286-9370

⚓ Portland Sailing Center
Portland, OR
Phone: (503) 281-6529

Washington

⚓ Bellhaven Charters
Bellingham, WA
Phone: (360) 733-6636, (800) 542-8812
www.pacificrim.net/~belhaven

⚓ Island Sailing Club
Kirkland, WA
Phone: (425) 822-2470
www.islandsailingschool.com

⚓ Northwest Cruising Academy
Seattle, WA
Phone: (206) 623-8123

⚓ Puget Sound Sailing Institute
Tacoma, WA
Phone: (253) 383-1774, (800) 487-2454
Fax: (253) 274-8703
www.pugetsoundsailing.com

⚓ San Juan Sailing
Bellingham, WA
Phone: (360) 671-4300, (800) 677-SAIL
Fax: (360) 671-4301
www.sanjuansailing.com

⚓ Seattle Sailing Club
Seattle, WA
Phone: (206) 782-5100

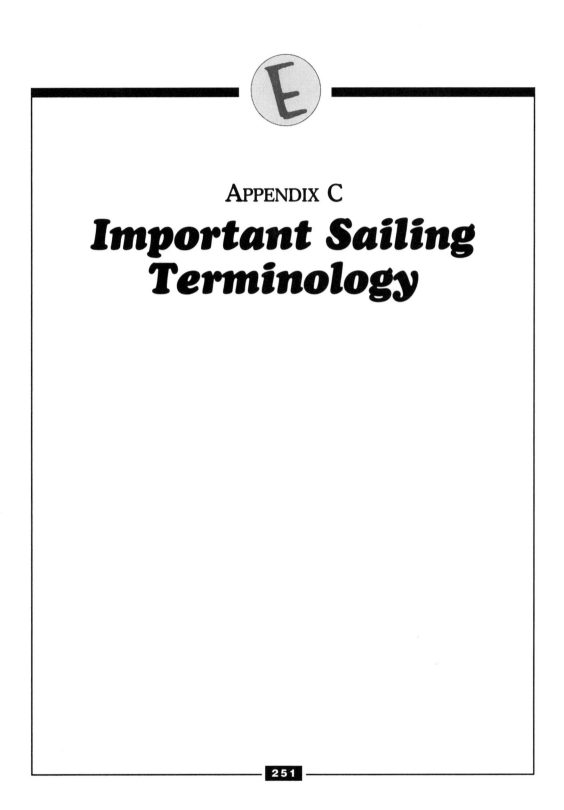

Important Sailing Terminology

aback: Wind on the wrong side of the sails.

abaft: Toward the rear of the boat, behind the boat.

abeam: At a right angle to the length of the boat.

abreast: Off the side, even with the boat.

admeasure: Formal measurement of a boat for documentation.

admiralty law: The "law of the sea."

adrift: Floating free with the currents and tide, not under control.

aerodynamic: Having a shape that is not adversely affected by wind flowing past it.

aft, after: Toward the stern of the boat.

after bow spring line: A mooring line fixed to the bow of the boat and leading aft where it is attached to the dock. This prevents the boat from moving forward in its berth. Its opposite, the forward quarter spring line, is used to keep the boat from moving aft in its berth.

aground: When a boat is in water too shallow for it to float in; i.e., the boat's bottom is resting on the ground.

aid to navigation: Any fixed object that a navigator may use to find his or her position, such as permanent land or sea markers, buoys, radiobeacons, and lighthouses.

amas: The outboard hulls of a trimaran.

anchor: (1) A heavy metal object designed such that its weight and shape will help to hold a boat in its position when lowered to the sea bottom on a rode or chain. (2) The act of using an anchor.

anchor bend: A type of knot used to fasten an anchor to its line.

anchor light: A white light, usually on the masthead, visible from all directions, used when anchored.

anchor locker: A locker used to store the anchor rode and anchor.

anchor windlass: A windlass used to assist when raising the anchor.

anchorage: A place where a boat anchors, usually an established and marked area.

anemometer: A device that measures wind velocity.

aneroid barometer: A mechanical barometer used to measure air pressure for warnings of changing weather.

astern: Toward the stern of a vessel, or behind the boat.

athwart, athwartships: Lying along the ship's width, at right angles to the vessel's centerline.

auxiliary: A second method of propelling a vessel. On a sailboat this could be an engine.

aweigh: To raise an anchor off the bottom.

backing (wind): The changing of the wind direction, opposite of veering. Clockwise in the Southern Hemisphere, counterclockwise in the Northern Hemisphere.

backsplice: A method of weaving the end of a rope to keep it from unraveling.

backwinded: When the wind pushes on the wrong side of the sail, causing it to be pushed away from the wind. If the lines holding the sail in place are not released, the boat could become hard to control and heel excessively.

bail: To remove water from a boat, as with a bucket or a pump.

ballast: A weight at the bottom of the boat to help keep it stable. Ballast can be place inside the hull of the boat or externally in a keel.

bar: A region of shallow water usually made of sand or mud, usually running parallel to the shore. Bars are caused by wave and current action and may not be shown on a chart.

barge: A long vessel with a flat bottom used to carry freight on rivers. Barges are usually not powered, being pushed or towed by a tugboat instead.

barograph: An instrument used to keep a record of atmospheric pressure, such as on a paper drum.

barometric pressure: Atmospheric pressure as measured by a barometer.

batten: (1) A thin strip of hard material, such as wood or plastic. (2) Battens are attached to a sail to stiffen it to a more preferred shape. They are placed in pockets sewn into the sail called batten pockets.

batten pockets: Pockets in a sail where battens can be placed to stiffen the sail.

bay: An enclosed body of water with a wide mouth leading to the sea.

beam: The widest part of a boat.

beam reach: Sailing on a point of sail such that the apparent wind is coming from the beam (side) of the boat at about a 90-degree angle. A beam reach is usually the fastest point of sail. A beam reach is a point of sail between a broad reach and a close reach.

bear away, bear off: To fall off. A boat falls off the wind when it points its bow farther from the eye of the wind. The opposite of heading up.

beating: Tacking, to sail against the wind by sailing on alternate tacks (directions).

Beaufort wind scale: A method of measuring the severity of the force of wind, named after Admiral Beaufort who created the system. 0 is no wind, whereas 12 would be a hurricane.

becket: A loop at the end of a line.

bend: A type of knot used to connect a line to a spar or another line. Also the act of using such a knot.

berth: (1) A place for a person to sleep. (2) A place where the ship can be secured. (3) A safe and cautious distance, such as "We gave the shark a wide *berth*."

binnacle: The mount for the compass, usually located on the wheel's pedestal.

bitt: A sturdy post mounted on the bow or stern to which anchor or mooring lines may be attached.

bitter end: The end of a line. Also the end of the anchor rode attached to the boat.

block: One or more wheels with grooves in them (pulleys) designed to carry a line and change the direction of its travel. A housing around the wheel allows the block to be connected to a spar or another line. Lines used with a block are known as *tackle*.

block and tackle: A combination of one or more blocks and the associated tackle necessary to give a mechanical advantage. Useful for lifting heavy loads.

boatswain: A crew member responsible for keeping the hull, rigging, and sails in repair.

bollard: A thick post on a ship or wharf, used for securing ropes.

bolt rope: A line (rope) sewn into the luff of a sail. The bolt rope fits in a notch in the mast or other spar when the sail is raised.

boom: A long spar extending from a mast to hold or extend the foot of a sail.

boom vang: Any system used to hold the boom down. This is useful for maintaining proper sail shape, particularly when running or on a broad reach.

bow: The front of the boat.

bow and beam bearings: A set of bearings taken from an object with a known position, such as a landmark, to determine the ship's location. A type of running fix.

Bowditch: A reference book named after the original author, Nathaniel Bowditch. Updated versions contain tables and other information useful for navigation.

bowline: A knot used to make a loop in a line. Easily untied, it is simple and strong. The bowline is used to tie sheets to sails.

brace: A guy. A line used to control the movement of the object at the other end, such as a spar.

breakers: A wave that approaches shallow water, causing the wave height to exceed the depth of the water it is in, in effect tripping it. The wave changes from a smooth surge in the water to a cresting wave with water tumbling down the front of it.

breast line: A line attached laterally from a boat to a dock, preventing movement away from the dock.

bridge: (1) The room from which a ship is controlled. On a smaller boat this is usually not a room, is outside, and is known as a cockpit. (2) A manmade structure crossing a body of water, usually for the use of automobiles or trains. A boat intending to pass under a bridge needs to make sure that it has sufficient vertical clearance unless it is a swinging bridge or a drawbridge.

brightwork: Pieces of wood trim and also any polished metal on a vessel.

broaching: The unplanned turning of a vessel to expose its side to the oncoming waves. In heavy seas, this could cause the boat to be knocked down.

broach to: An undesirable position in which a vessel is turned to expose its side to the oncoming waves.

broad on the beam: The position of an object that lies off to one side of the vessel.

bulkhead: An interior wall in a vessel. Sometimes bulkheads are also watertight, adding to the vessel's safety.

burgee: A type of flag used to identify a boater's affiliation with a yacht club or boating organization.

cabin: A room inside a boat.

camber: The curvature of an object such as a sail, keel, or deck. Usually used when referring to an objects, aerodynamic or hydrodynamic properties.

cam cleat: A mechanical cleat used to hold a line automatically. It uses two spring-loaded cams that come together to clamp their teeth on

the line, which is placed between them. Also see *jam cleat.*

canal: A manmade waterway used to connect bodies of water that do not connect naturally. Canals use locks to raise and lower boats when connecting bodies of water have different water levels. The Panama and Suez canals are two of the most famous.

can buoy: A cylindrical buoy painted green and having an odd number, used in the United States as a navigational aid. At night, they may have a green light. Green buoys should be kept on the left side when returning from a larger body of water to a smaller one. Nun buoys mark the other side of the channel. Also see *green* and *red daymarks.*

canoe stern: A pointed stern, such as on a canoe.

canvas: Tightly woven cloth used for sails, covers, dodgers, and biminis. Typically made from cotton, hemp, or linen. Modern sails are made out of synthetic materials generally known as sailcloth.

capsize: When a boat falls over in the water so that is no longer right side up.

captain: The person who is in charge of a vessel and legally responsible for it and its occupants.

car: A sliding fitting that attaches to a track allowing for the adjustment of blocks or other devices attached to the car.

cardinal points: The points of north, south, east, and west as marked on a compass rose.

carlins: Structural pieces running fore and aft between the beams.

carrick bend: A knot used to tie two lines together.

catamaran: A twin-hulled boat. Catamaran sailboats are known for their ability to plane and are faster than single-hulled boats (monohulls) in some conditions.

catboat: A sailboat rigged with one mast and one sail.

catenary: The sag in a line strung between two points.

caulking: Material used to seal the seams in a wooden vessel, making it watertight.

celestial navigation: A method of using the stars, sun, and moon to determine one's position by measuring the apparent altitude of one of these objects above the horizon using a sextant and recording the times of these sightings with an accurate clock. That information is then used with tables in the *Nautical Almanac* to determine one's position.

celestial sphere: An imaginary sphere surrounding the globe that contains the sun, moon, stars, and planets.

centerboard: A moveable keel in a sailboat that can be pivoted upward to reduce the boat's draft in shallow water.

center line: The imaginary line running from bow to stern along the middle of the boat.

certificate: A legal paper or license of a boat or its captain.

chafing gear: Tape, cloth, or other materials placed on one or more parts that rub together so that the chafing gear will wear rather than the parts that it is protecting.

chain locker: Storage for the anchor chain.

channel: A navigable route on a waterway, usually marked by buoys. Channels are similar to roads where the water is known to be deep enough for ships or boats to sail without running aground.

chart datum: The water level used to record data on a chart. Usually the average low tide water level.

chart table: A table designated as the area in the boat where the navigator will study charts and plot courses.

cheek block: A block with one end permanently attached to a surface.

chine: The location where the deck joins the hull of the boat.

chockablock: When a line is pulled as tight as it can go, as when two blocks are pulled together.

chop: Small, steep disorderly waves.

cleat: A fitting to which lines can be easily attached.

close reach: Sailing with the wind coming from the direction forward of the beam of the boat. A close reach is the point of sail between a beam reach and a close haul.

close up: A flag hoisted to the top of a flagpole.

clove hitch: A type of knot typically used when mooring. It is easily adjustable, but it may work loose.

club: A boom on a jib or staysail.

coastal navigation: Navigating near the coast, allowing one to find one's position by use of landmarks and other references.

Coast Pilots: Books covering information about coastal navigation, including navigational aids, courses, distances, anchorages, and harbors.

cockpit: The location from which the boat is steered, usually in the middle or the rear of the boat.

cockpit sole: Sole (floor) of the cockpit.

cold front: Used in meteorology to describe a mass of cold air moving toward a mass of warm air. Strong winds and rain typically accompany a cold front.

cold molding: A method of bending a material into an appropriate shape without heating or steaming to soften the material first.

colors: The national flag and or other flags.

compass card: A card labeling the 360 degree of the circle and the named directions such as north, south, east, and west.

compass course: The course as read on a compass. The compass course has added the magnetic deviation and the magnetic variation to the true course.

compass rose: A circle on a chart indicating the direction of geographic north and sometimes also magnetic north. Charts usually have more that one compass rose. In that case, the compass rose nearest to the object being plotted should be used as the geographic directions and magnetic variations may change slightly in different places on the chart.

composite construction: An object made with more than one type of material.

continental shelf: A region of relatively shallow water surrounding each of the continents.

counter: The part of the stern aft of where it leaves the water line.

courtesy flag: A smaller version of the flag of the country being visited. It is flown from the starboard spreader.

cowls: Scooplike devices used to direct air into a boat.

CQR anchor: Also called a plow anchor. Short for coastal quick release anchor. An anchor that is designed to bury itself into the ground by use of its plow shape.

crest: The top of a wave.

cringle: A fitting in a sail that allows a line to fasten to it.

crosstrees: Spreaders. Small spars extending toward the sides from one or more places along the mast. The shrouds cross the end of the spreaders, enabling the shrouds to better support the mast.

cunningham: A line used to control the tension along a sail's luff in order to maintain proper sail shape.

current: The movement of water, due to tides, river movement, and circular currents caused by the motion of the earth.

cutter: A sailboat with one mast and rigged a mainsail and two headsails. Also see *sloop*.

daggerboard: Similar to a centerboard, except that it is raised vertically. Like a keel, daggerboards are used to prevent a sailboat being pushed sideways by the wind.

davit: A device that projects beyond the side of the boat to raise objects from the water. Typically, a single davit is used on the bow of a vessel to raise an anchor, and a pair are used on the side or stern of the vessel to raise a dinghy.

daybeacon, daymark: A navigational aid visible during the day. In the United States and Canada, square red daybeacons should be kept on the right, and triangular green daybeacons should be kept on the left when returning from a larger to smaller body of water. Also see *can* and *nun buoys*.

day sailer: A small boat intended to be used only for short sails or racing.

dayshape: Black diamond, ball, and cone shapes hoisted on vessels during the day to indicate restricted movement ability or type. For example, three balls means aground.

deadlight: Fixed ports that do not open, placed in the deck or cabin to admit light.

deadrise: The measurement of the angle between the bottom of a boat and its widest beam. A vessel with a 0 degree deadrise has a flat bottom; high numbers indicate deep V-shaped hulls.

deck stepped: A mast that is stepped (placed) on the deck of a boat rather than through the boat and keel stepped. The mast of a deck-stepped boat is usually easier to raise and lower and is usually intended for lighter conditions than keel-stepped boats.

deckhead: The underside of the deck, viewed from below (the ceiling).

depth sounder: An instrument that uses sound waves to measure the distance to the bottom.

deviation: See *magnetic deviation, compass error*.

dismast: The loss of a mast on a boat. Generally, this also means the loss of some or all of the ability of the boat to sail.

displacement: The weight of a boat measured as the weight of the amount of water it displaces. A boat displaces an amount of water equal to the weight of the boat, so the boat's displacement and weight are identical.

displacement speed: Also hull speed. The theoretical speed that a boat can travel without planing, based on the shape of its hull. This speed is 1.34 times the length of a boat at its water line. Because most monohull sailboats cannot exceed their hull speed, longer boats are faster.

distance made good: The distance traveled after correction for current, leeway, and other errors that may not have been included in the original distance measurement.

distress signals: (1) Any signal that is used to indicate that a vessel is in distress. Flares, smoke, audible alarms, electronic beacons, and others are all types of distress signals. (2) The alpha flag is the legal requirement for boats with divers in the water. Boats should probably display both flags when they have divers in the water.

dividers: (1) A navigational tool used to measure distances on a chart. (2) The act of entering a dock.

downwind: (1) In the direction the wind is blowing. (2) A term describing the amount of curvature designed into a sail.

draft: Depth of a vessel's keel below the water line, especially when loaded.

drag: The resistance to movement.

drogue: Any object used to increase the drag of a boat. Typically shaped like a parachute or cone opened underwater, drogues slow a boat's motion in heavy weather.

dry dock: A dock where a boat can be worked on out of the water. The boat is usually sailed into a dry dock and then the water is pumped out.

dry storage: Storing on land. Many small boats are placed in dry storage over the winter.

ducts: Tubes used to move air, such as to ventilate an enclosed area.

DWL: Design water line. Also length water line or load water line (LWL). This is the length of the boat where it meets the water when loaded to its designed capacity.

ease: To slowly loosen a line while maintaining control, such as when loosening the sails.

ease the sheets: To loosen the lines that control the sails.

east wind, easterly wind: A wind coming from the east.

ebb, ebb tide: The falling tide when the water moves out to sea and the water level lowers.

echo sounder: An electrical fish finder or depth sounder that uses sound echoes to locate the depth of objects in water. It does so by timing the sound pulses.

electronic navigation: The use of echo sounders, radio, and various electronic satellite and land-based position finders to determine a boat's location.

emergency tiller: A tiller that is designed to be used in the event that wheel steering fails.

EPIRB: Emergency Position Indicating Radio Beacon. An emergency device that uses a radio signal to alert satellites or passing airplanes to a vessel's position.

eye splice: A splice causing a loop in the end of a line, by braiding the end into itself or similar methods. It may or may not be reinforced by a metal fitting known as a thimble.

fairlead: A fitting designed to control the direction of a line with minimal friction.

fall off: Also bear away or bear off. A boat falls off the wind when it points its bow farther from the eye of the wind. The opposite of heading up.

feathering: A propeller that can have the pitch of its blade changed to reduce drag when not in use. Also see folding and *variable pitch* propellers.

feet: More than one foot. A foot is a unit of measurement used primarily in the United States. One foot equals 30.48 centimeters.

fender: A cushion hung from the sides of a boat to protect it from rubbing against a dock or another boat.

fetch: (1) The distance that wind and seas (waves) can travel toward land without being blocked. In areas without obstructions, the wind and seas can build to great strength; but in areas such as sheltered coves and harbors; the wind and seas can be quite calm. (2) The act of sailing to a location accurately and without having to tack.

fid: A pointed tool used to separate strands of rope.

fiddle: A small rail on tables and counters used to keep objects from sliding off when heeled or in heavy seas.

Figure of Eight: A type of knot that can be used to stop a line from passing through a block or other fitting.

finger pier: A small pier that projects from a larger pier.

fin keel: A keel that is narrow and deeper than a full keel.

fisherman anchor: Kedge anchor. A traditionally shaped anchor having flukes perpendicular to the stock of the anchor and connected by a shank. These are less common than modern anchors, such as the plow and lightweight anchors.

flake: To fold a sail in preparation for storage.

flame arrester: A device used to prevent or stop unwanted flames.

flashing: Used to describe a light that blinks on and off in regular patterns.

flotsam: Debris floating on the water surface.

following sea: A sea with waves approaching from the stern of the boat.

foot: (1) The bottom edge of a sail. (2) Sailing slightly more away from the wind than close hauled to increase the boat speed.

fore: Toward the bow of the vessel.

fore and aft sail: The more common position of the sail with its length running along the ship's length as opposed to a sail such as a square sail that is mounted across the width of the vessel.

forecabin: The cabin toward the front of the vessel.

forecastle: The most forward below decks area of a vessel.

foremast: The forward mast of a two or more masted vessel.

foresail: A sail placed forward of the mast, such as a jib.

forestay: A line running from the bow of the boat to the upper part of the mast designed to pull the mast forward. A forestay that attaches slightly below the top of the mast can be used to help control the bend of the mast. The most forward stay on the boat is also called the headstay.

forestaysail: A sail attached to the forestay as opposed to a jib, which is attached to the headstay.

foretriangle: The space between the mast, the deck, and the headstay.

fractional rig: A type of rig in which the jib attaches below the top of the mast.

front: Used in meteorology to describe boundaries between hot and cold air masses. This is typically where bad weather is found.

full keel: A keel that runs the length of the boat. Full keels have a shallower draft than fin keels.

fully battened: A sail having battens that run the full horizontal length of the sail.

fully stayed: A mast supported by the use of lines known as stays and shrouds.

gaff: (1) A spar that holds the top of a four-sided gaff sail. (2) A pole with a hook at the end used to get a fish onboard.

gaff sail: A four-sided sail used instead of a triangular main sail. Used on gaff-rigged boats.

gale: A storm with a wind speed between 34 to 40 knots.

gale force winds: Wind speeds strong enough to qualify the storm as a gale.

galley: The kitchen area on a boat.

gallows frame: A frame used to support the boom.

gasket: Ties used to tie up the sails when they are furled.

gennaker: A large sail that is a cross between a spinnaker and a genoa. Hoisted without a pole, the tack is attached at the bottom of the headstay.

genoa: A large jib that overlaps the mast. Also known as a *jenny*.

geographic position: The position of a boat on a chart.

Global Positioning System: GPS for short. A system of satellites that allows one's position to be calculated with great accuracy by the use of an electronic receiver.

GMT: See *Greenwich Mean Time*.

go about: To tack.

grab rail: See *hand rail*.

great circle route: A course that is the shortest distance between two points, following a great circle. Great circle routes usually do not look like the shortest route when drawn on a flat map due to deviations caused by trying to draw a flat map of a round object such as the earth.

green buoy: A can buoy. A cylindrical buoy painted green and having an odd number, used in the United States as a navigational aid. At night, they may have a green light. Green buoys should be kept on the left side when returning from a larger body of water to a smaller one. Nun buoys mark the other side of the channel. Also see *green* and *red daymarks*.

green daymark: A navigational aid used in the United States and

Canada to mark a channel. Green triangular daymarks should be kept on the left when returning from a larger to a smaller body of water. Red daymarks mark the other side of the channel. Also see *can* and *nun buoys*.

Greenwich Mean Time: GMT for short. Coordinated universal time is a newer standard. A time standard that is not affected by time zones or seasons.

grommet: A ring or eyelet normally used to attach a line, such as on a sail.

ground swells: Swells that become shorter and steeper as they approach the shore due to shallow water.

ground tackle: The anchor and its rope or chain and any other gear used to make the boat fast.

gunkholing: Cruising in shallow water and spending the nights in coves.

gunwale: The upper edge of the side of a boat.

guy: Also called a brace. A line used to control the movement of the object at the other end, such as a spar.

gybe: See *jibe*.

gypsy: A windlass or capstan drum.

gyres: A large circular ocean current.

hail: To attempt to contact another boat or the shore, either by voice or radio.

half hitch: A simple knot usually used with another knot or half hitch.

halyard: A line used to hoist a sail or spar. The tightness of the halyard can affect sail shape.

hand: Someone who helps with the work on a boat.

hand-bearing compass: A small portable compass.

hand lead: A weight attached to a line used to determine depth by lowering it into the water.

hand rail: A hand hold. Usually along the cabin top or ladder.

handsomely: To do something carefully and in the proper manner, such as when stowing a line.

handy-billy: A movable block and tackle.

hanging locker: (1) A locker big enough to hang clothes. (2) Using such slips to attach a sail to a stay.

harbormaster: The individual who is in charge of a harbor.

hard-a-lee: A command to steer the boat downwind.

hard-chinned: A hull shape with flat panels that join at sharp angles.

hatch: A sliding or hinged opening in the deck, providing people with access to the cabin or space below.

hauling part: The part on the object which is hauled upon.

haul out: Remove a boat from the water.

hawse hole: A hole in the hull for mooring lines to run through.

hawsepipes: Pipes to guide lines through the hawse hole. On large vessels, anchors are stored with their shanks in the hawsepipes.

hawser: A rope that is very large in diameter, usually used when docking large vessels.

hazard: An object that might not allow safe operation. A group of rocks just under the water or a submerged wreck could be a navigational hazard.

head seas: Waves coming from the front of the vessel.

head up: To turn the bow more directly into the eye of the wind. The opposite of falling off.

head: (1) The front of a vessel. (2) The toilet and toilet room in a vessel.

headsail: Any sail forward of the mast, such as a jib.

headway: The forward motion of a vessel through the water.

heaving to: Arranging the sails in such a manner as to slow or stop the forward motion of the boat, such as when in heavy seas.

heavy seas: When the water has large or breaking waves in stormy conditions.

heel: Tilt of a boat to one side.

heeling error: The error in a compass reading caused by the heel of a boat.

high tide: The point of a tide when the water is the highest. The opposite of low tide.

hiking stick: An extension to the tiller allowing the helmsman to steer while hiking. This may be desired for improved visibility or stability.

hitch: A knot used to attach a line to a cleat or other object.

holding ground: The type of bottom that the anchor is set in. "Good *holding ground.*"

holding tank: A storage tank where sewage is stored until it can be removed to a treatment facility.

horizon: Where the water and sky or ground and sky appear to intersect.

horseshoe buoy: A floatation device shaped like a U and thrown to people in the water in emergencies.

hull: The main structural body of the boat, not including the deck, keel, mast, or cabin. The part that keeps the water out of the boat.

hurricane: A strong tropical revolving storm of force 12 or higher in the Northern Hemisphere. Hurricanes revolve in a clockwise direction. In the Southern Hemisphere, these storms revolve counterclockwise and are known as typhoons.

hydrography: The study of the earth's waters.

ICW: See *Intercoastal Waterway.*

inboard: (1) Toward the center of the boat. (2) An engine that is mounted inside the boat.

inboard cruiser: A motorboat with an inboard engine.

inches of mercury: A unit used when measuring the pressure of the atmosphere. 33.86 millibars. Inches of mercury is used because some barometers use the height of mercury in a sealed tube as a measuring device.

inflatable: A dinghy or raft that can be inflated for use or deflated for easy stowage.

in irons: A sailboat with its bow pointed directly into the wind, preventing the sails from filling properly so that the boat can move. It can be very difficult to get a boat that is in irons back under sail. An old square rigger could take hours to get underway again.

Intercoastal Waterway: A system of rivers and canals along the Atlantic and Gulf Coasts of the United States allowing boats to travel along them without having to go offshore.

International Code of Signals: A set of radio, sound, and visual signals designed to aid in communications between vessels without language problems. It can be used with Morse code, with signal pennants, and by spoken code letters.

irons: In irons. A sailboat with its bow pointed directly into the wind, preventing the sails from filling properly so that the boat can move. It can be very difficult to get a boat that is in irons back under sail. An old square rigger

could take hours to get underway again.

isobars: Lines drawn on a weather map indicating regions of equal pressure. When the lines are close together, this indicates a rapid change in air pressure, accompanied by strong winds.

isogonic line: A line connecting points of equal magnetic variation on a map.

jack line, jack stay: A strong line, usually of flat webbing, or a wire stay running fore and aft along the sides of a boat to which a safety harness can be attached.

Jacob's ladder: A rope ladder.

jam cleat: A cleat designed to hold a line in place without slipping. It consists of two narrowing jaws with teeth in which the line is placed. Also see *cam cleat.*

jaws: A fitting holding a boom or gaff to the mast.

jenny: A genoa jib. A large jib that overlaps the mast.

jetty: A manmade structure projecting from the shore. May protect a harbor entrance or aid in preventing beach erosion.

jibe: Also spelled gybe. To change direction when sailing in a manner such that the stern of the boat passes through the eye of the wind and the boom changes sides. Prior to jibing the boom will be very far to the side of the boat. Careful control of the boom and mainsail is required when jibing in order to prevent a violent motion of the boom when it switches sides. Jibing without controlling the boom properly is known as an accidental jibe. Tacking is preferred to jibing because the boom is not subject to such violent changes. Jibing is usually needed when running with the wind and tacking is used when close hauled.

jib netting: A rope net to catch the jib when it is lowered.

jib stay: The stay that the jib is hoisted on. Usually the headstay.

jib topsail: A small jib set high on the headstay of a double headsail rig.

jiffy reefing: A method of lowering the sail in sections so that it can be reefed quickly.

junction buoy: Also known as a preferred channel buoy. A red and green horizontally striped buoy used in the United States to mark the separation of a channel into two channels. The preferred channel is indicated by the color of the uppermost stripe. Red on top indicates that the preferred channel is to the right as you return, green indicates the left. Also see *can* and *nun buoys*.

kedging: (1) To kedge off. A method of pulling a boat out of shallow water when it has run aground. A dinghy is used to set an anchor, then the boat is pulled toward the anchor. Those steps are repeated until the boat is in deep enough water to float. (2) A traditionally

shaped anchor having flukes perpendicular to the stock of the anchor and connected by a shank. These are less common than modern anchors, such as the plow and lightweight anchors.

keel: A flat surface built into the bottom of the boat to reduce the leeway caused by the wind pushing against the side of the boat. A keel also usually has some ballast to help keep the boat upright and prevent it from heeling too much. There are several types of keels, such as fin keels and full keels.

keelson: A beam attached to the top of the floor to add strength to the keel on a wooden boat.

keel stepped: A mast that is stepped (placed) on the keel at the bottom of the boat rather than on the deck. Keel-stepped masts are considered sturdier than deck-stepped masts.

ketch: A sailboat with two masts. The shorter mizzen mast is aft of the main mast, but forward of the rudder post. A similar vessel, the yawl, has the mizzen mast aft of the rudder post.

king plank: The center plank on a wooden deck.

king spoke: The top spoke on a wheel when the rudder is centered.

knocked down: A boat that has rolled so that she is lying on her side or even rolled completely over. A

boat with appropriate ballast should right herself after being knocked down.

knot: (1) A speed of one nautical mile per hour. (2) A method of attaching a rope or line to itself, another line, or a fitting.

labor: Heavy rolling or pitching while underway.

lacing: A line used to attach a sail to a spar.

laid up: A boat in dry dock.

land breeze: A wind moving from the land to the water due to temperature changes in the evening.

landlocked: Surrounded by land.

lanyard: A line attached to a tool.

lash: To tie something with a line.

lateral resistance: The ability of a boat to keep from being moved sideways by the wind. Keels, daggerboards, centerboards, and leeboards are all used to improve a boat's lateral resistance.

latitude: Angular distance north or south of the equator, measured in degress along a meridian, as on a map or globe.

launch: (1) To put a boat in the water. (2) A small boat used to ferry people to and from a larger vessel.

lay: A small aft storage space for spare parts and other items.

lazy guy: A line attached to the boom to prevent it from accidentally jibbing.

lazy sheet: A line led to a sail but not currently in use. The line currently in use is known as the working sheet. Usually the working and lazy sheets change when the boat is tacked.

leading marks: Unlit navigational aids for use during the day. Like leading lights, they mark a bearing to a channel when they are lined up one above the other.

lead line: A line with a weight on the end used to measure depth. The lead is dropped into the water and marks on the line are read to determine the current water depth. The lead usually has a cavity to return a sample of the bottom type (mud, sand, and so on).

league: Three nautical miles.

leech: The aft edge of a fore and aft sail.

leech line: A line used to tighten the leech of a sail, helping to create proper sail shape.

leecloths: Cloths raised along the side of a berth to keep the occupant from falling out.

leeward: The direction away from the wind. Opposite of windward.

leeway: The sideways movement of a boat away from the wind, usually unwanted. Keels and other devices help prevent a boat from having excessive leeway.

life jacket: A device used to keep a person afloat. Also called a life preserver, life vest, PFD, or personal floatation device.

lifeline: A line running between the bow and the stern of a boat to which the crew can attach themselves to prevent them from being separated from the boat.

life raft: An emergency raft used in case of serious problems to the parent vessel, such as sinking.

life vest: See *life jacket.*

light: A lit navigational aid such as a lighthouse that can be used at night or in poor visibility.

light list: A list of lights arranged in geographical order.

lightship: A light placed on a ship. The ship remained in a fixed position. Most lightships have been replaced by lit buoys or other structures.

linestoppers: A device used to keep a line from slipping, such as a jam cleat.

liquid petroleum gas: LPG or propane for short. Propane is a common fuel used for cooking and heating. CNG (natural gas) is considered safer because propane is heavier than air and will sink into the bilge if it leaks, creating the potential for an explosion. Propane is more easily available throughout the world than CNG, however; so it is used for most boats outside North America.

list: A leaning to one side when not underway. Usually the result of an improperly loaded boat. Heeling is different from a list because it's caused by the forces of wind acting upon a sailboat that is underway. When a boat changes tacks, the direction of the heel will change sides, whereas a list is a continual leaning to the same side under any condition.

log: (1) A device used to measure the distance traveled through the water. The distance read from a log can be affected by currents, leeway, and other factors, so those distances are sometimes corrected to a distance made good. Logs can be electronic devices or paddle wheels mounted through the hull of the boat or trailed behind it on a line.

longitude: Imaginary lines drawn through the North and South Poles on the globe used to measure distance east and west. Greenwich England is designated as 0 degrees with other distances being measured in degrees east and west of Greenwich. For example; the center of California is approximately 120 degrees west and the center of Australia is around 135 degrees east. Also see *latitude.*

lookout: A person designated to watch for other vessels and hazards.

LORAN: An electronic instrument using radio waves from various stations to find one's position. The LORAN system is being replaced by the GPS system and will be obsolete in a few years. Many LORAN stations have already stopped providing service.

LPG: See *liquid petroleum gas* or *propane*.

lubber line: A mark on a compass used to read the heading of a boat.

luff: The edge of a sail toward the bow of a boat.

lugs: Metal or plastic pieces attached to a sail's luff that slide in a mast track to allow easy hoisting of the sail.

lying ahull: A boat that is letting herself be subjected to prevailing conditions without the use of sails or other devices. Lying ahull is usually not preferred to other actions because a boat may tend to lie with her beam to the waves and the wind (parallel to the waves). This can cause a boat to roll excessively and even become knocked down.

magnetic bearing: The bearing of an object after magnetic variation has been considered, but without compensation for magnetic deviation.

magnetic course: The course of a vessel after magnetic variation has been considered, but without compensation for magnetic deviation.

magnetic deviation: Compass error. The difference between the reading of a compass and the actual magnetic course or bearing due to errors in the compass reading. These errors can be caused by metals, magnetic fields, and electrical fields near the compass. Prior to using a compass, magnetic deviation should be recorded for many different points on the compass because the error can be different at different points. The act of checking for magnetic deviation is called swinging.

magnetic north: The direction to which a compass points. Magnetic north differs from true north because the magnetic fields of the planet are not exactly in line with the North and South Poles. Observed differences between magnetic and true north are known as magnetic variation.

magnetic variation: The difference between magnetic north and true north, measured as an angle. Magnetic variation is different in different locations, so the nearest compass rose to each location on a chart must be used.

main mast: The tallest (or only) mast on a boat.

mainsail: The main sail that is suspended from the main mast.

mainsheet: The line used to control the mainsail.

main topsail: A topsail on the main mast.

make fast: To attach a line to something so it will not move.

make way: Moving through the water.

marina: (1) A place where boats can find fuel, water, and other services. Marinas also contain slips where boats can stay for a time. (2) A buoy or other object used to mark a location.

marl: To wrap a small line around another.

marline: A small line used for whipping, seizing, and lashing.

marlinespike: A pointed tool used to separate the strands of a rope or wire.

mast: A tall vertical spar that rises from the keel or deck of a sailing vessel to support the sails and the standing and running rigging.

mast boot: A protective cover wrapped around the mast at the deck on a keel-stepped boat to prevent water from entering the boat.

masthead: The top of a mast. Wind direction indicators and radio antennas usually collect on the masthead.

masthead light: Also known as a steaming light. The masthead light is a white light that is visible for an arc extending across the forward 225 degrees of the boat. When lighted, the masthead light indicates that a vessel is under power, including sailboats with engines running. Masthead lights are usually located halfway up the mast rather than at the top.

mast step: The place that supports the bottom of the mast. The mast step usually has a built-in pattern fitting a matching pattern on the bottom of the mast, enabling the mast to be accurately positioned.

mast track: A track or groove in the back of the mast to which the sail is attached by means of lugs or the bolt rope.

MAYDAY: An internationally recognized distress signal used on a radio to indicate a life-threatening situation. Mayday calls have priority over any other radio transmission and should only be used if there is an immediate threat to life or vessel.

mean low water: A figure representing the average low tide of a region.

measured mile: A course marked by buoys or ranges measuring one nautical mile. Measured miles are used to calibrate logs.

Mediterranean berth: A method of docking with a boat's stern to the dock.

messenger: A small line used to pull a heavier line or cable. The messenger line is usually easier to throw, lead through holes, or otherwise manipulate than the line that it will be used to pull.

midchannel buoy: A red-and-white vertically striped buoy used in the United States to mark the middle of a channel. Midchannel buoys may be passed by on either side. Also see *nun* and *can buoys*.

midships: A place on a boat where its beam is the widest.

mil: Distance at sea is measured in nautical miles. See *nautical mile*.

millibar: A unit of pressure used to measure the pressure of the atmosphere. One millibar equals 0.03 inches of mercury.

mizzen sail: The sail on the aft mast of a ketch or yawl-rigged sailboat.

monkey fist: A large heavy knot usually made in the end of a heaving line to aid in accurate throwing.

moor: To attach a boat to a mooring, dock, post, anchor, and so on.

mooring: A place where a boat can be moored. Usually a buoy marks the location of a firmly set anchor.

mooring line: A line used to secure a boat to an anchor, dock, or mooring.

motor: (1) An engine. (2) The act of using an engine to move a boat.

mount: An attachment point for another object.

mushroom anchor: A type of anchor with a heavy inverted mushroom-shaped head. Mushroom anchors are used to anchor in mud and other soft ground.

natural gas: Short for compressed natural gas or CNG. A type of compressed gas used as fuel for stoves and heaters. CNG is stored in metal cylinders prior to use. It is considered safer than other types of fuel such as propane (LPG) because it is lighter than air and may rise into the sky in the event of a leak. Caution should still be used because CNG can collect near the cabin ceiling, potentially causing an explosion. Propane is available in more areas around the world than CNG, so CNG is not often used outside North America.

nautical: Having to do with boats, ships, or sailing.

Nautical Almanac: An annually published book that contains information about the position of the sun, moon, planets, and stars. This information is used for celestial navigation.

nautical mile: Distance at sea is measured in nautical miles, which are about 6067.12 feet, 1.15 statute miles, or exactly 1,852 meters. Nautical miles have the unique property that a minute of latitude is equal to one nautical mile (there is a slight error because the earth is not perfectly round). Measurement of speed is done in knots where one knot equals one nautical mile per hour. A statute mile is used to measure distances on land in the United States and is 5,280 feet.

navigable water: Water of sufficient depth to allow a boat to travel through it.

navigation: The act of determining the position of a boat and the course needed to safely move the boat from place to place.

navigational aid: Any fixed object that a navigator may use to find his or her position, such as permanent land or sea markers, buoys, radiobeacons, and lighthouses.

navigation lights: Lights on a boat to help others determine its course, position, and activity. Boats underway should have a red light visible from its port bow, a green light on the starboard bow, and a white light at its stern. Other lights are required for vessels under power, fishing, towing, and so on.

neap tide: The tide with the least variation in water level, occurring when the moon is one quarter and three quarters full. The lowest high tide and the highest low tide occur at neap tide. The opposite is the spring tide.

noon sight: A sighting taken for celestial navigation at noon, when the sun is at its highest point in the sky.

north: One of the four cardinal compass points. North is the direction toward the North Pole and is at 0 degrees on a compass card.

North Pole: The "top" point of the line about which the earth rotates.

North Star: Polaris, the North Star, is visible in the Northern Hemisphere and indicates the direction of north. In the Southern Hemisphere, the Southern Cross is used to find the direction of south.

north wind, northerly wind: Wind coming from the north.

oar: A stick with a blade at the end used to row a rowboat. Oars are different from paddles because they have a provision to be secured to the rowboat for rowing, such as an oarlock.

oarlock: A device to attach oars to a rowboat, allowing the operator to row rather than paddle the boat.

observed position: A position or fix determined by observing landmarks or other objects to find the position.

occulting lights: A navigational light which turns on and off in a regular pattern, but is on more than it is off. The opposite of a blinking light.

ocean: (1) The large body of salt water covering 70 percent of the earth. (2) The Atlantic, Pacific, Indian, and Arctic Oceans.

offshore: Away from land, toward the water.

off the wind: Sailing with the wind coming from the stern or quarter of the boat.

on the bow: To the bow of the boat, forward of the beam.

on the wind: Sailing close hauled. Sailing toward the wind as much as possible with the wind coming from the bow.

open: A location that is not sheltered from the wind and seas. An open location would not make a good anchorage.

outboard: On the side of the hull that the water is on. Outboard engines are sometimes just called outboards.

outhaul: A line used to tension the foot of a sail, used to maintain proper sail shape.

out of trim: Sails that are not properly arranged for the point of sail that the boat is on. The sails may be luffing or have improper sail shape, or the boat may be heeling too much. These conditions will slow the boat down.

outrigger: A flotation device attached to one or both sides of the hull to help prevent a capsize.

overboard: In the water outside of the vessel.

overfall: Dangerously steep and breaking seas due to opposing currents and wind in a shallow area.

overhang: The area of the bow or stern that hangs over the water.

owner's flag: A boat owner's private pennant.

paddle: (1) A stick with a blade in the end of it used to propel a small boat through the water. (2) The act of using a paddle to propel a boat.

pad eye: A small fitting with a hole used to guide a line.

painted water line: A painted line on the side of a boat at the water line. The color usually changes above and below the water line as the boat is painted with special antifouling paint below the water line.

painter: A line attached to the bow of a dinghy and used to tie it up or tow it.

palm: A tool worn on the hand with a thimble-shaped structure on it and used when sewing sails.

Pan-pan: An urgent message used on a radio regarding the safety of people or property. A Pan-pan message is not used when there is an immediate threat to life or property, instead the Mayday call is used. Pan-pan situations may develop into Mayday situations. As with a Mayday, Pan-pan messages have priority on the radio channels and should not be interrupted.

parachute: Sometimes used to describe a spinnaker.

parachute flare: An emergency signal flare that will float down on a parachute after launch, improving its visibility.

parallax error: Error that can be introduced when not reading an instrument directly from its front, due to the separation of the indicator and the scale being read.

parallels: Latitude lines.

partners: Supporting structures used to support areas where high loads come through openings in the deck, such as at the mast boot.

passage: A journey from one place to another.

pay out: To let out a line.

pedestal: The column that the wheel is mounted on.

pelorus: A card marked in degrees and having sightings on it that is used to take bearings relative to the ship, rather than magnetic bearings as taken with a compass.

pennant: (1) A small flag, which can be used for signaling. Flags can be used together to spell words or individually as codes, such as the quarantine flag. (2) A small line attached to a mooring chain, sometimes called a pendant.

PFD: See life jacket.

pile, piling: A pole embedded in the sea bottom and used to support docks, piers, and other structures.

pilot: An individual with specific knowledge of a harbor, canal, river, or other waterway, qualified to guide vessels through the region. Some areas require that boats and ships be piloted by a licensed pilot.

pitch poled: (1) When a boat's stern is thrown over its bow. (2) A material used to seal cracks in wooden planks.

planing: A boat rising slightly out of the water so that it is gliding over the water rather than plowing through it.

planing speed: The speed needed for a boat to begin planing.

planking: Wood strips used to cover the deck or hull of a wooden vessel.

plug: A tapered device, usually made from wood or rubber, which can be forced into a hole to prevent water from flowing through it. Plugs should be available to fit every through hull.

point: To sail as close as possible to the wind. Some boats may be able to point better than others, sailing closer to the wind.

Polaris: See the *North Star*.

pole: (1) A spar. Such as a pole used to position a sail. (2) One of the two points around which the earth spins, known as the North and South Poles.

poop deck: A boat's aft deck.

pooped: A wave that breaks over the stern of the boat.

port: (1) The left side of the boat from the perspective of a person at the stern of the boat and looking toward the bow. The opposite of starboard. (2) A porthole. A window in the side of a boat, usually round or with rounded corners. Portholes can be opened or fixed shut. Also see *hatch*.

porthole: A port.

pram: A type of dinghy with a flat bow.

preferred channel buoy: Also known as a junction buoy. A red and green horizontally striped buoy used in the United States to mark the separation of a channel into two channels. The preferred channel is indicated by the color of the uppermost stripe. Red on top indicates that the preferred channel is to the right as you return. Also see *can* and *nun buoys*.

prevailing winds: The typical winds for a particular region and time of year.

privileged vessel: The vessel that is required to maintain its course and speed when boats are approaching each other according to the navigation rules. Also known as the stand-on vessel.

prop: Slang for propeller.

propeller: An object with two or more twisted blades that is designed to propel a vessel through the water when spun rapidly by the boat's engine.

prow: The part of the bow forward of where it leaves the water line.

pulpit: A sturdy railing around the deck on the bow.

pump out: Removing waste from a holding tank.

purchase: Two or more blocks connected to provide a mechanical advantage when lifting heavy objects.

quadrant: A device connected to the rudder that the steering cables attach to.

quarantine flag: The Quebec pennant is flown when first entering a country, indicating that the people on the ship are healthy and that the vessel wants permission to visit the country.

quarter: The side of a boat aft of the beam. There are both a port quarter and a starboard quarter.

quartering sea: A sea that comes over the quarter of the boat.

quarters: Sleeping areas on the boat.

quick flashing light: A navigational aid with a light that flashes about once per second.

radar: Radio detection and ranging. An electronic instrument that uses radio waves to find the distance and location of other objects. Used to avoid collisions, particularly in times of poor visibility.

radar arch: An arch to mount the radar, usually at the stern of the boat.

radar reflector: An object designed to increase the radio reflectivity of a boat so that it is more visible on radar. Many small boats are made with fiberglass and other materials that do not reflect radar very well on their own.

radio: An instrument that uses radio waves to communicate with other vessels. VHF (very high frequency) radios are common for marine use, but are limited in range. Single sideband (SSB) radios have longer ranges.

radio beacon: A navigational aid that emits radio waves for navigational purposes. The radio beacon's position is known and the direction of the radio beacon can

be determined by using a radio direction finder.

radio waves: Invisible waves in the electromagnetic spectrum that are used to communicate (radio) and navigate (radar, RDF).

raft: A small flat boat, usually inflatable.

rail: The edge of a boat's deck.

rake: (1) A measurement of the top of the mast's tilt toward the bow or the stern. (2) The difference between high and low tides.

ratlines: Small lines tied between the shrouds to use as a ladder when going aloft.

RDF: Radio direction finder. An instrument that can determine the direction that a radio transmission is coming from. The RDF is used with a radio beacon to find a radio bearing to help determine the vessel's position.

reaching: Any point of sail with the wind coming from the side of the boat. If the wind is coming from directly over the side, it is a beam reach. If the boat is pointed with its bow more directly into the wind, it is a close reach. If the wind is coming from over the quarter, it is called a broad reach.

reciprocal: A bearing 180 degrees from the other. A direction directly opposite the original direction.

red buoy: A nun buoy. A conical buoy with a pointed top, painted red, and having an even number, used in the United States for navigational aids. At night, they may have a red light. These buoys should be kept on the right side of the boat when returning from a larger body of water to a smaller one such as a marina. Can buoys are used on the opposite side of the channel. Also see *green* and *red daymarks*.

reef cringles: Reinforced cringles in the sail designed to hold the reefing lines when reefing the sail.

reefing lines: Lines used to pull the reef in the sail. The reef line will pass through reef cringles, which will become the new tack and clew of the reefed sail.

reef knot: Also known as the square knot. This knot is an unreliable knot used to loosely tie lines around the bundles of sail that are not in use after reefing.

reef points: (1) Points where lines have been attached to tie the extra sail out of the way after reefing. (2) A line of rock and coral near the surface of the water.

reeve: Leading a line through a block or other object.

relative bearing: A bearing relative to the boat or another object, rather than a compass direction.

rhumb line: A line that passes through all meridians at the same angle. When drawn on a Mercator chart, the rhumb line is a straight line. However, the Mercator chart is a distortion of a round globe on a flat surface, so the rhumb line will be a longer course than a great circle route.

rig: A combination of sails and spars.

roach: A curve out from the aft edge (leech) of a sail. Battens are sometimes used to help support and stiffen the roach.

roller furling: A method of storing a sail usually by rolling the jib around the headstay or the mainsail around the boom or on the mast.

roller reefing: A system of reefing a sail by partially furling it. Roller furling systems are not necessarily designed to support roller reefing.

rope: Traditionally, a line must be over 1 inch in size to be called a rope.

row: A method of moving a boat with oars. The person rowing the boat faces backward, bringing the blade of the oars out of the water and toward the bow of the boat. They then pull the oars through the water toward the stern of the boat, moving the boat forward.

rowboat: A small boat designed to be rowed by use of its oars. Some dinghies are rowboats.

rudder: A vertically hinged plate of wood, metal, or fiberglass mounted at the stern of a boat for directing its course.

rudder post: The post that the rudder is attached to. The wheel or tiller is connected to the rudder post.

run aground: To take a boat into water that is too shallow for it to float in; i.e., the bottom of the boat is resting on the ground.

running backstay: Also known as runners. Adjustable stays used to control tension on the mast.

running bowline: A type of knot that tightens under load. It is formed by running the standing line through the loop formed in a regular bowline.

running fix: (1) A fix taken by taking bearings of a single object over a period of time. By using the vessel's known course and speed, the location of the vessel can be found. (2) Used to describe a line that has been released and is in motion.

safe overhead clearance: A distance that needs to be kept between the mast and overhead electrical lines to prevent electrical arcing.

safety harness: A device worn around a person's body that can be attached to jack lines to help prevent a person from becoming separated from the boat.

safety pin: A pin used to keep the anchor attached to its anchor roller when not in use.

sail: A large piece of fabric designed to be hoisted on the spars of a sailboat in such a manner as to catch the wind and propel the boat.

sailboat: A boat that uses the wind as its primary means of propulsion.

sailcloth: A fabric, usually synthetic, used to make sails.

sailing directions: Books that describe features of particular sailing areas, such as hazards, anchorages, and so on.

sail shape: The shape of a sail, with regard to its efficiency. In high winds, a sail would probably be flatter. Other circumstances can cause a sail to twist. Controls such as the cunningham, boom vang, outhaul, traveler, halyards, leech line, sheets, and the bend of the mainmast all can affect sail shape.

sail track: A slot into which the bolt rope or lugs in the luff of the sail are inserted to attach the sail. Most masts and roller reefing jibs use sail tracks. Systems with two tracks can allow for rapid sail changes.

sampson post: A strong post used to attach lines for towing or mooring.

scend: The distance that the trough of a wave is below the average water level. With large waves in shallow water, the scend is important to help determine whether a boat will run aground.

schooner: A sailboat with two or more masts. The aft mast is the same size or larger than the forward one(s). Also see *ketch* and *yawl*.

scow: A boat with a flat bottom and square ends.

screw: A propeller.

scupper: An opening through the toerail or gunwale to allow water to drain back into the sea.

sea: (1) A body of salt water. A very large body of fresh water. (2) Any body of salt water when talking about its condition or describing the water around a boat. Heavy seas, for example.

sea buoy: The last buoy as a boat heads to sea.

sea cock: A valve used to prevent water from entering at a through hull.

sea kindly: A boat that's comfortable in rough weather.

sea level: The average level of the oceans, used when finding water depths or land elevations.

seamanship: The ability of a person to motor or sail a vessel, including all aspects of its operation.

sea room: Room for a boat to travel without danger of running aground.

secondary port: A port that is not directly listed in the tide tables but for which information is available as a difference from a nearby standard port.

sector: An arc of a circle in which certain types of navigational lights known as sector lights are visible.

secure: To make fast. To stow an object or tie it in place.

semaphore: A method of signaling using two flags held in position by the signaler.

separation zone: A region drawn on a chart to separate two lanes that have shipping vessels moving in opposite directions.

serve: (1) To wind small line around a rope to protect it from chaffing and weather. (2) The direction that a current is moving.

shake out: To remove a reef from a sail.

sheathing: A covering to protect the bottom of a boat.

sheepshank: (1) A knot used to temporarily shorten a line. (2) A sudden change of course.

ship: (1) A large vessel. (2) To take an object aboard, such as cargo or water. (3) To put items such as oars on the boat when not in use.

shoal: (1) Shallow water. (2) An underwater sand bar or hill that has its top near the surface.

shore: The edge of the land near the water.

shroud: Part of the standing rigging that helps to support the mast by running from the top of the mast to the side of the boat. Sailboats usually have one or more shrouds on each side of the mast.

side lights: Green and red lights on the starboard and port sides of the boat required for navigation at night. Each light is supposed to be visible through an arc of 112.5

degrees, beginning from directly ahead of the boat to a point 22.5 degrees aft of the beam.

sideslip: The tendency of a boat to move sideways in the water instead of along its heading due to the motion of currents or leeway.

single sideband: (1) A type of radio carried on a boat to transmit long distances. (2) To cause an object to go to the bottom of the water.

skiff: A small boat.

slide: (1) Also called a lug. Metal or plastic pieces attached to a sail's luff that slide in a mast track to allow easy hoisting of a sail. (2) The act of using such lines to hoist heavy or awkward objects. (3) Ropes used to secure the center of a yard to the mast.

sloop: A style of sailboat characterized by a single mast with one mainsail and one foresail. Also see *cutter.*

slot: The opening between the jib and the mainsail. Wind passing through this opening increases the pressure difference across the sides of the mainsail, helping to move the boat forward.

snap hook: A metal fitting with an arm that uses a spring to close automatically when connected to another object.

snatch block: A block that can be opened on one side, allowing it to be placed on a line that is already in use.

snub: To suddenly stop or secure a line.

sound: Signals required by navigation rules describing the type of vessels and their activities during times of fog.

south: One of the four cardinal compass points. South is the direction toward the South Pole and is at 180 degrees on a compass card.

south wind, southerly wind: Wind coming from the south.

spar buoy: A tall buoy used as a navigational aid.

spar: A pole used as part of the sailboat rigging, such as masts, booms, and gaffs.

spherical buoy: A ball-shaped buoy marking a navigational hazard.

spill the wind: To head up into the wind or loosen a sail, allowing the sail(s) to luff.

spindle buoy: A tall cone-shaped navigational buoy.

spinnaker: A very large lightweight sail used when running or on a broad reach.

spinnaker halyard: A halyard used to raise the spinnaker.

spinnaker pole lift: Also spinnaker lift. A line running from the top of the mast, used to hold the spinnaker pole in place.

splice: The place where two lines are joined together end to end.

spreader: Small spars extending toward the sides from one or

more places along the mast. The shrouds cross the end of the spreaders, enabling the shrouds to better support the mast.

spring line: Docking lines that help keep the boat from moving fore and aft while docked. The after bow spring line is attached near the bow and runs aft, where it is attached to the dock. The forward quarter spring line is attached to the quarter of the boat, and runs forward, being attached to the dock near the bow of the boat.

square rigged: A sailboat having square sails hung across the mast.

SSB: See *single sideband.*

stability sail: A vertical pole on which flags can be raised.

stall: (1) To stop moving. (2) Air is said to stall when it becomes detached from the surface it is flowing along. Usually air travels smoothly along both sides of a sail, but if the sail is not properly trimmed, the air can leave one of the sides of the sail and begin to stall. Stalled sails are not operating efficiently.

standing rigging: The rigging of a boat that does not normally need to be adjusted.

starboard: The right-hand side of a ship as one faces forward.

starboard tack: A sailboat sailing on a tack with the wind coming over the starboard side and the boom on the port side of the boat. If two boats under sail are approaching, the one on port tack must give way to the boat on starboard tack.

steadying sail: Also stability sail or riding sail. Any small sail set to help the boat maintain its direction without necessarily moving, as when at anchor or in heavy weather.

steep seas: Tall and short waves caused by water current and wave directions being opposite to the direction of the wind.

steerage way: In order for the rudder to be able to properly steer the boat, it must be moving through the water. The speed necessary for control is known as steerage way.

stem: (1) The forward edge of the bow. On a wooden boat, the stem is a single timber. (2) The act of placing the foot of the mast in its step and raising the mast.

stepped: (1) A mast that is in place is *stepped*. (2) Where the mast is stepped, as in keel stepped or deck stepped.

stern: The aft part of a boat.

stern line: A line running from the stern of the boat to a dock when moored.

stern pulpit: Pushpit. A sturdy railing around the deck at the stern.

stiff: A boat that resists heeling.

stock: A crossbeam at the upper part of an anchor.

stopper knot: A knot used in the end of a line to prevent the end from running through a block or other narrow space. Stopper knots prevent a line that slips from unthreading itself and getting lost.

storm trysail: A very strong sail used in stormy weather. It is loose footed, being attached to the mast, but not the boom. This helps prevent boarding waves from damaging the sail or the rigging.

stow: To put something away.

strike: To lower.

stuffing box: A fitting around the propeller shaft to keep the bearing lubricated and to keep water out of the boat.

superstructure: (1) Cabins and rooms above the deck of a ship. (2) The sport of riding breaking waves on a board.

swab: (1) A mop made from rope. (2) To use such a mop.

swinging bridge: A bridge that swings away from the waterway so that boats may pass beside it.

swinging circle, swinging room: The distance a boat can move around its anchor. Swinging room is important because if other boats or objects are within a boat's swinging circle they may collide.

swivel: A rotating fitting used to keep a line from tangling.

tabernacle: A hinged support for the bottom of a mast so that the mast can be lowered easily when passing under bridges.

tachometer: A gauge that measures engine revolutions per minute.

tack: (1) The lower forward corner of a triangular sail (2) The direction that a boat is sailing with respect to the wind. See also *port tack* and *starboard tack*. (3) To change a boat's direction, bringing the bow through the eye of the wind.

tacking: (1) To change a boat's direction, bringing the bow through the eye of the wind. (2) To tack repeatedly, as when trying to sail to a point upwind of the boat.

tackle: Lines used with blocks in order to move heavy objects.

taffrail: A rail around the stern of a boat.

tail: (1) The end of a line. (2) To gather the unused end of a line neatly so that it does not become tangled.

take in: (1) To remove a sail. (2) To add a reef to a sail.

tall buoy: Also called a Dan buoy. A float with a flag at the top of a pole. Used to mark a position such as for a race or a man overboard.

tang: A metal fitting on the mast that the spreaders are attached to.

telltale: A small line free to flow in the direction of the breeze. It is attached to sails, stays in the slot, and in other areas, enabling the helmsman and crew to see how the wind is flowing. Proper use of the telltales can help sailors improve their sail trim.

tenon: The bottom of the mast, with a shape designed to fit into the mast step.

throat: The forward upper corner of a four-cornered sail known as a gaff rigged sail.

thwart: A seat running across the width of a small boat.

thwartships: Across the width of a boat.

tidal atlas: Small charts showing tidal stream directions and rate of flow.

tidal range: The difference between a tide's high and low water levels.

tide: The predictable, regular rising and lowering of water in some areas due to the pull of the sun and the moon. Tidal changes can happen approximately every six or twelve hours depending on the region. To find out the time and water levels of different tides, you can use tide tables for your area. The period of high water level is known as high tide and the period of low water level is known as low tide. In the Bay of Fundy, the tidal range exceeds 40 feet (13 meters).

tiller: A lever used to turn a rudder and steer a boat.

toe rail: A small rail around the deck of a boat. The toe rail may have holes in it to attach lines or

blocks. A larger wall is known as a *gunwale*.

tonnage: The weight or displacement of a ship.

top mast: A mast on top of another mast.

topping lift: A line running from the end of the boom to the top of the mast used to keep the boom from falling when the sail is not set.

topsail: A triangular sail set above the gaff on a gaff-rigged boat.

topsides: The sides of the hull above the water line and below the deck.

tow: To pull a boat with another boat, such as a tugboat *towing* a barge.

trailing edge: The aft edge of a sail, more commonly called the *leech*.

transit: Also called a range. Two navigational aids separated in distance so that they can be aligned to determine that a boat lies on a certain line. Transits can be used to determine a boat's position or guide it through a channel.

trapeze: A belt and line used to help a crew hike out beyond the edge of a boat to counteract the boat's heel. Usually used on small vessels for racing.

triatic stay: A stay leading from one mast, such as the main mast to another, such as the mizzen mast.

tricolor light: A running light allowed on some sailboats instead of the normal bow and stern lights. The tricolor light contains the red and

green side lights and the white stern light in a single fitting that is attached to the top of the mast.

trimaran: A fast sailboat with three parallel hulls.

trim tab: (1) An adjustable section of the rudder that allows the rudder to be corrected for lee helm or weather helm. (2) Sail trim; properly trimmed sails. (3) A properly balanced boat that floats evenly on its water line. Improperly trimmed boats may list or lie with their bow or stern too low in the water.

trip line: A line attached to the end of an anchor to help free it from the ground.

tropics: The region around the equator between the Tropic of Cancer and the Tropic of Capricorn. The tropics are known for their warm weather.

trough: The bottom of a wave, the valley between the crests.

truck: A cap for the top of the mast.

true wind: The speed and direction of the wind. The motion of a boat will cause the wind to appear to be coming at a different direction and speed, which is known as apparent wind.

turtle: A bag in which a spinnaker or other large sail can be stowed with the lines attached so that it can be rapidly raised.

two half hitches: A knot with two half hitches (loops) on the standing part of the line.

typhoon: A strong tropical revolving storm of force 12 or higher in the Southern Hemisphere. Typhoons revolve in a counterclockwise direction. In the Northern Hemisphere, these storms revolve clockwise and are known as hurricanes.

under bare poles: Having no sails up. In heavy weather, the windage of the mast and other spars can still be enough to move the boat.

under the lee: On the lee side of an object, protected from the wind.

undertow: Strong offshore current extending to the shore.

unfurl: To unfold or unroll a sail. The opposite of furl.

upwind: To windward, in the direction of the eye of the wind.

vane: A flat device that is affected by the wind. Vanes are used in wind direction indicators and some self-steering gear systems.

vang: A hydraulic ram or block and tackle used to hold the end of the boom down.

variable pitch: A type of propeller that has adjustable blades for varying speeds or directions, and may be able to reduce drag when under sail.

variation: Magnetic variation. The difference between magnetic north and true north measured as an angle. Magnetic variation is different in different locations, so the nearest compass rose to

each location on a chart must be used.

vector: A line drawn to indicate both the direction and magnitude of a force, such as leeway or a current.

veer: A shifting of the wind direction, opposite of backing. Clockwise in the Northern Hemisphere, counterclockwise in the Southern Hemisphere.

velocity made good: Also VMG. Actual boat speed after adjusting for such factors as current and leeway.

vertical clearance: The distance between the water level at chart datum and an overhead obstacle such as a bridge or power line.

VHF: (1) Very High Frequency radio waves. (2) A radio that transmits in the VHF range. VHF radios are the most common communications radio carried on boats, but their range is limited to "line of sight" between the transmitting and receiving stations. Also see *single sideband.*

visual fix: A fix taken by visually observing the location of known landmarks.

wake: Waves generated in the water by a moving vessel.

watch: (1) A division of crew into shifts. (2) The time each watch has duty.

water line: The line where the water comes to on the hull of a boat. Design water line is where the water line was designed to be,

load water line is the water line when the boat is loaded, and the painted water line is where the water line was painted. Actual water line is where the water line really is at any given time.

water line length: The length of the boat at the water line.

waterlogged: Completely filled with water.

waterway: A river, canal, or other body of water that boats can travel on.

way: The progress of a boat. If a boat is moving, it is considered to be "making way."

weather helm: The tendency of a boat to head up toward the eye of the wind. The opposite of lee helm.

west wind, westerly wind: Wind coming from west.

west: One of the four cardinal compass points. West is at 270 degrees on a compass card.

wet locker: A locker equipped with a drain so that wet clothes can be stored in it without damaging other objects in the boat.

whip: To bind the strands of a line with a small cord.

whistle buoy: A navigational buoy with a whistle.

wide berth: To avoid something by a large distance.

windlass: A mechanical device used to pull in cable or chain, such as an anchor rode.

wind scoop: A funnel used to force wind in a hatch and ventilate the below decks area.

wing and wing: A method of running before the wind with two sails set. Usually the mainsail on one side and a headsail on the other, or one headsail on each side.

working sheet: The sheet that is currently taught and in use to control a sail. The opposite of the *lazy sheet*.

yacht: A sailboat or powerboat used for pleasure, not a working boat.

yard: A spar attached to the mast and used to hoist square sails.

yaw: Swinging off course, usually in heavy seas. The bow moves toward one side of the intended course.

yawl: A two-masted sailboat with the shorter mizzen mast placed aft of the rudder post. A ketch is similar, but the mizzen mast is forward of the rudder post.

zenith: The point of the celestial sphere that is directly overhead.

zephyr: A gentle breeze. The west wind.

zulu: Used to indicate times measured in Coordinated Universal Time, a successor to Greenwich Mean Time. A time standard that is not affected by time zones or seasons.

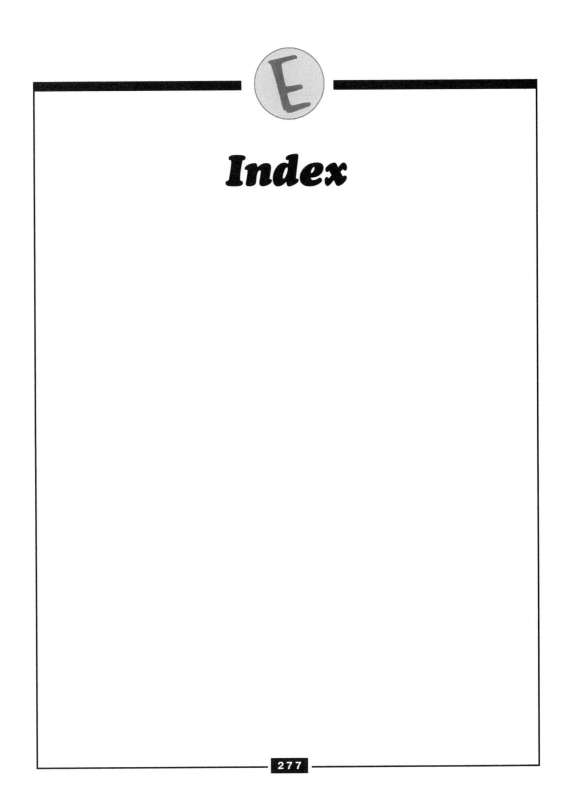

Index

We Have EVERYTHING!

Everything® **After College Book**
$12.95, 1-55850-847-3

Everything® **American History Book**
$12.95, 1-58062-531-2

Everything® **Angels Book**
$12.95, 1-58062-398-0

Everything® **Anti-Aging Book**
$12.95, 1-58062-565-7

Everything® **Astrology Book**
$12.95, 1-58062-062-0

Everything® **Baby Names Book**
$12.95, 1-55850-655-1

Everything® **Baby Shower Book**
$12.95, 1-58062-305-0

Everything® **Baby's First Food Book**
$12.95, 1-58062-512-6

Everything® **Baby's First Year Book**
$12.95, 1-58062-581-9

Everything® **Barbeque Cookbook**
$12.95, 1-58062-316-6

Everything® **Bartender's Book**
$9.95, 1-55850-536-9

Everything® **Bedtime Story Book**
$12.95, 1-58062-147-3

Everything® **Bicycle Book**
$12.00, 1-55850-706-X

Everything® **Breastfeeding Book**
$12.95, 1-58062-582-7

Everything® **Build Your Own Home Page**
$12.95, 1-58062-339-5

Everything® **Business Planning Book**
$12.95, 1-58062-491-X

Everything® **Candlemaking Book**
$12.95, 1-58062-623-8

Everything® **Casino Gambling Book**
$12.95, 1-55850-762-0

Everything® **Cat Book**
$12.95, 1-55850-710-8

Everything® **Chocolate Cookbook**
$12.95, 1-58062-405-7

Everything® **Christmas Book**
$15.00, 1-55850-697-7

Everything® **Civil War Book**
$12.95, 1-58062-366-2

Everything® **Classical Mythology Book**
$12.95, 1-58062-653-X

Everything® **Collectibles Book**
$12.95, 1-58062-645-9

Everything® **College Survival Book**
$12.95, 1-55850-720-5

Everything® **Computer Book**
$12.95, 1-58062-401-4

Everything® **Cookbook**
$14.95, 1-58062-400-6

Everything® **Cover Letter Book**
$12.95, 1-58062-312-3

Everything® **Creative Writing Book**
$12.95, 1-58062-647-5

Everything® **Crossword and Puzzle Book**
$12.95, 1-55850-764-7

Everything® **Dating Book**
$12.95, 1-58062-185-6

Everything® **Dessert Book**
$12.95, 1-55850-717-5

Everything® **Digital Photography Book**
$12.95, 1-58062-574-6

Everything® **Dog Book**
$12.95, 1-58062-144-9

Everything® **Dreams Book**
$12.95, 1-55850-806-6

Everything® **Etiquette Book**
$12.95, 1-55850-807-4

Everything® **Fairy Tales Book**
$12.95, 1-58062-546-0

Everything® **Family Tree Book**
$12.95, 1-55850-763-9

Everything® **Feng Shui Book**
$12.95, 1-58062-587-8

Everything® **Fly-Fishing Book**
$12.95, 1-58062-148-1

Everything® **Games Book**
$12.95, 1-55850-643-8

Everything® **Get-A-Job Book**
$12.95, 1-58062-223-2

Everything® **Get Out of Debt Book**
$12.95, 1-58062-588-6

Everything® **Get Published Book**
$12.95, 1-58062-315-8

Everything® **Get Ready for Baby Book**
$12.95, 1-55850-844-9

Everything® **Get Rich Book**
$12.95, 1-58062-670-X

Everything® **Ghost Book**
$12.95, 1-58062-533-9

Everything® **Golf Book**
$12.95, 1-55850-814-7

Everything® **Grammar and Style Book**
$12.95, 1-58062-573-8

Everything® **Guide to Las Vegas**
$12.95, 1-58062-438-3

Everything® **Guide to New England**
$12.95, 1-58062-589-4

Everything® **Guide to New York City**
$12.95, 1-58062-314-X

Everything® **Guide to Walt Disney World®, Universal Studios®, and Greater Orlando, 2nd Edition**
$12.95, 1-58062-404-9

Everything® **Guide to Washington D.C.**
$12.95, 1-58062-313-1

Everything® **Guitar Book**
$12.95, 1-58062-555-X

Everything® **Herbal Remedies Book**
$12.95, 1-58062-331-X

Everything® **Home-Based Business Book**
$12.95, 1-58062-364-6

Everything® **Homebuying Book**
$12.95, 1-58062-074-4

Everything® **Homeselling Book**
$12.95, 1-58062-304-2

Everything® **Horse Book**
$12.95, 1-58062-564-9

Everything® **Hot Careers Book**
$12.95, 1-58062-486-3

Everything® **Internet Book**
$12.95, 1-58062-073-6

Everything® **Investing Book**
$12.95, 1-58062-149-X

Everything® **Jewish Wedding Book**
$12.95, 1-55850-801-5

Everything® **Job Interview Book**
$12.95, 1-58062-493-6

Everything® **Lawn Care Book**
$12.95, 1-58062-487-1

Everything® **Leadership Book**
$12.95, 1-58062-513-4

Everything® **Learning French Book**
$12.95, 1-58062-649-1

Everything® **Learning Spanish Book**
$12.95, 1-58062-575-4

Everything® **Low-Fat High-Flavor Cookbook**
$12.95, 1-55850-802-3

Everything® **Magic Book**
$12.95, 1-58062-418-9

Everything® **Managing People Book**
$12.95, 1-58062-577-0

Everything® **Microsoft® Word 2000 Book**
$12.95, 1-58062-306-9

Everything® **Money Book**
$12.95, 1-58062-145-7

Everything® **Mother Goose Book**
$12.95, 1-58062-490-1

Everything® **Motorcycle Book**
$12.95, 1-58062-554-1

Everything® **Mutual Funds Book**
$12.95, 1-58062-419-7

Everything® **One-Pot Cookbook**
$12.95, 1-58062-186-4

Everything® **Online Business Book**
$12.95, 1-58062-320-4

Everything® **Online Genealogy Book**
$12.95, 1-58062-402-2

Everything® **Online Investing Book**
$12.95, 1-58062-338-7

Everything® **Online Job Search Book**
$12.95, 1-58062-365-4

Everything® **Organize Your Home Book**
$12.95, 1-58062-617-3

Everything® **Pasta Book**
$12.95, 1-55850-719-1

Everything® **Philosophy Book**
$12.95, 1-58062-644-0

Everything® **Playing Piano and Keyboards Book**
$12.95, 1-58062-651-3

Everything® **Pregnancy Book**
$12.95, 1-58062-146-5

Everything® **Pregnancy Organizer**
$15.00, 1-58062-336-0

Everything® **Project Management Book**
$12.95, 1-58062-583-5

Everything® **Puppy Book**
$12.95, 1-58062-576-2

Everything® **Quick Meals Cookbook**
$12.95, 1-58062-488-X

Everything® **Resume Book**
$12.95, 1-58062-311-5

Everything® **Romance Book**
$12.95, 1-58062-566-5

Everything® **Running Book**
$12.95, 1-58062-618-1

Everything® **Sailing Book, 2nd Edition**
$12.95, 1-58062-671-8

Everything® **Saints Book**
$12.95, 1-58062-534-7

Everything® **Selling Book**
$12.95, 1-58062-319-0

Everything® **Shakespeare Book**
$12.95, 1-58062-591-6

Everything® **Spells and Charms Book**
$12.95, 1-58062-532-0

Everything® **Start Your Own Business Book**
$12.95, 1-58062-650-5

Everything® **Stress Management Book**
$12.95, 1-58062-578-9

Everything® **Study Book**
$12.95, 1-55850-615-2

Everything® **Tai Chi and QiGong Book**
$12.95, 1-58062-646-7

Everything® **Tall Tales, Legends, and Outrageous Lies Book**
$12.95, 1-58062-514-2

Everything® **Tarot Book**
$12.95, 1-58062-191-0

Everything® **Time Management Book**
$12.95, 1-58062-492-8

Everything® **Toasts Book**
$12.95, 1-58062-189-9

Everything® **Toddler Book**
$12.95, 1-58062-592-4

Everything® **Total Fitness Book**
$12.95, 1-58062-318-2

Everything® **Trivia Book**
$12.95, 1-58062-143-0

Everything® **Tropical Fish Book**
$12.95, 1-58062-343-3

Everything® **Vegetarian Cookbook**
$12.95, 1-58062-640-8

Everything® **Vitamins, Minerals, and Nutritional Supplements Book**
$12.95, 1-58062-496-0

Everything® **Wedding Book, 2nd Edition**
$12.95, 1-58062-190-2

Everything® **Wedding Checklist**
$7.95, 1-58062-456-1

Everything® **Wedding Etiquette Book**
$7.95, 1-58062-454-5

Everything® **Wedding Organizer**
$15.00, 1-55850-828-7

Everything® **Wedding Shower Book**
$7.95, 1-58062-188-0

Everything® **Wedding Vows Book**
$7.95, 1-58062-455-3

Everything® **Weight Training Book**
$12.95, 1-58062-593-2

Everything® **Wine Book**
$12.95, 1-55850-808-2

Everything® **World War II Book**
$12.95, 1-58062-572-X

Everything® **World's Religions Book**
$12.95, 1-58062-648-3

Everything® **Yoga Book**
$12.95, 1-58062-594-0

Visit us at everything.com

OTHER *EVERYTHING*® BOOKS BY ADAMS MEDIA CORPORATION

EVERYTHING®

Trade Paperback, $12.95
1-55850-706-X, 320 pages

The Everything® Bicycle Book

Roni Sarig

Whether you're thinking about buying your first bike, or considering whether to enter the Tour de France, *The Everything® Bicycle Book* has all the information you need to steer you right! You'll learn about the different types of bicycles and how to choose one that's right for you, simple maintenance techniques to keep your bike ship-shape, repair techniques for when it falls apart, the rules of the road to keep you riding safely, as well as the latest in bike lingo and style tips to keep

Trade Paperback, $12.95
1-55850-814-7, 336 pages

The Everything® Golf Book

Rich Mintzer and Peter Grossman

Packed with information about the game of golf, its rich history, the great players and outstanding personalities, tours and tournaments, and proper etiquette, as well as anecdotes, trivia, and jokes, *The Everything® Golf Book* really does have it all! You'll find helpful hints and time-tested techniques on improving your game, creative visualizations that focus on the mental aspects of golf, golfing communities and international vacation destina-

Available wherever books are sold!
To order, call 800-872-5627, or visit everything.com
Adams Media Corporation, 57 Littlefield Street, Avon, MA 02322. U.S.A.